Diary of an Escape

T0048441

For Paola

Diary of an Escape

Antonio Negri

Translated by Ed Emery

polity

Published in French as *L'Italie rouge et noire*, 1985 and in Italian as *Diario di un'evasione*, 1986. Copyright © Antonio Negri, 1985. This translation copyright © Polity Press, 2010.

This English edition © Polity Press, 2010

Polity Press
65 Bridge Street
Cambridge CB2 1UR, UK

Polity Press
350 Main Street
Malden, MA 02148, USA

All rights reserved. Except for the quotation of short passages for the purpose of criticism and review, no part of this publication may be reproduced, stored in a retrieval system, or transmitted, in any form or by any means, electronic, mechanical, photocopying, recording or otherwise, without the prior permission of the publisher.

ISBN-13: 978-0-7456-4425-7
ISBN-13: 978-0-7456-4426-4(pb)

A catalogue record for this book is available from the British Library.

Typeset in 10.5 on 12 pt Plantin
by Servis Filmsetting Ltd, Stockport, Cheshire
Printed and bound in Great Britain by MPG Books Group Limited, Bodmin, Cornwall

Index by Ed Emery

The publisher has used its best endeavours to ensure that the URLs for external websites referred to in this book are correct and active at the time of going to press. However, the publisher has no responsibility for the websites and can make no guarantee that a site will remain live or that the content is or will remain appropriate.

Every effort has been made to trace all copyright holders, but if any have been inadvertently overlooked the publisher will be pleased to include any necessary credits in any subsequent reprint or edition.

For further information on Polity, visit our website: www.politybooks.com

Contents

Abbreviations

API	The 'beer' – Red Brigaders in Trané prison
BR	Brigate Rosse/The Red Brigades (Marxist–Leninist militant group founded in 1970 and broken up in 1980)
CSM	Consiglio Superiore della Magistratura/The Superior Council of Magistracy (self-governing constitutional body in civil and criminal matters)
DIGOS	Divisione Investigazioni Generali e Operazioni Speciali/ The Division of General Investigations and Special Operations (law enforcement agency charged with the investigation of organized crime and terrorism)
FLM	Federazione Lavoratori Metalmeccanici/Metalworkers' Union (trade union federation formed in 1973)
GAP	Gruppi di Azione Partigiana/Partisan Action Groups (Italian terrorist group founded by Giangiacomo Feltrinelli in 1970)
OCC	organizzazioni comuniste combattenti/communist combatant organizations
OS	*ouvrier spécialisé*
OVRA	Organizzazione per la Vigilanza e la Repressione dell'Antifascismo/The Organization for Vigilance and Repression of Antifascism (Mussolini's secret police, founded in 1927)
PCI	Partito Comunista Italiano/The Italian Communist Party (founded in 1921, outlawed during the Fascist regime and re-founded in 1943)
PdUP	Partito di Unità Proletaria/The Proletarian Unity Party (party of the extreme Left, founded in 1972)
UCC	Unione dei Comunisti Combattenti/The Union of

Combatant Communists, or Red Brigades–UCC (one of the two factions into which the Red Brigades split in 1984)

UNURI   Unione Nazionale Universitaria Rappresentativa Italiana/ The Italian National Representative Union of Universities (organ representing Italian students, 1948–68)

Author's Introduction

As the dates show, this diary was finished about two years ago. Immediately, a major Italian publishing house asked me if they could publish it. The publishing house was in receivership at the time, which meant that an independent editor had space to distance himself from the cowardliness of the majority. However, the publisher had hardly emerged from receivership when the new owners cancelled my contract. And, as if that was not enough, they also began attacking me and slandering me through the publisher's own daily and weekly newspapers. Since then things have gone from bad to worse, to the point where I had the pleasure of reading in *Corriere della Sera* a few weeks ago that, in the name of freedom of the press, my books should not be published at all! It does not surprise me to see journalists rallying to the cause of censorship, given that, in the name of defending the institutions, they are already prepared to be the servants of new fascist entities, lodges and corporations. I am proud of having obliged them to censor me, these same people who not so many years ago thought that they had succeeded in burying me beneath kilometres of lead, and who had accused me of being the assassin of the Republic – and then, when I was found to be innocent, reported the fact in a couple of column inches and forgot about it. Like hypocritical dogs who shit on the pavement and then make to bury it with a couple of paw strokes. At that point a major French publisher broke this united front of silence and dishonour and went ahead and published the volume. I thank him, and here I would also like to thank the people who, amid extraordinary difficulties and with great generosity, are now publishing this diary in Italian. They are showing once again that *chez nous*, that liberty which is detested and crushed by the state and by the big institutions, is nurtured and defended and given a high social value by ever-new figures and ever more intelligent subjects.

I wrote this diary to tell the truth about what was happening to me. Four years of preventive imprisonment, followed by election to Parliament and then by the experience, made *in corpore vili* ['on a body of no value'] – my own, in this instance – of the cruelty of the special laws and of the 'truth' of the *pentiti* [members of armed organizations who 'recant', collaborate with the authorities and receive state protection and/or a reduced sentence in return. Gradually two themes became central: my lack of any kind of confidence in the magistracy and the political class; and my declaration of innocence, hence my right to escape. I was (and am) literally pursued by a group of magistrates (supported by a compact set of political 'lobbies') who have interpreted in reactionary forms the struggle of the institutions against terrorism. This interpretation has removed the right to justice, has very seriously poisoned the democratic political system, and has constructed brothels of corporative infamy within the state. So much for the general picture. As regards my own personal position, a few basic facts will suffice to show the extent to which I have fallen prey to the system's madness. I have been accused, and must defend myself, in six separate trials, which have since become eighteen, bearing in mind the three levels involved in each trial; and now, six years after my arrest, only one and a half have been carried through. That leaves me (for the next twenty years, I imagine) with sixteen and a half trials in which I have to defend myself, find the money to pay lawyers, mobilize journalists and so on.

As for the political class: from Right to Left without exception, including what remains of the far Left – which had been backtracking politically to the point of indecency – it has accepted this degradation of the law without batting an eyelid. At least this has been the case for a long time. Now, in the course of the past two years – and particularly in recent months – there has been something of a reawakening, so that many of the accusations which I, as an innocent man and as an elected member of Parliament, bring here against these magistrates, political cliques and journalistic mafias have acquired resonance today through statements made by certain authoritative representatives of the state. Obviously this fact gives me a degree of pleasure – and it prompts me to confess (comforted by those declarations) that, if I had many doubts when I made my escape from Italy (as my diary confirms), today, when I think back, I can only thank the heavens for having inspired me to do so. If at that time I was in doubt, today I consider myself the subject of a miracle for not having let those doubts stand in the way of my escape.

An escape which has been a symbol of truth and liberty. No, 'our only claim to eternity will not be the contents of our police files', nor the ravings of Calogero and his like, nor the malevolence and cynical determination of the lodges! It will not be possible for the ruling class to cancel out the memory of our revolution, as they did on other occasions in Italy – for instance when, after 1870, they resorted to ferocious repression against the social movement of the revolutionary peasantry to destroy the movement for radical transformation which had traversed the Risorgimento; when they dissolved, through wars and fascism, the practice of working-class counter-power, which had accompanied the industrial revolution; or when they used restructuring, state massacres and emergency laws to crush the struggles which the exploited had opposed to the new and fierce rules of mature capitalism. No, you will not manage to cancel the memory of the 1960s and 1970s by applying the label 'terrorism'. We are not 'terrorists', just as our fathers were not 'deserters' or our grandfathers 'bandits'. We are stubborn people – who want, and who continue to want, from generation to generation, a radical transformation of society and a thoroughgoing political revolution. This is the reason why I published, and am now republishing, this diary – then in French, now in Italian. Because on this basis my feeling of innocence and the demand for justice which have jointly guided my action (and which are continually renewed and fed by the memory of the heroic and very sweet period of development of communist autonomy) now drive me to propose, with coherence, that I should return to Italy. Returning so as to confirm my freedom, just as they drove me to escape in order to preserve that freedom. Returning to Italy so as to resume the communist political struggle. Directly, immediately.

Because, in the first place, the precarious political equilibrium which was established in Italy around the defeat of terrorism has shown its limits: the ability to defeat terrorism was not accompanied by the intelligence needed to dissolve the reasons for it, or to recover its radical albeit ingenuous motivations. Because, secondly, not only have we seen a complete paralysis in the transformation and political modernization of the country, but we have also seen a barbarizing of its civil structures – a barbarizing paradoxically brought about by the extension of emergency laws and by the ways in which the parties have made use of these laws against each other. I do not criticize only the emergency laws; what I criticize also is their extraordinary extension, and the fact that they have become a huge disfigurement

of law and of the rules of simple human cohabitation. All these ugli-
nesses can only be cancelled by a programme of renewal which, in a
democracy, sees the social subjects who were formed in the struggles
of the 1960s and 1970s becoming protagonists again. Returning to
protagonism. The hope of a return is thus articulated with the claim
which, for all the mistakes made, my generation can broadly make:
that of being the only ones who tried to give body to the reform of
culture, to the modification of the democratic institutions and to
the development of liberty. The only generation in the forty years
since the end of the Second World War. Today we are in a position to talk about a return. A return of the exiles to their country,
a return of the prisoners to their families, a return of the generation of social struggles to democratic political life. We have to talk
about this return, because the country needs us and needs our will
and capacity for transformation. It needs our culture, the fact of our
differentness.

As for us, it does us no good to be scornful of the generation of
the Resistance and of the period of antifascism which preceded us.
Gradually, over the course of time, that generation has completely
abdicated all commitment to transformation. It rebuilt the country
after the war – rebuilt it so well that it gave us a country which was
almost the same as it was during the years of fascism. No dynamic
response was given to the enormous modification of the economic
and cultural base that the struggle of the world proletariat had
brought about. We have a political constitution which, contradic-
torily, combines both feebleness and rigidity. We have a political
class which is clinging onto power – a rotting ivy on structures that
are disintegrating. So a return is not only a desire for us; it is also a
necessity for the country. Our struggle has in fact been the genea-
logy – certainly not of the present, but – of the possible future of our
country. We have no intention of ending up in a situation where,
in Milan Kundera's words, our only claim to posterity will be the
contents of our police files. Our defeat has been only one episode,
and not even among the most important ones, in the struggle which,
in the world and in Italy, has been developing for a century for the
appropriation of the enormous productive forces that development
has created. Our generation is the only one to have a political culture
which is matched to the enormity of this technological revolution,
and one with a productivity and an invention-power to match. Thus
the notion of return derives its political strength from the ontological
force of a radical change that has already taken place in people's consciousnesses. We do not need memory in order to be able to declare

it. We do not need anything other than the fact of our existing, of our being present – of our return.

I feel that all this is near. And I feel that in the whole of Europe – and maybe even a bit further afield – many things are changing. Finally, it should be said that ours is a return which bears the scars of transformation. How much time have we spent working on this, how much suffering have we undergone – and yet this return appears so bright that I have no pain at the thought of that past; the only pain which I have now is the restlessness of a wait which, as of today, I hope will be very brief.

1

The Trial

24 February to 24 May 1983: Folios 1–37

Folio 1

24 February. Thursday. Morning wake-up call at 6.30. I am very tense. For four years I have been waiting for this fateful – is that the word? – day. I am already tired as I come to wakefulness. The sky is dark, but you can see that it is a cold crystalline blue, as often happens in Rome at this time of year. We come down to the disgusting narrow little cells. We wait. I read the graffiti on the walls. The body searches begin. Then we're chained together, four at a time, and we're loaded into the vans. The helicopter arrives. Buzzing overhead. A barking of military-style orders. Swarms of motorcycle police. We wait in the trucks. A joke or two among the comrades. Then our very noisy convoy moves off. Roads blocked off, guns pointing everywhere, one truck with a soldier in a kind of armoured turret, ready to shoot. Continuous stream of radio babble, the kind of thing you hear in the movies: 'Panther calling Eagle . . . Swan replying . . .' We've left the quiet of prison behind us. Now we're caught in the trappings of war. We stretch to peer out of the windows of our van. People look alarmed as we pass. Green grass along the outlying roads where they're taking us. Then, finally, the bunker, the infamous Foro Italico. Again we wait. By 10.30 a.m. we are in court. It's taken four hours to get here. Is it going to be like this every time? I'm done for. We enter the specially built cages in the courtroom, with the cameras and TV crews homing in on us. *'Cheese, cheese.'* Do you know what it's like to have spent a year, a month, even a day, in prison? *'Cheese, cheese.'*

Enter the judges. The repressive machine seems to thrive on this concocted routine. The stage-setting is antiquated, and the spectacle of force does nothing to remove the sense of anachronism. The machine, however, enjoys its airs and graces. Silence – apart from the continuing click, click of the cameras. *'Cheese, cheese.'* No, this court is a useless add-on. This trial is already a foregone conclusion for the institutions. Why carry on the pretence? How can there be any hope of finding justice in this trial, prejudiced as it is by four years of preventive detention? The cameras click and the film cameras whir. *'Cheese, cheese.'* It's hard to take in everything that's going on. Right at the back of this huge armed encampment we can see friends, relations and comrades. I'm terribly short-sighted, so the comrades point people out to me: 'Look, there's X, and there's Y . . .'. An equation with too many unknowns. However, in this feverish excitement I pretend that I too can see. Greetings, emotion. Santiapichi, the judge, starts. Giuliano, my lawyer, also starts. They exchange formalities, which seem like mafia signals. The problem this morning is how we are going to get out of a particularly absurd situation: today, apart from being on trial in Rome, I am also supposed to be on trial in Milan. The formality of their exchanges does nothing to conceal the fierce irrationality of the whole proceedings.

The court adjourns. We go down to the cells. We wait there for hours and hours. The machine grinds away, the handcuffs cut into your wrists, the court decides . . .

You might wonder how the court can make a decision in a situation like this. But it will decide, that's for sure. It *has* to decide. And thus the decision will conclude this imbalanced – I would say incoherent and ferocious – trial dialectics. So we won't go to Milan – we'll stay in Rome? We'll see tomorrow. Ah, mysterious decisionism [*decisionismo*], what a vulgar situation you have fallen into! We return to prison, physically exhausted. I experience a strange and horrible happiness at being back in my cell. I throw myself onto my bed. I want to sleep. The other comrades ask how it went. Finally I take a book, in the hope of getting off to sleep. Starobinski, *Transparency and Obstruction.* I can't sleep. My mind is caught up in the plot of the story. Rousseau as a Hölderlinian hero – but this trial of ours, is it not in reality a persecution of the 'beautiful soul' of the movement? Enough! Thought cannot stoop to concern itself with this trial. Reaching out, I pick up another book from the floor, the first that comes to hand. It is an issue of the German journal *Alternative*, the latest to arrive and also the last of the series. The comrades are saying '1968 is finished'. *Alternative* ran for more than ten years as a sourcebook within the movement. Now the story has come to an end, gentlemen, and another story is starting.

This picking up of a book from the pile is somehow symbolic. I laugh. It's like Erasmus picking out a page of the Bible at random, or myself as a child opening random pages of Leopardi. So the party is starting over, says the casual soothsayer. Maybe that is the case in Germany. But here everything's carrying on just the same. Including this infamous trial. I read, distractedly. The caricatural machine of justice is writ large before me, and I see how it is shored up by the daily torment of prison and the ferocious stage-setting of the trial. Four long years. And then, all of a sudden, I see the faces of Paola and Rossana, of those faithful old witnesses to truth. A sudden doubt rises in me. Maybe in this trial truth cannot win. This enlightenment of ours, this communist hope of ours, which does not surrender. Tell the truth, shout the truth. But what is truth in a political trial? On the one side – the stage-setting, the machinery, the dramatization. On the other – this wounded humanity of ours. Four years of preventive imprisonment. A great heap of memories, passions and suffering. And, first and foremost, a revolutionary passion lived to the limit, the joy of transformation. Two worlds. This trial is pitting two worlds against each other. It is recomposing life in the form of legality. No, this cannot be done . . . *'Cheese, cheese.'* They, too, know that it's not possible. That's the reason why nothing surrounding this trial has any rationality to it. The courtroom cages, the handcuffs, the hours and hours of waiting in the cells. No, they don't want the truth. They want the ritual. They want a sacrifice. Legality is restored in the symbolic, not in the rational. Paola, Rossana, why are you there, loyal, full of reason and beautiful? Go away! This is Aztec justice. Giuliano, why do you continue playing the lawyer, you who know about these things? At last I drop off to sleep. Just for a while. I dream that I am sleeping on a mattress full of knives and spears. The density of the institutions? How many times have you recalled me to that? *'Merde. Cheese.'* And yet I am serene. I smile. Pietro wakes me with a kiss. I sit down to write. (G12 Rebibbia – 24 February)

Folio 2

Second day of the trial. It's going to be postponed until 7 March. In other words, until Milan decides to release me from the trial that I am supposed to be undergoing up north. What looked at first like a great procedural mess has been sorted out and becomes insignificant. But the fact remains that I still have to undergo two trials – one here in Rome, for insurrection and for having supposedly set up an armed band, and the other in Milan, for crimes (demonstrations, robberies and so on) which, according to the prosecution, substantiate and demonstrate both the 'armed band' charge and the charge of insurrection. First the sentencing in Rome, and then the proofs in Milan. There's always something new to learn – absurdity is never sufficiently appreciated in our life. To arrive at this crazy result, which presumably he thinks is a neat operation, the president of the court is playing for time. He wants to wind up today's proceedings without having the charges read out, so as to delay the formal opening of our trial; he wants to avoid a situation in which we end up being judged 'simultaneously' in both Rome and Milan. The likelihood is that this would make one of the two trials collapse: most probably the one in Rome, under his jurisdiction. In short, two trials on the same evidence is fine, but those two trials taking place simultaneously is not fine. The contradiction within the system has to be controlled and contained, so that 'systemic circulation' is maintained. The contradictory fact is put out of the way. However, this operation of systemic logic is happening in the most banal fashion. Sometimes the spectacle is downright comical. For Santiapichi, it is a question of ownership: he has a property to be defended. For Abbate, the assistant judge, the problem is how to get into a position where he can pass the sentence he already has in his pocket, ready-made. Great confusion in court, a fluttering of robes and continuous sharp interchanges on all sides: between the court president and the lawyers, between the lawyers and the aggrieved parties, between the lawyers and the prosecuting counsel, and between the latter and the president. Our friends – Massimo, Giacomo, Marco – watch the scene in a state of consternation. Myself much less so. In fact (and I see and feel it more and more) there is a reversal in my way of seeing things, a complete reversal of perspective. They – the friends, the comrades on the outside – look at me in the cage and see me as if suspended in another reality, in another time. But I have the same sensation when I look at them – and I appreciate how much this happens in the continuity of my reversed perception. I see them in suspension. They come into the courtroom and, albeit with a degree of scepticism, they do believe in the idea of justice. They hope to tear down these damned bars and to win me back into the real-time of life. I know that this hope is irremediably lost, here, in this trial – the trial is purely and simply a continuation of prison. I look at them and I look at their hopes, as if I see everything projected onto a screen, far in the distance. Whereas my own 'real' is constituted by my ability to live the continuity between prison and trial. Certainly it is an absurd continuity, a constrained world, a substitution of the world – but it is nonetheless real for that. Thus there are different identities, counterposed. In this instance, my refusal to identify myself in the law and in the trial permits me to construct for myself, in prison, a way of surviving which is a force of resistance, an intellectual and ethical concentration. Thus the suspension of time, which the friends on the outside are denouncing, is for me a substitution of time: being-for-prison is the only form of resistance possible. It is, on the one hand, existence as an appendage. They do everything they can to remind you of it – a day of trial is ten or twelve hours of work. I find a desire insinuating its way into my head – that they should stage the trial directly in prison, lock, stock and barrel. But there is also a continued sense of internal freedom, of irreducible resistance. Freedom! That's certainly not something that the trial will give me. Here inside, and through those mechanisms, the word appears to have no meaning. No, freedom has nothing to do with the dimension of time involved in the trial. So don't look at me as if this trial is going to win me back into life. The trial is only dragging me into the abyss of an injustice that has turned itself into institution and machine. How can a monster generate freedom? By now my freedom is already stronger than any illusion, than any trial. It will make me something other. *Inglan' is a bitch* (LKJ) [Linton Kwesi Johnson]. (G12 Rebibbia – 25 February)

Folio 3

Much nervousness in prison. Enea and Pietro have suddenly been transferred, one to Volterra and the other to Fossombrone. For the moment they are in the isolation cells in those prisons. We hear that the authorities are possibly planning to clear out Rebibbia. A general state of hysteria. I spend these days of the suspended hearing going over the trial in my mind. I ask myself continually, what exactly is a political trial? Certainly not a process designed to arrive at a truth. Rather it is one of the forms which exhibit the ongoing restructuring of the equilibrium of constitutional powers. The life of the law is the law of the jungle. What is happening here is that justice is advancing and organizing, within the totality of constitutional powers, its powers of political exclusion. A political trial is thus the pivotal point around which, through the medium of the magistracy, all the powers of the state re-consolidate their mutual loyalty and exclude the forces of difference. They formalize the exclusion of the forces of renewal. Thus a political trial becomes very much an act of state. It is here that law is formed – constitutional law of exclusion, of banning from the *polis*. I am frightened by the compactness of this power which, in judging me, rediscovers and reformulates its own identity. I am blinded by the strength of its presence. It seems to me impossible to resist it. I begin to think about the past. Was it not against precisely this overbearing presence that we were struggling – against this continuous, latent and efficacious overdetermination of the constitution? Against this perversion of democracy? Against the narrow-minded and closed character of its institution? Here instead we have power in the final instance. Juridical exclusion. I have been re-reading my *Pipeline*, which has just been published: in my view the concept of exclusion relates to that of poverty. The person who is excluded is like the person who is poor. In the great ceremony of repression I experience myself as a poor person [*unpovero*]. In my mind's eye I see again images of our struggles and conquest of a revolutionary consciousness. A delirium? No, I am simply reconfirming a passion for justice – in the social, in reality, and in poverty. A *chasseur noir*, as Vidal-Naquet says. (G12 Rebibbia – 26–27 February)

Folio 4

How is it possible for an ethical totality – like the one represented by us, the defendants in this trial – to constitute itself in the presence of another figure, which also presents itself as a totality? Logic excludes the co-presence of two totalities. Such a relationship can exist only if one of the two totalities is a nothing, is unreal. But I cannot accept this – I claim the ethical totality of our project, of our existence. Our adversary is power. But power cannot accept to be stripped of its value either. In this clash there is no possibility of transcendence. So how can there be any meeting point here, how is any dialectics possible in a trial? Aristotle sees this clash of absolutes as the essence of tragedy. Paul Ricoeur in his latest book, which I am reading, relates the polarity of the dramatic plot to the absolutization of the time of consciousness as Augustine describes it in his *Confessions*. In the unfolding of the plot, every actor lives the absoluteness of consciousness. However, recognizing this and saying it is not the same as overcoming the irreducible split. Here dialectics is not possible. Particularly not in the postmodern scenario we inhabit. All the contradictions have lost any hierarchical dimension. Conflict takes place on the surface – a surface that is flat. The trial is therefore not a hierarchical function – it is simply a terrain on which absolutes rebound off each other. One against the other. The impermeability is complete. And yet consciousness does not remain content with the plot. Sometimes, on the basis of my studies and my beliefs, I think that our ethicity is Spinozan *potenza* [potentiality] and imagination, and that the ethicity claimed by the adversary is a tendency to nullification – to the unitary and nullifying appropriation of being. I fear my metaphysical presumption, but I don't know how to lessen its fascination and its grip. I understand that hard objectivity of relationship, by virtue of which every character is affected by the irresoluteness of the plot and every form of awareness is relative. But, having said that, I am not able to convince myself that our witnessing the real has been, and is, less than absolute. I think of the trial; of how this ethical content of ours has rendered our language – within the trial – entirely specific and untranslatable; and of how, in consequence, no dialogue will be possible. Thus our trial will be a rolling-out of life and of its truths, one against the other, but with an impossibility of finding a middle way, a mode of confrontation. The passages become invisible – mine to them, and theirs to me. The determinations become impossible to define – mine to them and theirs to me. Perhaps this tragedy of ethics that we are living is no longer resolvable: neither in ourselves nor in the globality of the drama. I regard with extreme bitterness this obligation of mine to move within the ethical. In its extreme hardness. I do not understand how this trial can be resolved. Or rather, there is only one way: that of frontal clash, that of the affirmation of our humanity. In postmodernity, in a world which roots values singularly in a horizon with a flat surface, how would a trial, a judgement, a restoration of power be possible? The only thing possible is my, or our, capacity to assert the truth – without illusions, without any claim to reconquer any dialectic of recomposition. And yet this ethical affirmation of ours is, in essence, radical and given. Without presumption I live this irresolvable paradox of separation. (G12 Rebibbia – 28 February)

Folio 5

Everyone is saying that Negri is not to be forgiven. I am the unpardonable one. Strange rumours are reaching me from Milan, where the trial has begun in my absence. In Milan the situation is dominated by the ideology of the 'evil teacher' ['*cattivo maestro*']. This was constructed by the chroniclers of the Historic Compromise – and pliable judges, armed with that horrible Machiavellianism which makes their thinking so antiquated, have happily taken it on board. The lawyers, from what I understand, are having a hard time getting to grips with the reality of the trial in its twisted complexity, in its dis-levels and in the articulation of its various layers, in the ruinous direction it has taken – that of attributing moral responsibility for everything that has happened to me and my comrades. They employ ferocious murderers as ideological accusers, and with this they attempt, almost furiously, to cancel out the history of the class struggles – and also the empirical history of the party struggles that produced the killing of Tobagi. This horrific crime must be covered by an ideological smokescreen. The restorative function that the political trial fulfils in the composure of domination has to run its full course. So I am the unpardonable one. I read Girard, on sacrifice, on the scapegoat: among so many vague points, the only truly restorative function of this sacral act is that of enabling the ensemble of power to regain its composure. And in the present-day repetition of this drama, in the Milan trial, I feel the heavy inertia of a power which is incapable of liberating itself from similar expiatory and recompositional [*ricompositiva*] imaginings – materially incapable of anything other than a mystifying and falsifying identity, as if it were a force of gravity, a black hole. (I have written to the socialists, urging them not to accept in Milan this fundamental mystification and providing evidence to unmask the operation under way. I hope they will have the courage to act.) It seems, however, that I am to all intents and purposes unpardonable. I believed, and I still believe, that only a great mass awakening can lead us out of a situation in which justice is restoration rather than truth – not an allocation of responsibility but a repetition of power. This dialectical fetish: what you have removed you must give back, what you have taken you must restore. No, life is not this. I am not an evil teacher – and I am not the evil teacher by antonomasia, as the press would have me appear. I have lived, and I still live, a process of liberation that is exhausting, continuous, non-linear, but fairly oriented. There is no doubt that it breaks with consolidated being, both as ethics and as a relation of power – but that it is capable of blowing it apart is more difficult to say. You run through the internal fissures of this being; others want to find the cell into which to lay the mine. I have taught how to follow the deep veins of being, not how to place bombs. There is no place from which this world can be made to explode. It has to be extinguished. Just as there is no justice, there is no juridical place on which articulations of a new life, which are liberated, can be recomposed.

'We're di forces af vict'ry / an' wi' comin' rite through / we're di forces af vict'ry / now wat yu gonna do' (LKJ). So do what you like . . . Don't pardon me – I am guilty of having put myself in unison with being. For that, and only for that, am I responsible. And happy. And my hands are clean of blood. Facing me I have insane killers who have now become 'repentants' – and, on the other side, the heroes of the restoration, men whose hands are red with the blood of the scapegoat. Who knows why the analysis of the ritual maintains itself always so high and rarefied, so theoretical, and does not reconstruct instead Foucauldian small histories and genealogical life stories of the executioners . . . (G12 Rebibbia – 1–3 March)

Folio 6

In Milan they have cut me out of the Rosso–Tobagi trial. A temporary suspension. What does this mean concretely? It means that they will try me first in Rome and then in Milan. I assume they are thinking – or rather making the insane supposition – that, if by some chance I am found not guilty or set free for any reason, they will be able to keep me in prison anyway, awaiting the trial in Milan. In fact the preventive detention coming from Milan starts later than the Rome version. Two trials, two preventive detentions, two sentences, two punishments: and I'm going to have to go through all this, this tortuous Calvary, before I can even begin to think about living again. What barbarism! This is how this Milanese decision avoids a situation of having two trials going on at the same time. It solves problems of etiquette – but the net result is a jail sentence for me, just like that, out of the blue, without the case even being argued. This system really does stink. This little Milanese manoeuvre reveals its whole deeper nature. No use in summoning you to higher principles – this is another world. Sometimes even I find myself protesting: all this is completely Kafkaesque! But it's not true; all this is only vulgar, clapped-out, caricatural. It is not that the suffering and torment are distributed by processes of bizarre and irrational logic: what we have here is just dirty dealing and the sniggering of those who are in power. In Italy the penal legislator and the magistrate observe the old rules of agrarian power, which lies somewhere between despotism and the mafia. The undoubted repressive functionality of penalties and, above all, of procedures smacks of hatred for the adversary, the enemy, the subversive and the marginal, a hatred which has the dry transparency of the midday sun. Nothing is tortuous and tormented here: the intrigue of the legal system is played out with cruel and devious cunning. There is brutality and brutality: the wooden, mechanical brutality of the Anglo-Saxon sovereign, the perverse brutality of the regimes of realized socialism, and then this Mediterranean brutality, which is both a bit Levantine and a bit Islamic. When I think of the magistrate who uses these standards of doubling the number of imprisonments and penalties, I cannot imagine him other than as a cat sitting and picking his teeth after having eaten the mouse. A ferocity which is entirely natural. They say that legality and enlightenment were supposed to soften and rationalize this kind of Sultan's justice. But in Italy they have perfected – and now in this state of emergency they exalt – the liminary characteristics, the combination of class hatred, cunning and force. (G12 Rebibbia – 4 March)

Folio 7

The first review of *Pipeline*, in Montanelli's *Giornale*, written by Arpino. An avalanche of libel and insult. Against the 'Babel of jargon' which I allegedly represent, the purist calls for a 'restoration of language'. Restoration – that magic word. So now poor Santiapichi is asked to take on another task – which anyway is entirely at one with his institutional task – that of restoration. Bringing back order to things that have become disordered. Does language have the sacral function of preserving, reproducing and transmitting the fetishism of culture? Arpino's opinion on this is entirely clear. I avoid the sarcasm of a possible reply, considering the pathetic nature of the criticism – no point in using sarcasm against a culture that is terminally sick and isolated, incapable of passion and clinging to banalities. On the other hand it is true that I have a soft spot for Babel – but language, and our pursuit of it in what it produces, is indeed what introduces us into the phenomenology of this divided and plural world. They, on the other hand, would like language to be, like norms and command, in the form of a narrow and wretched unity – whereas in fact there are many languages and norms and commands. And yet here in Italy this is not expressed. Dull tradition is rather conjugated with a timid realism, which is ideological and from the start impoverished. As for the literary avantgarde, it has been fascinated more by technologies than by the struggles and the riotous realities of the ghettos and factories. Even the revolt of music has been kept within the realm of polite decency – Dalla as Arpino, Battisti as Montale. The fact is that the marriage between culture and power is indissoluble in this country of happy slaves, which calls itself Italy. (G12 Rebibbia – 5 March)

PS An additional page about other reviews. Probably a good idea to keep all this material together.

16 March In *La Stampa* Vattimo deals intelligently with the controversial polemic about a Babel of languages. The metropolitan dissolution of life cannot be lived except in the form of a disaggregation of language. There are analogies between *Pipeline* and what Negri most abhors – the rosy disaggregation which someone like Arbasino exercises over the real of culture. Heliogabalus as a representation of expression, of imagining today. But (and here is my first objection to the self-satisfied mysticism of Vattimo) the problem is that of poetry – in other words, of arriving at, and not of mystifying; of putting into red, and not into pink, the material determinations of the disaggregration of the world and of language. Today, even in destructive ways, poetry, desire and love can and must penetrate the dynamic of this disaggregation. A truly Leopardian function.

27 March Zucconi, writing in *Il Giorno*, sets out to do a political critique of *Pipeline*. A splendid book, he says, when it talks about prison, but the book's philosophy – a philosophy of searching for absolutes – is unacceptable when Negri talks about anything else. Beware of searching for truth – *cave canem!* It is paradoxical that the politician Zucconi understands the Babel of languages as a search for absolutes. The politician is intelligent – more so than the rosy litterateur – and almost as intelligent as the nihilist. I am reading Heidegger these days, where he writes about Hölderlin. This poetry, which ploughs being in order to reproduce its desperate meaning – what thing is capable of living outside of absoluteness? But how could anyone think that the crisis we are living is not absolute, in the whole array of its causes and effects? It is hypocritical to deny it. And then, why overload the term 'absolute'? – it expresses being in the reference, in the tendency, in the given onticity; this is not metaphysics but materialist rigour in the recognition of things.

4 April It is Ruggero Guarini's turn to express an opinion about *Pipeline* – in today's *Espresso*. The communist *refoulé* moves on the same terrain as the catholic Zucconi. Once again, it is the absolute that worries him. But not, as in the case of the Catholic, because the absolute is a backdrop for relativity (and thus, in short, I am lacking a sense of sin – which is unforgivable!) – but because the great culture of modernity, from Hobbes to Spinoza, from Max Weber to Simone Weil, has reconstructed only a relative horizon of values for man. *Pipeline* = *bricolage* = extraneity to the course of negative thought. I could explain to him – in the manner of the good Guarini – many things about these writers, who have been my bedside reading for the past thirty years. But what's the point? There is also a pavement of culture, and there are street corners where dogs piss. Here, in the face of communists *refoulés* and of *nouveaux philosophes* of all disciplines, what is being brought into question is materialism – in other words the absoluteness of the given fact, the absoluteness of struggle. To avoid this relationship, to elude it, means putting on priestly clothing and conceiving of the function of criticism as the disciplinary mediation of an unknown transcendental. It is ridiculous. No, no – not the unknown, but the truth of this struggle of ours, of this certain absolute: this is what we should prove ourselves on. *Pipeline* has gone some way in experimenting with this. Others, however, convinced themselves that communism has betrayed them, which means that they view any attempt to concern oneself with the torments of humanity as being indecent, and the preservation of their own skins as being sacred.

17 April Forcella, in *Il Messaggero* – against the removal, in Italy, of the 1970s, in culture and in everyday thinking. This brings me back to my topic. Because it is precisely the theme of the behaviour of culture in the face of struggles, of repression, of 7 April, that is fundamental here. A *trahison des clercs*. A betrayal that has been corporeal, heavy and hypocritical – when (at one and the same time) reality had presented itself as a Babel, ideology had collapsed, and the search for revolutionary transformation had become, for substantial layers of the movement, an immediate passion. This was the big problem. So why renegue on this immediacy of the desire for the absolute, this passage through chaos which alone could have produced renewal? And then why suddenly forget the need and – often – the memory of having taken part in all of this? Why reject a body of which one had asked – and from which one had received – contact and caress? Why isolate oneself? Why accept the state of emergency, the state of exception, the repentance of prisoners, and the whole disgrace of the thing? Why not seek and declare the truth in the face of this provocation? Why not recompose, in poetry, that split which everyone lived in their being? A large part of the Italian intellectuals spent the 1970s as if they were desiring – timid and excited, in struggles, in the new movements – a woman whom they could not touch. When she went off about her own business they started calling her a whore. Thus they projected onto their conscience the poverty of their relationship with the world – and out of that chaos and disquiet, which poetry should have traversed and dominated, they made instead the dough for their own impotence.

24 April Ceronetti – raging – in *Corriere della Sera*, against Braudel and all those who see Marxism as a sound foundation of science. Amusing! And he ends by exclaiming: 'And then they write so badly, all these Marxists!' Probably it is precisely in the arid pretentiousness of the likes of Ceronetti that we find the reason for the *trahison des clercs* – for this refusal of being, for this stretching outside the limits of the relativity of values, which lies in their opportunism. A pure and simple love of death, a nostalgia for the nul state. But the mummy will answer him politely, just as it replied to Federico Ruysih: 'We too were once alive.' (G12 Rebibbia – Written at various times)

Folio 8

Back in court again. The same wearisome ritual – getting up very early, and then the wrist-irons, and then from the cells into the courtroom cage, where we sit for hours and hours. The third day of trial activity. The real trial is now beginning. I sit and watch, with a genuine curiosity to see how the machine operates. Today is taken up with hearings of the major presentations: the civil parties at the debutantes' ball. But this is not what interests me most. The central element is the intervention by the Public Prosecutor. Finally I understand fully what is meant by the phrase 'accusatory trial'. The absolute pre-eminence of the prosecution, of accusation, as the driving force of the trial. A kind of structural straitjacket, a rigid predetermination. The accusation is already a fact, irreversible – as represented in that pile of papers, which the prosecution has accumulated and which the Public Prosecutor has been waving around from the start, like an avenging angel. There is no search for truth, and therefore no debate among equals in order to arrive at it. There is an accusation, which has full freedom in the expression of its force, and there is your right to defend yourself from it. The one who does the accusing is a public power; the one who defends represents a subjective right. The court stands in the middle between the two – it would be more appropriate to say at mid-height, because it is not there to resolve the problem in terms of truth, on the horizon of what is true and going behind the surface of the conflict, but rather it mediates the overbearing nature of the accusation in relation to the low height of the defendant. The court has to guarantee that the game between the cat and the mouse plays out fairly. The Public Prosecutor stands on a step which is higher than the defendants, on a raised bench that is on the same level as the court and markedly separate from the lawyers. The stage-setting well expresses the relations of power. But that is not all. We are tired, we are not used to all this, and in some senses we are infuriated by all the ceremonial (the cage – we want to be together, but there's no space to move – there's an enormous tension between freedom and brotherly love, which only increases the lump in the throat); in this situation, in the reverential game that the contending parties imagine, we are forced to sit and listen as the accusation unfolds in its bizarre extremity. Arrogant, offensive, prejudiced: this is the way the law wants it. I had almost forgotten that I was being accused of armed insurrection against the powers of the state, because the thing seemed so ridiculous to me. But I am called out of my illusion, summoned back to this sordid reality, by the voice of the assistant public prosecutor – a voice that is carefully modulated, sometimes cracked, sometimes thundering, like that of a fairground barker, in no sense worthy of this supposed sophisticated fiction of justice, but a good match for the strident tone of the accusation. A high-level accusation, sustained by lies, and one which cannot be criticized once it has been consecrated by justice. *Mama, don't cry.* The genetic processes of the sacred, which anthropologists display in the continuous process of their formation over long centuries, are here repeated in the insubstantiality of a *mise en forme* which moves so fast as to make them objects of consumption. Subordination of justice to the temporal rhythms of fashion, of superficial communication, of low-grade information? Almost. Certainly, subordination to the timescales of the mass media. But it becomes evident that this is immediately false and almost scurrile when differing forms of awareness, people and forces intersect. Hence the accusation has to heighten even more – in the face of this slight durability and relative inertia of the mass media – its own position of institutional overdetermination. The result is an uncertain equilibrium – between pre-constituted and inertial authority on the one hand and, on the other, the abyss of ridiculousness and implausibility to which the media are constrained at the end of their arc of efficacy. I am living the pre-eminence of the accusation with this intellectual suspicion. I wait for it to burn down like a match, until it burns the fingers of the person holding it. I have the impression that, were it not for the servility of the journalists, we would very soon see the efficacity of this machine reduced to nothingness. But it is amazing to see how it works, this dirty intermeshing between institutional pre-eminence and the owners of the media. Now I am in prison. I am writing – I have drunk a bit of wine, and one of the Bach cello concertos is restoring calm to the evening – a very strong wind is blowing outside and the prison is extremely silent. I feel an urge to scream. I am hungry and thirsty for truth. I wish the trial were capable of expressing a possibility – just one possibility – of life. I would be prepared to gamble everything on such a margin of hope. But this is not possible. It is difficult and terrible to recognize the effectuality of an event of whose necessity you have always been theoretically aware. It is impossible, quite impossible, to alter anything here; the trial is the extension of prison, just as prison is the extension of society at large. This is the structure of the state. Of justice. A declaration of truth cannot destroy it. How solid is the inertia of power. How poor is truth. (G12 Rebibbia – 7 March)

Folio 9

The fourth, fifth and sixth days of the trial. I am tired beyond measure. But it's worth writing a word or two – on the unfairness of the rules of combat. The lawyers have been good for once. Giuliano has been on the attack, arguing that the tribunal in Rome has no competence to judge us. A lucid and passionate speech. He dismantled and deconstructed a trial logic which, in bringing us to Rome, has stitched us into the uniforms of prisoners for life. For a moment I am breathing better, a lot better. Tommaso, with sharp intelligence and his experience in civil law, homed in on the problem of the extraditions and showed how some of the *pentiti* will not even be able to appear in court, and how the charges against us are based on cheap horsetrading. Then Beniamino, Pino and the others. The overall process of the trial has been attacked, the charges have been taken apart, and the whole set-up can be seen for the unbelievable ludicrous thing it is. What good will it do us? None. But at least we are showing the unfairness of the trial proceedings – the arrests based on mere pretexts, the insane logic of the *pentiti*, the overriding of proper territorial jurisdictions, the illegality of the procedures, etc.

And behind all that: the special prisons, the isolation, the brutal interrogations, the never-ending preventive imprisonment. What will we get out of it? Nothing. But the iniquity of Italy's trial processes does not apply only to us – it is an intrinsic part of the whole legal system. As in Aesop's fable, there is no point in the lamb bleating its innocence before the wolf. Increasingly we are discovering that, from our side, the only possible course of action is to fight this hopeless situation to the bitter end, not with any expectation of obtaining justice, because that is impossible, but in order to contribute what we can to breaking and transforming this machine of oppression. This is not a question of justice but of politics pure and simple. For the moment the main difficulty is being able to handle it physically. An enormous tiredness has come over me. The machinery of the trial, at this level of political abstraction and bellicose crudeness, crushes you. During four years of imprisonment I have found ways of building a personal physiological rhythm, a kind of intellectual and physical microclimate. My prison years have accentuated, almost like a defence instinct in a wild animal, the inner presence of a sense of intelligence, of a force of love. But now I am hurled into the storm, and sometimes I find myself losing my bearings. A kind of physical enervation gets the upper hand. I only hope that within this different, changing rhythm of life the bodily dimension of intelligence will help me to survive and will increase, in spite of tiredness, my intuition of the movements of the enemy machine. (G12 Rebibbia – 8/9/10 March)

Folio 10

On the outside (in prison 'outside' means 'the world'). On the outside, then, the crisis is raging. This week's elections in France and Germany have seen a consolidation of the forces of the Right. Monetary chaos. The European Monetary System is wobbling. American pressures – the dollar continues its headlong rush – capitalism command shows the same irrational arrogance as our judges – I imagine them wishing that they could be paid in dollars at least! The big capitalists seem to have entirely recovered from the blowback of last year (1982, the fateful date, the closing of the cycle initiated with the unlinking of the dollar from gold in 1971, and the oil crisis of 1973 . . . remember all that), when the refusal by Mexico and Brazil to pay their international debts revealed the irreversibility of the level of struggles in the countries of the third world. Then everyone was trembling. And they are still trembling. Entirely possible that Reagan will become a

Keynesian. We need to study and pay attention . . . Europe is the one who risks paying a heavy price. The movement seems to have disappeared – if it existed now, in its movement towards transformation, it would have come and surrounded our prison. I look at things with alarm. *Erkenntnistheorie*: praise of the absence of memory. But, that said, one still has to count on deep strata of composition. On ontology. Everyone pretends not to know what the term means, but everyone knows the meaning of this solid resistance, which configures structures and possibilities of regulation. However, there is no sign of a politics, a new politics, entering the arena. What will be produced by these new, irreducible and irreversible layers of awareness of one's social class? The only serious new force appears to be the German 'greens'. On our side, the fact that we have to live our hopes of getting out of prison in the absence of a movement is difficult to handle – it suggests that the situation outside is dramatic and very heavy. It was from that point – from the moment when terror extinguished the movement and the state internalized its barbarities – that the 'Years of Lead' began. Not just for us, but for everyone. Chaos has penetrated into the structure of the state. Who could have foreseen such a massive turnaround even just a few years ago?

Clashes between the Consiglio Superiore della Magistratera [Upper Council of the Magistracy] (supported by the President of the Republic) and the Procura di Roma [Prosecutor's Office in Rome]. Our good Gallucci is at last in the eye of the cyclone – I remember him, wily, vulgar, damp with sweat, in the days when he was accusing me of being the killer of Aldo Moro. I wish him a visitation by the good old punitive Olympian gods of classical theology. Maybe Luciano is right when he says that one day we shall see the bodies of our enemies floating past on the great river of history. Our days pass in a state of hysteria. Rossana is writing an apocalyptic letter: the timings of a solution to the institutional problem are speeding up, new constitutional equilibria of forces are in the making. I don't think so: it will always be the same old Italian shit. They've shouted too much about an Italian *coup d'état* which never came, but which in fact is happening all the time. Paola keeps me informed about the business of my standing as a candidate for the Radical Party – this was offered to me a year ago. It's not clear what prospects such a project might offer. I don't expect much to come of it – but I am not giving up hope either. This transit across institutions as a way of gaining freedom and of continuing the fight feels very much like Lenin's train journey to Finland. I have always been a firm believer in these kinds of tactical transitions.

Now, these transit possibilities are gathering with decisive intensity, they are punching holes in the fabric of this deep-seated crisis: 'For all that I find myself in "financial distress", not since 1849 have I felt so cosy as in this "outbreak".' I wouldn't go along with Marx in defining our present crisis as 'marvellous' – but what is certain is that, things being as they are, and given the Years of Lead that we are living, this degeneration of the political forms of the mediation of power, together with the revelation of the decisive contradictions within the system, constitute my – our – only possibility of gaining our freedom. I am tired, but I am heartened by the crisis into which these honourable gentlemen are falling. In the trial we are achieving nothing: all we can hope to obtain – and that may turn out to be precious little – will be won by coming out and attacking at the political level.

Important to stress the crisis – the emptiness of the capitalist response, its inability to touch on the substance of the crisis, and finally the fact that both the inability to pose the problem of a political solution to the Years of Lead and the possibility that someone will begin to confront the problem – both are based in this degradation.

This ambiguity is very deep and insoluble. For them. All that we need to do is make intelligent use of their dirty crisis. Outside, outside the prison, in the world – that's where the solution lies, the only possible solution. If not a solution brought by our movement, it will at least be woven by our healthy political realism. Finland's train needs to get under way. For all the difficulties. Go on . . . on your way . . . (G12 Rebibbia – 13 March)

Folio 11

The seventh and eighth day of the trial: now they are rolling out in a rhythm which becomes evermore ritualistic. The disproportion between the contending parties and the unfairness of the game are becoming ever more obvious. Alberto is very good at putting forward procedural objections and points of order – in volleys, one after the other. Hearing him speak, it really does not seem possible that the trial can stand up on such foundations – but that is what will happen, and we all know it. The machine grinds and crunches. Then Giangi and the others raised their own procedural objections. Finally, in the last couple of days, the state lawyers and the civil parties have also had their say. A real Brechtian lesson in the workings of the law – a few technical–formal quibbles, the odd reference to articles of law, and insistent reference to decisions by the Supreme Court – and then the fundamental argument: the law is our law, the procedures are our procedures, just as we are the only ones able to draw their conclusions. An enormous arrogance, combined with a mafiotic sense of power and of how it works. Law reveals itself to be what Benedetto Croce, phenomenologist and unashamed apologist of his class, claimed that it should be: on the one hand, a technical instrument of command; on the other, an ethical means of social ordering geared to the requirements of the parties in society who exercise command. The function defines the organ. It is certain that the administration *chez nous* has become somehow reconciled to this general conception and to a practice that derives from it. The crudeness of its ways of proceeding is ethically legitimated, and the method can even endow itself with a certain finesse in sustaining the violence of its rulings. The shortcomings of my ability to understand the enemy have never been as great as they are in this case. I have underestimated power's capacity to adapt its force and its inertia to the vulgarity of the actors – I have underestimated the cunning agility which governs the tactics of the big institutions. I have never grasped very well the movements of the python. It would take a sensuous, feminine logic, to rearticulate the violence of the antagonism – if one is to understand these crossings of power. An acid logic, capable of dissolving, like the oily violence of the family, this bitumen of the juridical institution. I try and try again. I do not succeed – I cannot bring myself to accept that the truth of our protest is not going to be recognized and that the hard and damnable violence of the court procedures is going to package all the injustices committed into one bundle, preparing them for a tacit reabsorption within the trial. A certain intellectual extremism is in play in my protest – but instead I should be more sensitive, more astute, more sensuous. More feminine. Sylvie comes to mind – the way she makes use of intelligence, of a powerful critique based in women's liberation, of a subtle understanding of both fact and concept – first she takes it on board, accepts it, understands it, almost caressingly, and then, having taken it in, she dismembers it and dissolves it – in order to destroy the appearance of any consolidated figure of power. Using these parameters of understanding, one could construct a critique of cynical reason – after all, what else is it, if not cynicism, this instrumental conception of the law, a conception articulated to the arrogance of power? (at the moment I am reading Peter Sloterdijk on the subject). I wish you were here with us, Sylvie, in these days of the trial, helping me to resolve my anger into a critical understanding. I wish you could be here to understand how irony and disillusionment can feed a great passion for justice. And to destroy this baleful situation – of a tacit and normative subjection, and of a domination which is so strong as to express itself as logic. To learn how feminine wisdom might free us from all homology with what has started to happen in that courtroom of injustice: the building, or rather the rebuilding, of an instrumental apparatus in relation to truth, a claim to knowledge which develops by assuming power as its criterion – this is truly masculine, even before being juridical, despotic, capitalist! I wish you could be here, as you have been during many of the days of my imprisonment, to explain to me how I should not accept their plan of conflict and of destruction – but that only an independence founded on love and on intelligent sensibility can enable us to survive, to seek liberty, to reconquer freedom. To exclude the knowledge which is based on power, together with any other cognitive or institutional function that makes of power the reason of its own legitimacy. To seek knowledge, in feminine manner, in love and in the practice of a critical dissolving of the ties of dependence. But, really, what is there left for me to do in this trial? (G12 Rebibbia – 17–18 March)

Folio 12

Power for them is a thing – their thing. They have a taste for practising it, sharing it, imposing it – a physical taste. This manipulability is for them corporeal. Like with a woman. And for that reason every woman becomes a whore in their hands. Today Montanelli has published in *Giornale nuovo* – which is exemplary as a medium for the communication of power, as an alcove where things are manipulated – he has published an interview with me. It is accompanied by a commentary just as boorish and cynical as it is good-natured – against preventive detention. Thus my protest was banalized on this last margin: that of the territory of the polemic about civil liberties. This is what is bound to happen in the coming months – one can see this clearly by now. Given the impossibility of upholding this monstrous disgrace which is known as the 7 April case, they will try to save form by feeding the polemic against the enormity of preventive detention. For them this represents a weak point – and we ourselves have too easily accepted to be used, and to use this terrain. In this way we have become a kind of appendage to other concerns. In this Gomorrah of the law, with the refined manners of a ladykiller [*donnaiolo*], Montanelli knows that a little present has to be given to the prostitute every once in a while. What continues to amaze me, in this reality I am living, is his vulgarity. Men in power feel the thing in which they participate as if it were their own. Solidly so. Sometimes power is given a metaphysical (albeit vague and malodorous) reading, but in this instance the commodity fetishism is never anything other than sordid.

The intellectual, who is extraneous to power, is often brought to apply to it an imagination which, even in combating it, in some respects exalts it. No, what we are living is not a drama of metaphysics – but a very painful banality, a poverty of ideas and ethics. In the world of the thing. One time power might have meant slave hunts, or the piratical capturing of riches – drunkenness of war, or capitalist voracity – but here, for us, in our trial and in its surroundings, it is only a corrupt representation of the thing. Buñuel. Law has lost all contradictoriness with the real – it preconstitutes it. It is not a repressive force, but the function of a reality that is repressed – a symptom of the thing. For this reason, when all is said and done, I can find even Montanelli likeable [*simpatico*] because, being aware of all this, he often plays out this vulgarity with a quizzical look. This is the sympathy that relieves you of the bare brutality of the executioner. How many brutes have I seen – sometimes policemen and prison guards – with the same sympathetic sensibility as our Indro . . . (G12 Rebibbia – 20 March)

Folio 13

Today, while listening to Tarsitano as he was raising points of order (today, the ninth day of the trial, late in the evening all our procedural points were rejected, and our requests for freedom – brought up again this morning by Luciano, in a fine and proud exposition – were completely ignored) . . . – today, as I say, I reviewed the entire political hinterland of this trial. The words of Tarsitano really did weigh like rocks. Rocks piled up against us, rocks which the history of the working-class movement is going to have to shift out of the way – because they obstruct the path of any possibility of critical thinking and renewal. Tarsitano, a small-time functionary of the Italian Communist Party, a modest lawyer, a great frequenter of courtrooms, and the prompter and mentor of the infamous Fioroni – an acid political religiosity, a resentful behaviour, a seeker of revenge. I knew him years ago, when, as a representative of the party, he was hanging around the movement. Now he has turned his back on all that, and has renegued. A cowardly breed! So, when did this whole affair begin? How many years have passed now? Four, five . . . Of imprisonment for me, and of political defeat for them. At the time, they – the PCI – imagined that they were on the brink of coming to power. We continued to hate power. So then they decided to embark on this big repressive operation which was represented by 7 April. And they betrayed every duty of bearing witness to the truth, every duty of defending liberty. The Calogero theorem, and the emergency laws between 7 April and 21 December 1979, which were its practical consequence, were the fruit of an intense hatred, of a Jacobinism turned upside down, towards defending reaction – of the illusion that it could put an end to it through an uncontainable history of Italian proletarian struggles and that it could use other means to penetrate into the Palace – which they imagined to be rich and at the disposal of their corresponding vices. Political stupidity went hand in hand with the betrayal of principles. The outcome was a lurid liberticidal operation. The path of the movement was blocked by thousands of arrests, and with this any political dialectic and any hope of transformation were closed. Today Tarsitano is here, and he holds forth in legalistic jargon about our imprisonment – in contraposition, precisely, to his defeat and that of his party in the general collapse of the conditions of freedom and struggle. Procedure is, in terms of the trial, an ambiguous material; in an event of such long duration and complexity as ours, it makes it possible – in fact it makes it necessary – to retrace the whole historical genesis of the thing. Especially when things begin to loosen up and the contradictions can be seen for what they are. So now we witness the disintegration of the character and of the climate of ideas in which he was created: Tarsitano has lost the security of the first years of the trial, when, with holy fury, he was feeding lies to the first *pentiti* and granting them freedom. Little is left now of that Stalinist pride. Only a dark resentment. He even resorts to the weapons of prudence every now and then – but the words fail him: a paranoiac delirium, immediately corrected as if it were some kind of mental lapse. In reality he is a man destroyed, a scoundrel who has repented, a former generosity that has been perverted and is now incapable of recycling itself rationally. Little by little, as the words fly around the tired courtroom, I too become tired, and I let myself drift off into imaginings. I recall the sectarian simple-mindedness with which these gentlemen thought that they had things in the bag and could manipulate power. And then the long sleep of reason in which they were caught up – incapable as they were of understanding how power, real power, making use of the spaces of juridical illegality and of the political stereotypes offered, transferred repression from the vanguards to the struggles – right into the heart of the working-class neighbourhoods and the factories. I remember the hatred that used to pour out of the so-called communist press. I remember the hired witnesses [*testimoni prezzolati*] in the Federation. But then I also warn that infamy does not pay and that bad politics, like bad paper money, drives out the good. I remember the number of people who tore up their party cards, the crisis of the party's rank and file organisers, the landslide electoral defeat and the senility of the leadership. And how all this put an end to the incredible history of Italian-style communism – a singular and heroic phenomenon, destroyed by stupidity and betrayal. So here we have Tarsitano, standing in front of me, still talking – a pitiful symbol of a situation of which, when all is said and done, he too is a victim. Let us liberate ourselves from all this, from these utterly base representations of a tragedy that has run its course. It is not in the trial, but in political struggle that perhaps we have a possibility, maybe our last chance, to rebuild a terrain of renewal. In the tiredness of the evening I try to discuss this again with the comrades. (G12 Rebibbia – 21 March)

Folio 14

The comrades. Today the cross-examinations began. Cecco was the first to be examined – strong and dignified in standing by his experiences of 1968 and Potere Operaio. I see them go up one by one onto that damned stand, under the spotlights, after so many years lived in common. The comrades. This evening we had supper together – eight of us – the prison rules allow it – all of us from 7 April. I look at my comrades with the sweetness that these years of brotherhood permit me. Every evening we have a strong discussion – always the pleasure of life has the upper hand over the discomforts of prison – the pleasure of life, of discussion, of searching. They are all abstract, these comrades – not at all because they don't have passions and a powerful humanity, but because they enjoy the abstraction of concepts. They are all intellectuals, in the best sense of the word and of the reality it expresses. Real figures of intelligence. If they were not that way in the beginning, they were obliged to become so – and they have enjoyed the discovery. As characters they are very strong – with a taste for polemic, for individual contradiction, even for exotericism, hysteria and strangeness – and all this builds a community. A community which succeeds in being efficacious, both internally and in relation to the rest of the world, to the extent that it is abstract, reasoning and conceptual. The paradox of our existence together as a community is extreme. The community becomes stronger the more abstract it becomes, the more it is political in the sense that this term defines a real mediation of vocations and potentialities. *Politik als Beruf.* What crazy happenstance created the situation which has brought about this communitarian possibility within the randomness of the myriad options of the prosecution? We are the fruits of this case. The '7 April' case is a most fortuitous combination of possibilities, an improvised gathering together of individuals – but we have transformed the case, turning it into a potentiality. A Lucretian paradox, this – in the fall of the atoms we have determined the communitarian *clinamen.* With my mind I caress the minds of each of the comrades in front of me. A Platonic symposium. I know that I couldn't lean over and stroke anyone's belly even if I wanted to – the sexual discipline is rigid among us. But I love them more than physically.

This transformation of the abstract into the more potent concrete is what characterizes our community. And this is what destroys prison. When I look at this community of men, and at that society, judgemental or delirious, which we have before us, then I laugh with joy. The abstraction of thought becomes a humorous distraction. I toy with the idea of swapping roles in the trial – of putting the defendants in the place of the prosecutors. Emilio as the president of the court – he would have the ability – but through humanity, only humanity – to make Severino confess. Franco as the prosecuting counsel – he would put Marini to shame, he would show the bizarre irrationality of all the mechanisms of the prosecution. In my screenplay Luciano would be a state lawyer – but from a democratic state: he would argue for the right to opposition, and, with a fair share of irony, he would propose even the absolution of Abbate and Tarsitano. Paolo P. and Chicco would be journalists. They would take the trial for what it is – a farce; but if even so much as a moment of truth were to appear, they would argue that it is an element of sincerity. Security services would be furnished by Oreste and Arrigo: the whole business would become so sportive that the disciplinary origins of sport, or the sportive and ritual origins of justice, would come completely to the fore, and prison could consequently be replaced by a sports field. Paolo V. would have the role of a lawyer. He argues for the possible as a place of subversion. (He remains a dangerous individual, even in a communist regime, because he is so materialist that he risks becoming Leopardian – tell me, Paolo, where does the verification of the concrete stop?) And so on. But leaving aside games, tonight we actually did it, at table. Marione was drawing, and is still drawing. There's something else in play. There is this incredible radicality of the reversal of values, of the separateness of our being. At this point an intelligent enemy, someone like Judge Sica, could protest: 'The Mafia are like that too.' It's true – but it is not absolutely true. Maybe we have mafia ways of behaving, just as institutions do, and well done to anyone who is capable of making formal distinctions – *Benedetto dixit*. It is not true without qualification, because the joy of the abstract is what triumphs with us. What joy there is in the abstract!

Abelard and Eloise. An abstract sensuality. A game which is more real than reality. A bureaucratic ritual reversed. A bureaucracy of charisma? Max Weber would spin in his grave. Go ahead and suffer, prophet of misfortune. Here something else is being played out: in prison, a prime example of a leadership group, capable of struggle, capable of antagonism, in the period of the real subsumption of the society of the state. In the cellar of the Palace we have perhaps invented, all by ourselves, the way to be free, enterprising and rationally inventive. But in the Palace *quand même*. This is the basis for our possibility of liberty – in the overturning of cynicism, in an overturning which has all the disenchantment of cynicism but functions in positive mode. Formidable desires for justice, equality and liberty. Gemisthius Pletho between Mistra and Florence. *Erasmus victor*. An ancient moment which prefigures and constructs the ontology of the present. Renaissance. This community of comrades has prepared, in poverty, what awaits it in the richness of victory, in the joy of liberation, in the enthusiasm of winning once again and of transformation. How I love my comrades! (G12 Rebibbia – 24 March)

Folio 15

I am ill. A bit of a fever. I spend the day studying. I am reading Leopardi. I have been working on him for a while now and he fascinates me. There are curious analogies between our personal situations – imprisonment in Recanati and the omnipresent wretchedness of the Italian provinces; also between our historical situations – the defeat of the revolution, the disaggregation and the lack in Italy of any centre of cultural production; and at the level of our metaphysical crisis – in solitude only the poetic voice makes it possible to live an ethical tragedy that is so fully under way; and all this constitutes itself into a desire for flight – this is the continuous dimension of Leopardi's poetry. I too would like to flee, and on the ashes of

Jacobinism live the heroism of a new positive proposition of liberty, building a weapon against the inertia of the system that oppresses me. I read left-wing interpretations – Luporini, Binni – no, he is not really a progressive but a libertarian in flight. Leopardi builds on disenchantment with progress and on the joy of liberation. These poor Leopardian progressives!

Those interpretations collapse into an inability to grasp the materialistic dimension of the flight – neither in aestheticism nor in utopia, then, but towards an infinity of possible worlds. In Leopardi, time dominates the poetic discourse and configures itself into this inexhaustible spiralling between the infiniteness of voice and of hope, and the return of a life bounded by sterility and historic defeat. A dialectical tension, a breaking of the useless indefinite rebounding of imagination and reality one against the other, impotently. This Leopardian voice builds alterity – a new possibility of existence. In catastrophe, thinking becomes bifurcated and the originary possibility of being proposes itself.

In crisis, the will to flee represents a reconstruction of the world. In prison I have worked a lot: I have written *Il comunismo e la guerra*, *Macchina-tempo*, *L'anomalia selvaggia* and *Pipeline*. All this has been a continuous meditation on dualism and on the end of dialectics – in short, on the possibility of twisting the separate human and proletarian condition into a constitution of liberty – of an 'other' liberty. Leopardi comes towards me at this extreme edge of the tragedy of the ethical and of the desire to overcome it. He comes towards me rendering the voice corporeal, materialist, constitutive – poetics, praxis, destroying the ontology of thought and working instead on that of practical being, playing it out on the temporal margin of the world – to return to the terms of Agamben's very fine book. I think about the trial again, about the extreme tension of the theoretical model it represents – an inert machine of repression, powerful inasmuch as it is deadly, and against it a heroism which can only constitute itself in flight, in alterity, in the proud independence of disenchanted reason and hope. Yes, Leopardi. (G12 Rebibbia – 26 March)

Folio 16

I am reading a photographic documentation of the struggles of young people in Germany against the building of the *Startbahn-West*. In the old nature, facing ranks of police transformed into angels of evil, a new nature – strong and generous – is moving, capable of bringing together resistance to the destruction of old values and construction of new values in the community. I enjoy looking at these photographs. Particularly when I take account of the fact that these struggles have been able to produce mediations and political force within and against the institutions. In Italy, that generation, which in Germany led the struggles, has been destroyed by repression and by terrorism. Here there is a void, a deep void – chilling. But for how long can this political condition stop the rebuilding of a revolutionary movement here too? I am not able to make forecasts – nevertheless I project onto this terrain of analysis a few of the ontological hypotheses that are dear to me. That urgency which I feel in people's consciousnesses, that urgency for an 'other' life, full of possibilities, that new ethics – it seems to me that these things cannot be built other than collectively. I am not able to make forecasts – I can't say how this will happen – for sure the rebuilding dynamic will be transversal, and it will insist essentially on the singularities of the movements – and the contents will be those of a distribution of wealth which refuses the logic and fetishism of commodity exchange. But who can add other elements of forecasting which will not function as forces of disaggregation and of impoverishment towards this subject, which is in the process of formation? Towards this rebuilding, which is innovation? Every now and then I receive letters from comrades on the outside, or from comrades who have been released from prison and are rebuilding a *rapport* with reality – and I note, albeit in the lack of concrete indications of struggle, the reappearance of a great enthusiasm to know and understand. Not yet committed in practical terms. In Italy, struggles like those against *Startbahn-West* have not yet been seen. Here the nascent movements, and most particularly the peace movement, have to be on their guard against the vultures – whose long shadows take life wherever they are reflected. Vultures, bureaucrats and parasites. They have shattered and buried the continuity of the movement and they have insulted and repressed its separateness. Now, in parasitic and hypocritical ways, they try to rebuild it, as a movement for peace, as a council movement [*movimento dei consigli*], in order to dominate it. Of this at least I am sure: they will not succeed. But what a huge waste of energies – thrown into passivity, while in the rest of Europe the new subjects of liberation are going through their apprenticeship. In our trial we need to succeed in arguing for this separateness. But perhaps this way of being is so internal to ourselves, so much our own, that anyway the adversary senses it – takes it as a characteristic sign of our existence. Nevertheless I would like to be in the woodlands of the *Startbahn-West* and I would like to be with my comrades – in the fullness of a political relationship of revolutionary reconstruction. Today more than ever I experience as an affront the bars, the prison, the never-ending cages of this mutilated existence. (G12 Rebibbia – 27 March)

Folio 17

Borromeo – the first *pentito* in the trial. Day eleven. We're plucking daisy petals – will he sing, won't he sing, will he, won't he . . . An absurd encounter/clash with the president of the court. Santiapichi asks for freedom as the price – meanwhile, just to give him a reminder, they had arrested him again. Nothing is explained. Borromeo tries to be clever, with that stupid air of his. Like [the buffoon] Bertoldo. He simply repeats the text of his interrogation. With obstinate, pedantic, bookkeeping attention. Word for word. He makes the court angry, and everyone else too. In this respect of not going beyond the initial ambiguity of the first interrogations, of sticking instead with that ambiguity, he drives everyone crazy. He remains cold, dumb, speaking in a monotone. It seems to me that, in his not particularly athletic consciousness, something approaching a drama may be unfolding – does he want perhaps to redeem himself morally? It is amusing to see someone who has sold out making an effort to regain human and social dignity. Certainly, with respect to the days of 1979, something must have changed on the outside too – in public opinion, infamy is once again being seen as infamy. However, for the moment not much seems to have changed. Apart from the shouting of the president, the scene in court is silent. The other prosecutors also dig around, but they can't get the spider out of his hole. The whole thing is ridiculous. Santiapichi is ridiculous, egged on by the unspeakable Abbate, trying to get to people's secrets and promising favours in return. As for the civil parties, they are extremely timid and nervous about getting their fingers burned. It is obvious that they don't trust each other. Not to mention the stupid yapping Public Prosecutor. The whole stage setting is ridiculous too. It's like a fortress in some Tartar desert. Now the court as such no longer exists – the public is no longer admitted, so the scenario consists solely of the mass media. Excited TV journalists, quantities of newspaper journalists, endless numbers of politicians, swarms of lawyers – the *pentito* has arrived – and all of them crowding into the courtroom. A great illusion. And, behind it all, an empty void. The court management system and the security checks have the effect of preventing the attendance of the public. Now, however, as often happens, the court's stage management is spinning in a vacuum. Borromeo continues to build on this vacuum. He admits very vaguely the existence of secret groupings in Milan. But he resists provocations and denies the existence of other levels of organization, unknown to him. Over and over again, to the point of becoming boring, he says he knows nothing about specifics. I intervene myself, denouncing the flattening logic of the proceedings (ten years conflated into a single breath), and the atemporal and theoremic form of the accusation and of the questions put to the defendants.

Major brouhaha. Court suspended. Franco comments: when the going gets tough, the tough get going. Maybe he's right, maybe he's wrong. I prefer the 'soft' approach. Then Borromeo finishes. A pitiful end. Boring and bitter. He has maintained a level of reticence throughout, tirelessly sticking to his guns. A reticence that is stupid and useless. Why not say the truth – why not tell what the movement really was? Opocher comes to mind, my good old teacher. The time of truth in a trial, the time of the crime, and the time of its trial-based ascertainment, he used to say, become one – the historical time of the fact can and must be subsumed within the time of judgement, to immobility and fixity, to abstract contemplation.

But is this really possible, my good old teacher? Here we have lived five years, ten years of struggles, of transformation of the real. How is one to verify this transformation? Inside that cage, faced with this infamy, I am like a caged animal. Ten years – my life, and the lives of others, the change. Here the machine is functioning like a forced rewind of the imaginary. The present imaginary is back-projected onto a past that is passed and gone. These translations of values not only betray/modify that reality, they actually reinvent it. What we have here is a reduction of the facts to the image of a crime – it is, precisely, only the image which creates the criminal fact, and which furthermore deprives it of all historicity. Certainly the image could lift the fact out of the brutality of the event; but, on the other hand, in our case it requalifies the event as brutal. No – no possibility remains of translating the event into image – the image of the present. Rather, one could examine and unfold the history of the present, cruel and stupid as it is: the imaginary of the judges. So, then, this so-called trial is simply a con trick. The contemplation and reconstruction of the fact have already been decided, in advance, and *against* the fact. Borromeo does not know this, but he suspects it. He senses the enormity of the thing. An emotional *pentito*, a good *pentito*. He is scared that the evil he is doing is going to rebound on him. He is scared that his falsity is definitively going to destroy him. A good *pentito* = the ghost of a man. (G12 Rebibbia – 28 March)

Folio 18

Day twelve. Nothing worth talking about. The tedious Borromeo continues. Personalities involved in this trial – that would be something worth talking about. Giuliano, my lawyer. I love him dearly. What does a lawyer represent for a political prisoner? He is more than just a human point of reference – he is the only person who arrives continuously from the outside world, like some kind of wise extra-terrestrial, with whom you can discuss politics, with whom you can compare past and present. The world of prison and that of the trial produce this simplification of the picture: if the lawyer is intelligent, he understands and performs this role. So the defence comes to be a critical evaluation of the relationship between past and present. With Giuliano there are no problems of trial technique – only problems of reality. And these are pursued by him with analytic intelligence and total participation at the level of ideas. For Giuliano, the fact of representing a political client is not a fiction – it is an identification with the client, a transformation. But here it is not a question of 'clients' – rather it is a relationship which becomes a common creation! For Giuliano, the 7 April trial is an act of moral fidelity and intellectual honesty. He is tired and he is working like a lunatic. My confidence in him is all the greater when his attitude is critical. Giuliano is good. Today Giuliano has been cross-examining, hitting at the core of the matter, uncovering the untruths and the omissions in the *pentito*'s account of things . . . There's shouting from the back of the courtroom – in the Tartar desert of the court a young DIGOS officer intimated to Paola Negri that she needs to behave more respectfully in court. I think Paola had her feet up on the bench in front of her. Poor little DIGOS, trying to give a disciplinary ticking-off to such a power of nature! Paola, you sweetest of creatures, why do you still rebel so noisily against this normative idiocy of power? For years and years you have known the humiliations and cruelties of prison guards – you have seen a lot worse than this – so just ignore the stupidity of the DIGOS – indignation does not pay in this society of slaves. But I know that you don't care about that donkey – what irritated you was just the rude interruption of your concentration. Concentration on me, and on the comrades, and on the trial proceedings. A love which has become an attentiveness, an attentiveness that is organized around a whirlpool of generosity, around a poetics of justice. Without Paola, without her smile filled with light and without her extraordinary strength I don't know how I would have survived all these years. She has travelled like a nomad, for days and days, for nights and nights . . . She came to find me wherever I was, without a pretence of serenity but with a powerful passion, with sincerity, wherever the prison authorities sent me – in that southern panorama of prisons which is a thousand kilometres from our northern cities. Every week, for four years. We have discussed politics, we have argued, she has given me advice, she has comforted me – and at the same time she has raised our children and she has gone out to work. But an enormous emotional feeling about the unacceptable injustice suffered has kept her close to me during these long years – and at the same time a passion that activates her intelligence – indeed a unique key to her seductiveness and to our relationship. An intelligence which never rests, which gets fired up in seeking and tracking down every possibility, every patch of blue sky. A sensibility which is sometimes fractious – because a proud intelligence accepts only a relationship of equality. Then, alternatingly, enthusiasms, depressions, reflections, normality in performing extraordinary duties. In short, have you ever wished for a perfect creature who is woman–lover, intellectual and mother? We have become adept, during the absurdity of prison visits, at saying many things to each other in few words – almost ciphers, which only a profound discipline succeeds in turning into discourses, indications of signals. A chronometric coincidence of pulsings. This is what it must be like in the world of nature.

In the courtroom today I know that she is there at the back, feeling, like me, the brutality of this whole affair – like me, she is irreligiously intolerant of the emptiness of ritual. And she sends the hapless DIGOS to take a running jump. Then Paola comes to visit me in prison, for forty minutes, like always, to discuss things that need to be done and problems that need to be solved. Difficulties, hopes. What is a wife? What is love? (G12 Rebibbia – 29 March)

Folio 19

In *Il Manifesto* today there's an article about the trial, written by Rossana. Basically she says: raise your sights, otherwise this trial is not going to lift off. Impose the political content that the court is trying to conceal, otherwise the trial is good for nothing. And she is right. She is right in her analysis of the tiredness, of the low profile of the trial as it has proceeded thus far, with its procedural quibbles and so on: small ridiculous stories of disorganized squabbling group-uscules, little stories which not even the pharaonic projections of the prosecution manage to render as anything other than banal. But she is also right from another point of view. Only by giving politics a central role in the trial, only by producing a strong political sub-jectivity, can the prosecution's game-plan be broken. We have to be capable of producing a mechanism opposed to that which has been set in motion by the prosecution. In the first place, it has captured, whether really or falsely it doesn't matter, a subversive movement – that of the 1970s and, by that act of enforcement which institutes power, it has made it into a show trial designed to exhibit the crime and to restore law and order. However, this aspect has to be con-cealed. The arbitrary nature of the operation must be veiled, and this is the second moment of the operation. And it is for this reason that the court, with such abiding hypocrisy, keeps separate the moment of ascertaining the truth and that of applying the law – it cannot afford to let it be seen that the repressive and normative dimension weighs so heavily on the formation and unfolding of this trial. This hypocrisy then rebounds on the defendants, who are obliged to engage in the ascertainment of the truth as if it were an operation of logic. (The cynicism of reducing to logic the ascertainment of the truth is the religion of judges – the habitual bastard rationalism which fancies itself as a modern behaviour! My God, just look at the harm that has been done by the formalist schools – the likes of Kelsen and Bobbio! See how they have polished up cynicism! Barbaric judge-ment would be preferable.) Then, in the third place, there is penal judgement – nothing scientific here – the science of penology is a kind of philosophy of universal analogy, or rather a kind of statistics – the nature of the judgement is based after all on the free synthesis which the conviction of the judge operates on the result of ascertaining the truth, in the face of a normative structure which he pre-selects with equal freedom . . . The subjective and political element of the trial is so very central and exhaustive that, were it not for the dramatic nature of the sentencing function, one could almost reduce the penal judgement to a ludic structure. Instead it is a lurid structure, performing dishonestly, always being so subjective as to constitute a tragedy in itself – a tragedy of abandonment to arbitrariness and of destructuration of the subject and of events. So what might it mean to produce an operation opposed to that which is conducted by power? It means unmasking the political redundancy of the moment of formation, or of the moment of ascertainment, or of the function of judgement – and counterposing to them another set of standards. Restructuring the real, where the judgement tries to destructure it. Destructuring the political judgement of the adversary and structuring the truth of the struggle. The trial becomes political – and not only on the side of the prosecution – when the political nature of the subjects transforms itself into the production of an alternative set of normative standards – when the synthesis involved in the trial can no longer develop on the vertical axis of one single set of standards, but is compelled to come to terms with a different set of standards. The so-called 'dialectics of the trial' [*dialettica processuale*] has to be transformed into antagonism. Antagonism of values, of stories, of life. Social self-valorization against juridical cynicism. So: does this bring us back to the guerrilla trial? Absolutely not. That has been defeated, and correctly defeated, because it was unintelligent, because it did not counter with alternative sets of standards, but simply tried to oppose different and counterposed powers. The lack of intelligence stemmed from utopianism, sectarianism and illusion. Here, on the contrary, we have to unmask the repressive dimension in the formation of the trial and reconstruct, in an alternative and politically pregnant way, the truth of our history and of our movement. And finally we have to counterpose a project of open and alternative justice, capable of destroying the political freedom of the judge and of his own arbitrary subjectivity, and strong and explicit in its declaration of the justice of our struggle. It is here and only here that we shall be able to establish another profile for the trial, from our own point of view. However, that said, I should also add a note: we have to criticize the civil liberties [*garantismo*] approach, which we have adopted thus far. This approach does not view the trial as a political terrain in which two separate sets of standards measure up against each other – rather it distinguishes authority from law and asks authority to use the law correctly. But is not this trial of ours (and probably all trials, whether political or not) characterized by an initial determined political intermixing of authority and law? So what sense does the civil rights argument make? (G12 Rebibbia – 1–2 April)

Folio 20

Very strange and horrible images characterize the world on the outside – all very postmodern. From today's newspapers: Reagan is talking of setting up gigantic laser umbrellas to protect the United States . . . In the Persian Gulf, during the course of the dirty Iran–Iraq war, there have been bombings of coastal oil wells, which resulted in an ecological disaster, and the sea is full of oil . . . These events de-nature the world. The enormity of it all is terrifying. And yet there is no difference from the de-naturing produced by an event like the 7 April trial, in the horrible systemic machinations that have created it and continue to feed it. It is a devastation of consciousnesses which is accompanied by a blunting of the sense of justice. The extreme character of the infamy and cruelty generates indifference. We live the indifference of others, of everyone. Thus the scenario becomes completely flat. The trial is certainly overdetermined by a political will, the trial is certainly qualified within a rigid transcendency of relations of power – but this is not enough to specify the real singularity it has. Its paradoxical singularity consists in the fact that the catastrophic diminution of justice which it represents is not perceived as a radical change for the worse, but as normality. An Arctic night – without seasons, without transformations. A world without light. (G12 Rebibbia – 3 April)

Folio 21

There is a ferocious attack on us in the Roman pages of *L'Unità*. A whole page of insults and reactionary opinions about how social peace is threatened by the very existence of the 7 April trial. Today, once again, there is alarming news of the possible closure of *Il Manifesto*, the only newspaper to have given our case front-page treatment. And today comes the news that, because they are centralized and operate at the national level, the radical radio stations are to be closed, by authority of the ministry. Then they talk about combating monopoly! This and other news is enough for me to characterize the dead superficiality of this wretched country of ours, in a scenario which recalls the unanimous consensuses of 1936 – the moment of triumph of a scabrous regime of illiberality. A party (which likes to call itself communist) is engaged, as if this were a battle of life or death, in the construction of repressive, fevered notions and fantasies within which to bring about its own political legitimation – and on the other hand the few voices that are still free – such as *Il Manifesto* and the radical radio stations – are being throttled. Why is it that the end of a republic, of the great passions which contributed to its formation and of the great struggles which bedecked its development has to offer a spectacle of such a fearsome inversion and distortion of values? The process of decay has certainly been continuous in recent years – progressively, corruption has undermined all values and every institution, and the repression of liberty has touched every sector and all social subjects. But why does this advance of the sickness not find, finally, at least some small hiccup of self-awareness and urgency of renewal? The sick body passively accepts its metastases and accepts to be reproduced in them. Those of us who are suffering in person the extreme consequences of this disaggregation would almost have cause to be cynically and sarcastically amused. But that's not the way it is, because our lives are on the line here. Life, life, life. (G12 Rebibbia – 5 April)

PS The article that follows was written up by Paolo V. on the basis of a collective discussion. It was published in *Il Manifesto*, 20 and 22 February 1983.

Do You Remember Revolution?

[Original text signed by Lucio Castellano, Arrigo Cavallina, Giustino Cortiana, Mario Dalmaviva, Luciano Ferrari Bravo, Chicco Funaro, Toni Negri, Paolo Pozzi, Franco Tommei, Emilio Vesce and Paolo Virno. Rebibbia Prison, Rome, January 1983]

Looking back once again to re-examine, with intellect and memory, the movement of the 1970s, we are certain of at least one thing. The history of the revolutionary movement, first of the extra-parliamentary opposition and then of the autonomy [*autonomia*], was not a history of marginals, fringe eccentricity or sectarian hallucinations from some underground ghetto. We think that it is justified to claim that this history (part of which has now become the subject of our trial) is inextricably woven into the history of the country, into the decisive changes and into the break-points that have characterized it.

Holding firmly to this point of view (which might seem banal, but which is bold and even provocative in these times we inhabit), we want to propose a historical–political bloc of theses on the past decade, which go beyond our own immediate defence concerns in the trial. The considerations that follow, often in the form of simply posing problems, are not addressed to the judges – who thus far have only been interested in the merchandizing of *pentiti* – but to all those who have been involved in the struggles of these years. To the comrades of '68, to those of '77; to those intellectuals who have 'dissented' (as we now say), judging rebellion to be rational. So that they may intervene in their turn to break the vicious circle of memory distortion and conformity. We think that the time has come for a realistic reappraisal of the historical truth of the 1970s. Against the pentiti we need truth. After and against the pentiti we need political judgement. An overall assumption of responsibility is today both possible and necessary. This is one of the functional steps towards the full affirmation of 'post-terrorism' as a dimension proper to the confrontation between the new movements and the institutions.

That we have nothing in common with terrorism is obvious. That we have been 'subversive' is equally obvious. Between these two truths lies the key issue at stake in our trials. But nothing can be taken for granted. The determination of the judges to equate subversion with terrorism is known to all, and it is intense. We shall conduct our defence battle with appropriate technical and political means. But it would be wrong for this reconstruction of the '70s to take place only in the courtroom of the Foro Italico. There needs to be a frank and wider debate in the movement, in parallel with the trial, among the social subjects who have been the real protagonists of the 'great transformation'. Among other things, or above all, this is a vitally necessary condition if we are to speak adequately of the tensions facing us in the '80s.

1

The specific characteristic of the 'Italian '68' was a combination of innovative and explosive social phenomena – in many ways typical of situations of mature industrialization – and the classic paradigm of communist political revolution.

The radical critique of wage labour, its refusal on a mass scale, was the main content of the movement of mass struggles, the matrix of a strong and lasting antagonism, the 'substance of things hoped for'. This gave food to the contestation of roles and hierarchies; to the struggle for wage egalitarianism; to the attack on the organization of social knowledge; to qualitative demands for changes in everyday life – in short, to the general striving towards concrete forms of freedom.

In other countries of the capitalist West (Germany and the USA for example), these same forces of transformation were developed in the form of molecular changes in social relations, without directly and immediately posing the problem of political power, of an alternative running of the state. In France and Italy, owing to institutional rigidities and to a very simplified way of regulating conflicts, the question of state power and of its 'seizure' immediately becomes central.

In Italy especially, despite the fact that in many ways '68 marked a sharp break with the labourist and state socialist traditions of the historical working-class movement, the classical political models of communism still found a real space in the new movements. The extreme polarization of the class confrontation and the lack of any real political mediation or adequate response at an institutional level (on the one hand, the 'internal commissions', and on the other, before the emergence of local bodies, an overcentralized structure) create a situation where the demand for a higher income and new spaces for freedom go hand in hand with the classic Leninist question of 'smashing the state machine'.

2

Between 1968 and the early 1970s the problem of finding a political outcome for the mass struggles was on the agenda of the entire Left, both old and new.

The Italian Communist Party [PCI] and the unions on the one hand, the extra-parliamentary groups on the other were counting on a drastic change in the balance of power, one which would carry through and consolidate the change in the relations of force that had already occurred in the factories and in the labour market. Regarding the nature and the quality of this political solution – generally held to be both decisive and necessary – there was a long and tortuous battle for hegemony within the Left.

The revolutionary groups, which had a majority presence in the schools and in the universities and also had roots in the factories and in the service industries, realized that the recent movement for social transformation coincided with a marked breakdown of the framework of legality that had hitherto existed. They emphasized this aspect of the situation, in order to prevent any institutional recovery of profit margins and capitalist command. The extension of the struggles to the entire metropolitan territory and the building of forms of counter-power were seen as necessary steps in resisting the blackmail of the economic crisis. The PCI and the unions, on the other hand, realized that '68 would lead naturally to the break-up of the centre-left government and to 'structural reforms'. A new 'framework of compatibility' and a more complex and articulated institutional mediation would, in their view, guarantee a kind of working-class protagonism in the relaunching of economic growth.

The most bitter polemics and divisions took place between the extra-parliamentary organizations and the historic Left. At the same time, however, the battles of ideas for defining the outcome of the movement also traversed these two political arenas horizontally. One need only recall, for instance, the Amendola [PCI right wing] criticism of the Turin FLM and against the 'new unionism' of the movement. Or the different – and often very different – interpretations which the components of the unitary trade union made of the nascent 'zone councils'. At the same time, within the far Left, there were the differences between the workerist current and the Marxist–Leninist organizations.

However, as we have said, these divisions of orientation revolved around a single basic problem: how to translate into terms of political power the upheaval in social relations that had developed in the period after '68.

3

In the early 1970s the extra-parliamentary Left imposed the problem of the use of force, of violence, in terms that were completely coherent with the classical communist tradition: in other words considering it to be one of the means necessary for any attack on the terrain of power.

There was no fetishism of the use of violence. On the contrary, it was strictly subordinated to the advancement of the mass movement. At the same time there was a clear acceptance of its relevance. The dense fabric of mass conflicts throughout society undeniably posed the question of political power in clearly discontinuous terms: it had a specific, non-linear character. After the violent clashes in Avola, Corso Traiano [in Turin] and Battipaglia, the 'state monopoly on the use of force' appeared as an unavoidable obstacle, which had to be systematically confronted.

Thus, from a programmatic perspective, the violent breaking of the law was conceived of in offensive terms, as the manifestation of a new counter-power. Slogans such as 'Take over the City' or 'Insurrection' captured this perspective, which was seen as being inescapable, if not immediate.

On the other hand, from a concrete perspective, organization in terms of illegality was a modest enough affair, with exclusively defensive and contingent goals: the defence of pickets, of housing occupations, of demonstrations; security measures intended to prevent possible right-wing reaction (which was no longer excluded as a possibility after Piazza Fontana [bombing provocation in Milan, December 1969]).

In short, there was a theory of attack and rupture, developed out of the intermeshing between communist culture and the 'new political subject' who emerged after '68; but its practical manifestations were minimal. It remains nevertheless a fact that, after the 'Red Years' of '68–9, for thousands of militants – including rank-and-file trade union cadres – getting equipped for the 'illegal' domain, for instance by debating in public the forms and timings of the confrontation with the repressive structures of the state, was completely a matter of commonsense discourse.

4

In those years the role of the first clandestine armed organizations – the GAP, and the Red Brigader [BR] – was completely marginal and extraneous to the general thematics of the movement.

Clandestine organization, the obsessive appeal to the partisan tradition [of the Resistance], the reference to the 'skilled' worker – these had absolutely nothing in common with the organization of violence on the part of class vanguards and revolutionary groups.

The GAP, taking as its reference point the old anti-fascist resistance and the Communist Party tradition of 'dual level' organizing (mass and clandestine), which dated back to the '50s, was proposing the adoption of preventive measures against what it saw as the imminent threat of a fascist coup. On the other hand, all throughout this early phase, the BR – which were formed from a confluence of Marxist–Leninists from Trento, ex-Communist Party members from Milan and ex-Communist Youth Federation personnel from Emilia – looked for support and contacts among the PCI rank and file, and not in the revolutionary movement. Anti-fascism and 'armed struggle in support of reforms' was how they labeled their operations.

Paradoxically, it was precisely the adoption, on the part of the communist vanguard, of a perspective on struggle which still included illegality and violence that gave an absolute and unbridgeable character to the gap between this perspective and the strategic option of clandestinity and 'armed struggle'. The sporadic contacts that existed between the groupuscules and the first armed organizations did not lessen but actually confirmed the irreconcilability of culture and political line between them.

5

In 1973–4 the political context within which the movement had developed for years began to disintegrate. Within a short period of time there were multiple ruptures of continuity in the movement, changes of political perspectives and behaviours, and changes in the very conditions of social conflict itself. These abrupt changes were due to a number of concomitant and interacting factors. The first was the PCI's change of policy towards the closure of political space at the international level, which it now saw as necessitating an immediate and urgent 'political breakthrough' of the given situation.

This led to a split, which became increasingly deep, within a line-up of political and social forces that had up to this time, in spite of internal differences, shared the common goal of finding, after '68, an alternative terrain of power, which would reflect the radical content of the mass struggles and their transformative content. A part of the Left (the PCI and their trade union confederation) now began to draw closer to the possibility of government and became opposed to wide sectors of the movement.

The extra-parliamentary oppositions now had to redefine themselves in relation to the PCI's '[Historic] Compromise'. This redefinition led to a crisis and a progressive loss of identity for the groups. In fact the struggle for hegemony on the part of the Left, which had to some extent justi-fied the existence of [revolutionary] 'groups', now seemed to have been resolved unilaterally, in a way that shut down and separated alternative perspectives and put an end to dialectics. From now on, the old question of 'finding a political breakthrough', an alternative management of the state, was to be identified with the moderating politics of the PCI. Those extra-parliamentary organizations that still followed this perspective were forced to try to go along with the PCI and to influence the outcome of the '[Historic] Compromise', setting up its extremist version (we recall the presentation of 'revolutionary' lists in the 1975 administrative [local] elections and in the 1976 political [national] elections). Other groups found instead that they had reached the limits of their own experience. Sooner or later they found no alternative but to dissolve themselves.

6

Secondly, as a result of the [union–employer] contracts of '73–4, the central figure behind the struggles – the assembly-line worker of the major factories, the mass worker – began to lose his offensive role for class recomposition. The restructuration of large-scale enterprises was beginning to take its toll.

The increasing use of lay-offs [*cassa integrazione*] and the first, partial changes in technology and work organization fundamentally altered the modes of production and blunted the thrust of preceding forms of strug-gle, including the mass strike. The homogeneity of the shop floor and its capacity to exercise power on the overall process of production were undercut by new machinery, systems of control, and the restructuring of the working day. The representative functions of the new 'Factory Councils', and hence the dialectic between left and right within them, had a paralysing effect on the unity and autonomy which had underlain the preceding struggles.

Not that the power of the line worker (the 'mass worker') was weak-ened by any reserve army or competition from the unemployed in the traditional sense. The point is that industrial reconversion tended towards investment in sectors outside the sphere of mass production. This brought other sectors of labour-power, which had been relatively marginal – such as women, youths, highly educated new strata and so on – to a central position in social production as a whole. These new strata had less history of organization behind them. Increasingly now the terrain of confronta-tion was shifting towards the overall mechanisms of the labour market, with public expenditure, with the reproduction of the proletariat and of young people, and in general with the distribution of incomes which are independent from remuneration for work.

7

In the third place, a change occurred along the internal dimension of the subjectivity of the movement, of its 'culture' and horizon of development. In a nutshell: a rejection was taking place of the entire tradition of the working-class movement, of the very idea of 'seizing power' with the classic goal of a 'dictatorship of the proletariat', of residual fantasies about 'the real socialism' [in eastern Europe], and of any project of management.

As for the links that had existed within the post-'68 movement between new qualitative goals and the old model of communist revolution, these were now totally broken. Power was now seen as an alien and inimical force, something to defend oneself against, but not something worth 'conquering' or 'taking over' – rather worth reducing and keeping at a distance. The key to this new outlook was the affirmation of the movement itself as an alternative society, as a richness of communication, of free productive capacities, of forms of life. To conquer and to control its own 'spaces' – this is becoming the dominant form of practice for the new 'social subjects', for whom wage labour is no longer the principal terrain of socialization but pure and simple 'episode', contingency and non-value.

The feminist movement, with its practices of community and separatism, with its critique of politics and power, with its deep mistrust of any institutional and 'general' representation of needs and desires, and with its love of differences, is emblematic for this new phase. It provided the inspiration, whether explicitly or not, for the new movements of the proletarian youth of the mid-'70s. The referendum on divorce [1974] is a very important indication of this tendency towards the 'autonomy of the social'.

From this point on, it becomes impossible to speak of a 'family album' – be it even a family in crisis! The new mass subjectivity is totally alien to the official labour movement. Their respective languages and objectives no longer have any common ground. The very category of 'extremism' no longer explains anything; it merely confuses things. One can only be an 'extremist' in relation to something similar; but it is precisely this 'similarity' that is disappearing fast. *Those who look for continuity, who care for a 'family album' can only turn to the separate and sectarian existence of the Marxist–Leninist 'combatant organizations'.*

8

All these three factors in the turning point which occurred between '73 and '75, but especially the last one, contributed to the birth of 'the workers' autonomy' [*l'autonomia operaia*].

The autonomy is formed against the project of the [Historic] 'Compromise', in response to the crisis and failure of the groups, apart from 'workerism', interacting conflictually with the restructuring of production. But above all it expresses the new subjectivity, the richness of its multiple differences, its being a stranger to formal politics and to the mechanisms of political representation. It does not seek a 'political breakthrough' but embodies a concrete and articulated exercise of power within society.

In this sense, localism is one of the defining characteristics of the autonomous experience. Rejecting any prospect of a possible alternative running of the state meant that there could be no centralized leadership of the movement. Each regional area of the autonomy follows its own concrete particularities of class composition, without seeing them as a limitation, but as its *raison d'être*. It is therefore practically impossible to reconstruct a unitary history of the *autonomia* movements between Rome and Milan, or between the Veneto and the south.

9

From '74 to '76, the practice of mass illegality and violence becomes more intensified and diffuse. But this phenomenon, unknown in the preceding period, has no overall 'anti-state' objective behind it. It is not a preparation for any 'revolutionary' rupture. This is the main point. In a metropolis, violence develops as a function of the need for an immediate satisfaction of needs, the conquest of 'spaces' that could be autonomously controlled – and largely in response to cuts in public spending.

In '74 the self-reduction of transport fares, organized by the unions in Turin, relaunched mass illegality, already experimented with, particularly during rent strikes. From now on, almost everywhere, and in relation to the whole range of public services, this special form of guaranteed income was widely put into practice. While the unions had intended this self-reduction to be a symbolic gesture, the movement transformed it into a generalized, material form of struggle.

But, more than self-reduction, it was above all the occupation of housing in San Basilio [Rome], in October 1974 that marked a turning point: a high level of spontaneous 'militarization' by the proletariat as a defensive mass response to bloody police aggression. A further step for the movement was the big Milan demonstrations in the spring of 1975, following the killings of Varalli and Zibecchi by fascists and policemen.

Violent street confrontations were the point of departure for a whole series of struggles against the government's economic 'austerity' measures – the first steps in the so-called 'politics of sacrifice'. Throughout '75 and '76 we experienced the transition – in many ways 'classic' in the history of welfare struggles – from self-reduction to appropriation; from a defensive behaviour in the face of continuous increases in prices and bills to an offensive practice of the collective satisfaction of needs, which aims to overturn the mechanisms of the crisis.

Appropriation – the best example of which was the night of the New York blackout – concerns all aspects of metropolitan life: free 'political shopping' and occupation of premises for free associative activities; the 'serene habit' of the young proletariat of not paying for the ticket at the cinema or concert; overtime bans; the lengthening of rest periods in factories. Above all, it represents the appropriation of 'life time', liberation from the constraints of factory command and a search for a new community.

10

By the mid-1970s, two distinct tendencies towards the extensive reproduction of violence had become apparent. These may be approximately defined as two different paths in the 'militarization of the movement'. The first path was the movement of outright resistance to the restructuring of production in the large and medium-sized enterprises.

Here the protagonists were numerous worker militants, formed politically in the period 1968–73, who were determined to defend at all costs the material basis on which their contractual strength had depended. Restructuring was lived as a political catastrophe. Above all, those factory militants who were most involved in the experience of the factory councils tended to identify restructuring with defeat; this was confirmed by repeated union sell-outs on work conditions. To preserve the factory as it was, in order to maintain a favourable relation of forces – this was the core of their position.

It was around this set of problems and among the personnel of this political/trade union base that the Red Brigades – [in their second phase] from '74– 75 – found support and were able to take root.

11

The second area of illegality, in many ways diametrically opposed to the first, was made up of those 'social subjects' who were the result of restructuring, of decentralization of production and of mobility; an absence of guarantees, of precarious part-time work, of fragmented forms of income and of the immediate impact of the overall territorial and social organization of capitalist command.

This new proletarian figure, emerging from the process of restructuring, violently confronted local governments and the administration of income transfers and fought for the self-determination of the working day. This second type of illegality, which we can more or less identify with the autonomous movement, was never an organic project. It was distinguished by the total fit between the form of struggle chosen and the attainment of its given objectives. This involved the absence of separate 'structures' or 'functions' specialized in the use of force.

Unless we accept 'Pasolinism' as an ultimate category of sociological understanding, it is impossible to deny that the diffuse violence of the movement in these years was a necessary process of self-identification and affirmation of a new and powerful productive subject, born out of the decline of the centrality of the factory and exposed to the massive pressure of the economic crisis.

12

The movement that exploded in '77, in its essentials, expressed this new class composition and was by no means a phenomenon of marginalized strata.

The 'second society' [Asor Rosa, PCI cultural spokesperson], this new class composition was already becoming a 'first society' from the point of view of its productive capacity, its technical–scientific intelligence and its advanced forms of social cooperation. The new social subjects reflected or anticipated in their struggles the growing identity between new productive processes and activities of communication – in short, the new reality of the computerized factory and the advanced tertiary sector.

The movement [of '77] was itself a richly productive force, independent and antagonistic. The critique of wage labour now took an affirmative direction, creatively asserting itself in the form of 'self-organized entrepreneurship' and in the partial running from below the mechanisms of the welfare system. This 'second society', which was centre stage in '77, was 'asymmetrical' in its relation to state power. No longer was there a frontal confrontation; rather there was a sidestepping or, in practical terms, a search for spaces of freedom and income in which the movement could consolidate and grow. This 'asymmetrical' state was a precious fact, and one which testified to the solidity of the social processes underlying it. But it needed time. Time and mediation. Time and negotiation.

13

However, the restoring operation of the Historic Compromise denied time or space to the movement and re-proposed a symmetrical relation of opposition between the struggles and the state.

The movement found itself subjected to a frightening process of acceleration, blocked in its potential articulation, in a total absence of margins of mediation. This was quite different from the process in other European countries, most obviously in the case of Germany, where the repressive operation was accompanied by forms of bargaining with the mass movements, and hence did not directly attack their reproduction. In the [Italian] 'Historic Compromise', the repressive net was cast exceedingly widely; legitimacy was denied to any forces developing outside of, and opposed to, the new corporative regulation of conflict. The repressive intention in Italy developed a generality that was aimed directly against spontaneous social forces. Thus it happened that the systematic adoption of political–military provisions by the government reintroduced 'exogenously' the necessity of general political struggle, often purely and simply as a 'struggle for survival', while it marginalized and ghettoized the emancipatory practices of the movement and its dense positivity at the level of quality of life and of the direct satisfaction of needs.

14

The organized autonomy movement [autonomia] found itself caught between ghettoization and direct confrontation with the state. Its 'schizophrenia' and its subsequent defeat can be traced to the attempt to close this space by securing a relationship between the rich social network of the movement on the one hand and, on the other, its own need to confront the state.

Within the space of a few months, this attempt proved to be quite impossible and failed on both fronts. The unprecedented acceleration of '77 caused the organized autonomy slowly to lose contact with those social subjects who pulled out of traditional political struggle and followed their own various solutions – at times 'individualist', at times of 'co-management' – in order to work less, live better, and maintain their own spaces for freely creative production. this same 'acceleration' led the autonomous organizations to break off relations with those militaristic drives which, being present within the autonomy movement itself, soon became a separate tendency pushing for the formation of armed organizations. At that point the autonomy movement discounted all the political weaknesses of its own political–cultural model, concentrating on the linear growth of the movement, on its continual expansion and radicalization. Struggles were often read by the autonomy as a negation of all political mediation rather than as a basis upon which political mediation could operate. Immediate antagonism was counterposed to any dialogue, any 'negotiation' and any 'use' of the institutions.

15

From the end of 1977 and throughout 1978 there was a growth and multiplication of formations operating at a specifically military level, while the crisis of the organized autonomy became more acute.

Many saw in the equation 'political struggle = armed struggle' the only adequate response to the trap in which the movement had been caught by the politics of the Historic Compromise. In a first phase – in a scenario repeated many times – numbers of militants within the movement made the so-called 'leap' from endemic violence to armed struggle, yet conceived of this choice and its heavy obligations as an 'articulation' of the movement's struggles, as the creation of a kind of 'servicing structure'. But a form of organization specifically geared to armed action revealed itself to be structurally lacking in homogeneity with the practices of the movement. Sooner or later, it could only go its own separate way. Thus the numerous 'combatant organizations' that proliferated in the period 1977–8 ended up either resembling the model of the Red Brigades, which they had initially rejected, or even joining them. The Red Brigades, as the historic guerrilla formation engaged in a 'war against the state' which was totally separated from the dynamic of the movement, ended by growing 'parasitically', in the wake of the defeat of the mass struggles.

In Rome especially, at the end of '77, the Red Brigades made a large-scale recruitment from the ranks of the movement, which was in deep crisis. During that year the autonomy had come up against all its own limitations, opposing state militarism with radical replays of street confrontations, which produced a dispersion of the movement's potential instead of consolidating it. The repressive straitjacket, and the real errors of the autonomists in Rome and some other areas, opened the way for the expansion of the Red Brigades. This organization, which had criticized harshly the struggles of 1977, was now, paradoxically, gathering remarkable fruits in terms of reinforcing its organization.

16

The defeat of the movement of '77 began with the kidnapping and killing of Aldo Moro in March–May 1978. In a kind of tragic parody of the way the official Left had operated in the mid-1970s, the Red Brigades similarly pursued their own separate 'political breakthrough' at the expense of currents of resistance in society at large.

The 'culture' of the Red Brigades – with its people's courts, prisons, prisoners and trials, and its practice of the 'armed fraction', totally within the logic of an autonomy of the political, were played against the new subjects of social antagonism as much as against the institutions and the state.

With the Moro operation the unity of the movement was definitively broken. A twilight zone of drifting began, which was characterized by frontal attacks launched by the autonomy on the Red Brigades and by the withdrawal of large sectors of youth and the proletariat from political struggle. The 'emergency', so loudly proclaimed by the state and by the PCI, was lashing out in the dark or, rather, tended to select its victims from among people known as 'subversives' and in the public view, who were used as scapegoats in a generalized witch-hunt. In the circumstances, the autonomy found itself facing a violent attack, beginning with a purge in the factories of the north. Thus the 'autonomous collectives' in factories were lambasted as pro-terrorist by the trade unions and by the PCI, and were weeded out and denounced. And when, in the very days of the Moro kidnap, the autonomists were launching a struggle at Alfa Romeo against working on Saturdays, they were branded by the historical Left in a militaristic, demonizing, 'anti-terrorist' campaign. Thus began the process of expulsion from the factories of the new generation of vanguard militants – a process which reached its climax with the mass sackings of sixty-one key militants at FIAT in the autumn of 1979.

17

After the Moro operation, in the desolate landscape of a militarized civil society, the state and the Red Brigades faced each other like opposite reflections in the same mirror.

The Red Brigades rapidly went down that irreversible path whereby the armed struggle became 'terrorism' in the true sense of the word. Their campaign of annihilation began. Police, judges, magistrates, factory managers, trade unionists were killed only on account of their 'function' – as the pentiti have subsequently revealed.

Moreover, the wave of arrests [rastrellamenti] against the movement of autonomy, in '79, eliminated the only political network which was in a position to fight against the logic of terrorism. Thus, between '79 and '81, the Red Brigades were for the first time able to recruit militants not only from the minor 'combatant organizations', but also directly from a scarcely politicized youth, whose discontent and anger were now deprived of any political and programmatic mediation.

18

As a mass phenomenon, the pentiti are only the other side, equally militaristic and equally horrible, of the terrorist coin.

The phenomenon of pentitismo [system of remission for state informers, set up by law in December 1979] is an extreme version of terrorism, its pavlovian 'conditioned reflex', the ultimate proof of its total abstraction and alienation from the fabric of the movement. The incompatibility between the 'armed struggle' and the new social subject is revealed in a distorted, horrendous way by these acts of verbal merchandizing.

Pentitismo is a 'logic of annihilation' of the whole judicial framework, an indiscriminate vendetta, a celebration of the absence of historical memory – precisely when it sets in operation, in a perverse and manipulated way, an individual 'memory'. The *pentiti* are false even when they tell the 'truth'. They unify what is divided, they abolish real motivations and context, they recall effects without causes, they establish hypothetical links, they interpret according to various theorems. *Pentitismo* is terrorism introjected into the institutions. There will be no post-terrorism without a parallel overcoming of the culture of *pentimento*.

19

The sharp, definitive defeat of the political organizations of the movement, at the end of the '70s, in no sense coincided with a defeat of the new political and productive subject, who has made his 'general test' in the eruption of '77.

This new social subject has carried out a long march in the workplace, in the organization of social knowledge, in the 'alternative economy', in local services and administrative apparatuses. This subject has proliferated by keeping close to the ground and avoiding any direct political confrontation, manoeuvering between the underground ghetto and institutional deals, between separateness and co-management. Although under pressure and often forced into passivity, this underground movement today constitutes – even more than in the past – the unresolved core of the Italian crisis.

The rearticulation of the working day; the pressure on public spending; the questions of protection of the environment and choice of technologies; the crisis of the party system; and the problem of finding new constitutional formulae of government – behind all these questions, the density of the mass subject, with her multiple demands for income, freedom and peace, remains intact.

20

Now, after the Historic Compromise and in the post-terrorist situation, the same question of '77 returns on the agenda: how to open spaces of mediation, which can allow the movements to express themselves and grow.

Struggles and political mediation; and negotiation at the institutional level. This prospect, here as well as in Germany, is rendered both possible and necessary not by the timidity and backwardness of the social conflict, but by the extreme maturity of its contents.

We have to pick up and develop the thread of '77 against the militarism of the state and against any tendency to relaunch the 'armed struggle' (there is no 'good' version of it, no alternative to the practices in Third International style á la Red Brigades: all versions end by being antithetical to the new movements). A productive force [*potenza*], both individual and collective, is placed outside of and against wage labour. The state is going to have to take this phenomenon into account, including in its administrative and econometric calculations. This *potenza* can be at one and the same time separate, antagonistic, and capable of seeking and finding its own mediations.

Folio 22

'Do you remember revolution?' Personally I have no difficulty in remembering it, and in keeping alive my hopes for it. But all this makes me so angry! Why? The tainted consciousness of the intellectuals, the 'nit-picking' of the far Left, the opportunism of the socialists, the hatred from the communists – all of this loads: the word – with suspicion, the concept – with contempt. In the trial today Luciano spoke in defence of revolution – with that lucid, impassioned and spiritually detached intelligence of his. The judges – Santiapichi and Abbate – responded provocatively, fed as they are by their conviction that they are in the right, by a sense of their role, by a mad presumption of good faith. The problem is perhaps banal: it lies in the fact that these Roman magistrates, in their isolation, really no longer know what we are talking about. Their class origins are rooted in the thin soil of the bureaucratic petty bourgeoisie, or in the arrogance of the agrarian bourgeoisie. Their culture does not extend beyond a regurgitated Croceanism. They are nervous of the new culture they see lining up before them. They respond to statements of reason with a preoccupied and foul-smelling belch of arrogance. There really is no way of discussing with them. The distance between our languages is the distance between simplicity and cynicism – our cool simplicity and their oily cynicism. This is what is not understood by the critics of our 'Do You Remember Revolution?' They don't understand that the clash, which is not beyond but right inside the struggle itself and inside the radical separation between autonomy and terrorism, has been a clash between two cultures: on the one hand the simplicity of needs; on the other, the world of politics. For the world of politics you can read state and terrorism – two sides of the same coin, monstrous figures of political alienation. On that clash, on that

separation, you then have the people saying 'Yes, but . . .'. Enough!
Come and listen to Luciano in court and you will understand the full
enormity of this provocation, this bastardization, this falsification.
It is on this terrain that all the misunderstandings accumulate. We,
for example, refer to ourselves as being 'dissociated' – but power has
tried to taint this word by making it equivalent to '*pentito*' or 'spy'.
Power understands that behind our dissociation from terrorism lies a
call for revolution and behind our reassertion of our identity, which
is irreducible to that of terrorism, lies a continuous desire for communism. Lucio, with some force and with a measure of hysteria, puts
all this out in the open again. And the response is provocation; what
comes back is stupidity and vulgarity. They are unable to understand
what is being talked about. They understand that it is about something inimical to them, which they are incapable of absorbing. You're
good, Lucio – in the way you have established a high profile for this
political battle, which we absolutely have to sustain. And win? That's
another problem – we all know that today it is impossible to win.
(G12 Rebibbia – 7–8 April)

Folio 23

I spend the day reading fresh transcripts of witness statements.
Today the statements of the latest wave of *pentiti* arrived. Bettini,
Virzo, Marocco, Coniglio. They are terrible in their dogged acceptance of the theorems and in their cold repetition of what has been
dictated to them by the public prosecutors. They try to lend credibility to the prosecution's most fantastical fabrications. But this is
not the problem – we shall be able to destroy the material content
of these allegations in court. The problem is rather the one raised by
this generation of *pentiti*. Why? Why this haemorrhage? One thing
is certain in this whole debate: the *pentito* is a character who breaks
with group loyalty and with the values that constitute his group, and
he makes this break not so much at the moral level (which would
be completely irrelevant, or at least secondary in terms of juridical
effects), as at the juridical level. He has to accuse if he is to be valued
as a *pentito*. And the more people he accuses, the more people he
sends to the gallows, the closer he comes to his own freedom. Thus
the fact of being a *pentito* becomes essentially a kind of barter. Today
I am trying to make the effort, in my own mind, to overcome the
contempt, the disgust and the infinite moral repulsion that all this
awakens in me and to understand it, if possible, *sine ira et studio*. So

there are two actors in this reduction of law to a bartering operation: on the one hand the judge and the juridical system, and, on the other, the *pentito* and the system of regulation of social loyalty. It seems to me that the juridical practice of *pentimento* obeys the conditions of balance of the social market only if it is considered as a relationship between the judge and the *pentito*, not if it is evaluated as one between the juridical system and the social system. To explain what I mean: it seems to me obvious that barter is taking the place of the rule of law [*diritto*] (which was once abstract, general and so on), and that this is happening increasingly and to such an extent that it is becoming the operational principle of the juridical system, albeit in the more sophisticated forms of contract, exchange and negotiation. This is how corporate entities react nowadays: their rigidities are such that a regulating mode can only be constructed through temporary sets of standards and conventions of barter. From this point of view, the phenomenon of *pentimento*/barter is one that fits this flat society, where there can be no transcendence of law, but only juridical procedures of transaction. However, we have here an explosive contradiction, because this way of proceeding, of barter through *individualization*, negates the substantial purpose of a postmodern contractual system of law. Such purposes come to be identified through the need of regulating the relationship between rigidities that are *collective*. The new contractual system of law has collective means and purposes; it is another name for social collective regulation. In the legislation on *pentimento*, on the other hand, the rules of the new system of law become banalized and reduced to individual acts of trading. Instead of a legal interplay of powers and counter-powers, we have what is effectively a practice of selling indulgences. Juridical reformism gives itself away by introducing norms for individual favours, and the judges who apply these norms thus place themselves on a terrain of fraud – in relation to the dynamism and the new teleology of their own system of rules. *Sine ira et studio*: in consequence, the indecency of the *pentitismo*-based and bandit-style system of crimes and penalties resides essentially in the gap between the new normativity, of a collective contract and regulation, and old, individualistic mercantile contents. As a system it is doubly barbaric, because on the one hand it destroys the old system of law, which could engage directly with individuals insofar as its normativity was general and abstract; on the other, it destroys the possibility of building a new system of law on a base of rules that match the circumstances, of administrative proceduralization, of engagement of the individual – *but only in the relationship between collective entities*. In this sense the juridical system contradicts or, even worse, sets itself up against the system of social loyalties. In doing this, the judge who constructs the *pentito* (in the sense of landing him with this juridical label and of recognizing him as such) is also carrying out an immoral operation, insofar as he frees him from those bonds of group loyalty which the law should, on the contrary, assume to be the foundation of its strength during the present phase of transformation. That said, it should be added that the judges have a field day: like drug dealers, they are performing an act of immorality – but it's clear that the drug-addict wants it. And that brings us to the subjective problem of the *pentimento*. Why this haemorrhage of *pentiti*? For the moment, just one point. In almost all cases, the *pentito* (assuming that he is not just some small-time turn-coat) belongs to the fringes of the movement. His participation in the political group was determined more by an evaluation concern-ing the efficacy of its fire-power and the relevance of his action for the conquest of power than by his adherence to a collective project of transformation. In other words, in the great majority of cases, the terrorist/*pentito* is part of the traditional political family – and not of the new breed of revolutionary subjects. The cynicism of the *pentito* is homologous with that of the judges and with that of the politicians who made the laws. So why this haemorrhage of *pentiti*? It is not the fruit of the defeat of terrorism – it is the fruit of the victory of terror-ism over the autonomous and communist wings and sectors of the movement. It is the fruit of the hegemony of terrorism, after 7 April 1979, over the whole movement. The homicidal infamy of terrorism had finally to be crowned with this judicial infamy – and on those moral and judicial homologies become the symbol of the entire moral and cultural system of power in Italy. On the other hand, this is just what one would expect: that corruption, dissolution and decadence should give each other a deformed reflection in this infamy. (G12 Rebibbia – 9 April)

Folio 24

When I think of my accusers – Santiapichi and Abbate, performing on stage in front of what is virtually a professional jury (it has already done the Moro case) and in front of Marini, seated as he is on the public prosecutor's dais – I can't avoid feeling a certain sympathy for them. Functional mediocrity of the magistracy – a poor level of culture, with strong old-style Italian resonances (Croce) and a smat-tering of reforming modernization (English law – sic!); a moderate level of politicization, with touches of sympathy for the national unanimity of the Historic Compromise and with the after-effects of a history of corruption (Severino and the mafia charges from which he managed to extract himself); a touch of paranoia (Abbate and his use of the pencil: it reminds you of Humphrey Bogart playing with the marbles, rhythmic and obsessive, in his performance as the commander in *The Caine Mutiny*); a strong degree of exhibitionism; administrative coldness and bureaucratic excess; extreme ritualization, offset by posturing attitudes and the occasional sly joke – and so on. However, this is not what elicits my sympathy; rather it is the lack of freedom and of intelligence. Everything always so predictable; never any unexpected behaviour. Their legitimacy, however, is not determined by the mediocrity of their culture and intelligence – rather their legitimacy derives entirely from the machine. They are appendages of the machine – I feel sorry for them on this account. But at the same time they scare me with the inertia they represent, the inertia they must represent. I cannot forget that their apparent (and somewhat relative) having nothing to do with prison, with its sufferings and with the preventive detention that we have endured, with torture and chains and prison escorts, is indeed only in appearance. In reality they are part of the whole package – and the denial they often display in dealing with it (and the irritation, sometimes even the contempt) does nothing to diminish but actually accentuates the fact of their central role in the machine. Their bad conscience does not negate this relationship but deepens it. I am struck and terrified by the sense of irresponsibility towards the real that these premises determine. I repeat: all the more so as they are people of bad conscience. Bad conscience generates resentment. In my silent contemplation of them I find nothing to awaken feelings of trust. The more they feel guilty about their subordination to this machine, the more they load that guilt onto us. Good sense as a corrective? But what room is there for it within a machine which has already programmed life imprisonment for us? No, the heaviness, the absolute negativity of this trial situation can only be resolved by some kind of driving force that can break the inertia. They are powerless to break with it, even if they wanted to. And we ourselves can only break it through our ethical resistance and through the heroism of our understanding – by surviving, constructing our community and demystifying the machine. And then? And then? (G12 – Rebibbia – 10 April)

Folio 25

This is not a trial, it is an execution. Days of cross-examination. I'm losing track of the days – seventeen, eighteen, nineteen. Lucio has been subjected to a string of charges which came from the new *pentiti*. The trial unfolds, against him, a truth which is already formed, established and fixed. But that truth – the truth of the prosecution – does not hold up. And so the preliminary hearing [*istruttoria*] is being re-opened, according to the Public Prosecutor Marini, to show that these people are guilty anyway. We are caught in a vicious circle. Arrigo has been on the stand and has now concluded his cross-examination. He puts forward a full account of the movements and political development of '68. They don't understand what he is saying. The judges are prisoners to one history and to one language: the history of the *pentiti* and the language of the Red Brigades. The outcome is a terrible confusion, which only the stereotypes such as those of 'Red Brigaders' can simplify. When Arrigo admits to a robbery, the court goes crazy: they want him to 'confess' [be a 'repenter', '*pentito*']. Arrigo may be a repenter, but he refuses to put quotation marks around it. He refuses to speak in Red Brigades language – a language which, in its limited instrumental rationality, seems to suit the judges very well; and he also refuses to tell anything other than the truth. Furthermore, he has no inclination to colour the movement's events in dark colours; he prefers to emphasize the real tragedies of opportunism (for himself) and of infamy (for the others). The *pentito* is a liar even when he is telling the truth. His story is always instrumental and overdetermined by the pardon he is going to receive from the bosses. When they become prisoners of *pentitismo*, the judges degrade the function they should fulfil. And they are fully caught up in this degradation. In fact, when you look at judges in this trial and you consider the mediocrity of their relationship with the truth, their crude functionalism and the hypocrisy of their approach to reality, you are forced to come to the conclusion that, if they were on the other side, they would be Red Brigaders. There really is an abyss between them and us, the comrades. On our side there is intelligence and doubt, passion and playfulness, hope and pain, and above all there is the attempt, continuous and tireless, to rebuild that history, that situation, with humility and enthusiasm, and always with truth. But when will the judges ever be able to understand that our mistakes belong in the context of changes taking place in generations and generations of political militants – and in the context of a hope for communism, of which we represented the renewal? (G12 Rebibbia – 11/12/13/14 April)

Folio 26

Days twenty, twenty-one, twenty-two and twenty-three of the trial. The situation is now as follows: after four years of trial, they are about to open new pre-trial proceedings [*istruttoria*] against us. The structure is still the one created by Calogero; but this particular goatskin is not filled with good old wine but with the depositions of the *pentiti*, which are now turning up after four years. The Milan trial has entirely spilled over here. All that one can say is that the madness of Calogero finds here its long-distance executors. Building the schema in a void, using the media to create a false national consensus, convincing people of our guilt, and *then* getting other people to find the evidence for you. Incredible but true. This is not a trial, it is purely and simply the construction of an intrigue. At this stage any defence becomes impossible. What is the point of trying to contest the structure of the accusation when this structure is de facto incontestable and the evidence is supplied not only a posteriori, but after a time lapse of four, five, ten years? I am writing this after the cross-examinations of Lucio and during that of Marione. With strength and with generosity, albeit from within a state of terrible tiredness, Marione succeeds in reconstructing an 'alternative' view of our history. He presents the historical truth against which the prosecution has built its case – a history of diffuse struggles and spontaneous acts of constructing the movement, a picture of great openness, of joy of living and of need to struggle. Marione speaks of the 'party of Mirafiori'; the Public Prosecutor replies by accusing him of the fact that, out of that movement, there emerged terroristic forces and organizations. And then follows list after list of *pentiti*. For him, the link is causal and we are the devil. I admire my comrades, and also myself, for the strength that we put in resisting this unequal battle. (G12 Rebibbia – 21 April)

Folio 27

There are going to be parliamentary elections. Long discussions among the comrades about the possibility of me standing as a candidate. I see Rossana, who tells me her doubts about it. We discuss at length – I am beginning to know her better. Seeing her again, after so many years, the old polemics came to mind – in reality all of us have lost out a bit, but it remains the case that those who lost most were those who believed in a linear operation of transformation of the working-class movement in Italy. Now, the claim for the values of liberty which Rossana and her people are carrying forward – this really does seem to be a new moment of convergence of forces. Reconstruction and transformation of the working-class and communist movement? I don't know. Perhaps – the first emergence of something absolutely original. I don't believe in transfigurations. Or, rather, I believe in them only when they are a result of death. Dialectical negation, with its infinite interweavings of continuity, is only an imbroglio. That's how we talk. Rossana takes pleasure in liberty, in liberation, and hates prisons and fraudulent trials; all this brings out the old communist in her. I recognize myself in this discourse and I know that it is what has made me what I am. But alongside that I also have other feelings – which are, I think, those of the new proletarians and new social subjects: a radicalism in my love of liberty which is deeper, more desperate and more bodily. In Rossana, the notion of civil liberties and respect for a state based on law is articulated together with the communist revolution. For me, this articulation is only negative – and the history of liberty is a history of counter-powers. Rossana places more hope in this trial than I could ever place. It is curious to see how positively utopian she can be and how many very generous illusions she can carry within her. Rossana's pessimism of the intellect. Today, at the moment when the tragedy of the trial begins to come close to (and perhaps even interweaves with) the proposal of travelling through the desert of the political, I ask myself, in a state of perplexity, what on earth I have to do with all this. I sense a big distance. Rossana is a most beautiful woman. She has a smile that comforts me. Rossana has many doubts about the forms in which my electoral candidacy should be presented – and she also has many suggestions. By the end of the discussion, she is more or less in agreement with the idea that I should do it anyway – but she has many suspicions about the people and the forces who are putting me forward. Little by little I begin to feel myself trapped in a discourse which is not my own. But it is also the case that this candidacy is the only 'chance' I have of getting out of prison. And perhaps it offers the only possibility to pluck this trial out of its destructive inertia. (G12 Rebibbia – 23 April)

Folio 28

Chicco has the capacity to show the court what it means to have a movement which is 'other' and a political awareness which is 'other'. Days twenty-four and twenty-five of the trial. He does so with great intelligence and with a remarkable capacity for putting concrete flesh on historical and conceptual data, even those which are completely external to the matter in hand. His argumentation is brilliant, and his delivery reaches heights of polemical vigour. As he speaks, he brings to life all the demonstrations, struggles, alternatives, contradictions. He talks about the movement of '77 in the streets of Milan and explains how, far from arming the youth, we were creating political proposals and the organization of a political project. He shows how hopes and expectations were flowing in our circles and how the education of political sentiments and our political discourse were strong. And then the anger of the working-class neighbourhoods, and the young unemployed, and the feminist movement, and the poor intellectuals. He explains how all this appeared on the stage of struggles and was articulated into a thousand different rivulets of organization. He carries on like this at length, for two, three days of hearings. Overriding the provocations of the judges and of the prosecution, he manages to expand the picture he is describing. Chicco is a great comrade. His imagination really does address, and in human terms, a reality which is 'other', which power cannot imagine as being anything but criminal. The history of the '70s, of a dream and practice of assailing the heavens, is here presented as a moment of life and hope. The recent days have shown the enormous gap that exists between our capacity to produce truth and the court's inert expression of its unbelievable desire to repress it. There is a wall between our two languages. A wall of horror. (G12 Rebibbia – 27–28 April)

Folio 29

It becomes increasingly obvious that the only way we can get anything out of this trial is by overturning the logic which has made the whole set-up possible – a logic of persecution, the attempt to make an example of us, and the construction of a show trial in order to put a repressive closure on fifteen years of struggles. This is what 7 April symbolizes. This logic has to be overturned. We have to show that the defeat of the movement of those years was only made possible through the denaturation of the formal constitution and through a blatant use of illegality – together with the attempt to found a new material constitution: a rigid relationship between the already existing party forces. The new could not be allowed to appear on the scene, because the new was subversive. In our trial we have to show that this operation has run onto the rocks, that the irreversible has happened and cannot be undone (*factum infectum fieri nequit*), that the new has rights of citizenship in Italian democracy. Hence the solution to our trial is a political solution to a problem which is unavoidable in terms of the constitution. For this reason, in the next phase of the trial we must opt for a high profile which is entirely polit- ical – and at the same time we must open a more articulated dialogue with the institutional forces which understand the centrality of the problem we represent. We also have to build a growing relationship between the 7 April trial and the forces – both those in prison and those in the movement – who are beginning to think seriously how to change the present political situation and how to emerge from the Years of Lead. All this is difficult, damnably difficult. But that is no reason for abandoning hope. When I think what we have been able to achieve in these years, in the worst situations – the inner depths of the special prisons, or the squalid basement of this Palazzo – I think I can be allowed moments of optimism. We are moving inside contra- dictions that cannot be broken apart. Too many things in the Italian situation suggest that the liberticidal bloc of forces which wanted to promote itself as the new material constitution cannot hold up. The rise of the Socialist Party is supported not so much by the strength of the party itself as by its constitutional positioning, by its need to break the advance of the new material constitution (through the Historic Compromise and partitocracy). The 7 April trial needs to be used in this direction. In juridical terms we can get nothing out of it, but politically we can get a lot. And we should pay attention to what is happening in Europe; to the resumption of struggles in Poland; and to the actions of the German Greens. There is news today of clashes involving Solidarnosc in Warsaw. Today two German friends came to see me, and our discussion kept returning to these themes over and over again. In our struggle against this trial, the key point for regaining a historical breathing space will be a redeployment of the programmatic contents of the communist autonomy movement within the newly developing struggles in Europe. I am very hopeful – the elements of the current political conjuncture are pushing in this direction. (G12 Rebibbia – 1 May)

Folio 30

Luciano has been fantastic in court – analytic, discursive, concise and optimistic, but also bitter – he is completely caught up in it, with his lucid intelligence, his proud sense of ethics and his juridical presence of mind. We are at the twenty-seventh, twenty-eighth and twenty-ninth days of proceedings. Faced with a prosecution machine which shows the highest levels of arrogance towards him – in the complete absence of any evidence – he resists, and does so with a touch of irony. The symbolic meaning of this trial consists in our throwing off the alleged moral responsibility for terrorism. Luciano is able to demonstrate that the central moments in the development of terrorism – the killing of Moro and the killing of Tobagi – were organized against the movement – against that continuity of struggles which we protest. Luciano is pursuing an abstract line of defence, without allowing himself to be distracted from the wicked concreteness of the charges. The inconsistencies in the documentation, the whole pettifogging process in action. Oh God, how I despise them! Luciano, so incapable of bad feelings, so incapable of intrigue, is a really positive figure in this revolting scenario. A limpid retaliation. The powerful lights of the courtroom seem to pass right through his slender figure. You judges, how can you not be frightened by the transparency of his commitment? In the course of the past four years Luciano has lived the worst that the prison system had to offer – including Favignana with its revolting dungeons, before the judicial authorities became so ashamed that they decided to close it. Then the revolt at Trani. Then he had to endure the hysterical and restless meddling of the justice department, which was sending him to different prisons up and down the length of Italy. With lucidity and contemptuous silences he defends his injured humanity before these raging dogs. He is a shining example of moral resistance to the abuses of power, transformed into a knowing alterity. This game, this digging out of an alternative truth, this irreducible desire for life (even to the extent of creating imaginary representations of community in the most desperate of situations) . . . Luciano has pursued all this with rigour. And always with a smile. He has become strong – physically strong and morally invincible. The ponderous inertia of this trial and of the prison system has not affected him. His heroism smiles out. Disarmingly. He always tries to make himself understood. And to make them change discourse. His innocence shines out like a living spark from the searing hatreds of this trial. He is a Papageno of our times – it is not from ingenuousness that truth is born; only reason knows how to create nature. Luciano, how are you able to maintain your coolness and to nourish your sense of humour? How much suffering has your soul had to endure for it to have become so full of virtue? I am tired this evening, and as I think of you I find no rest. Thinking of your proud stance. And yet it is incredible to see your innocence banged up there, after four long years, against these machine men! They are prisoners of the injustice they have committed, and this in turn is what keeps us in prison. All that is left is imagination. The good imagining of finding ourselves in a movement which is rebuilding the values of liberty and community. There remains a restless spirit which will never lie down, and a new life which will spring up with fresh vigour from under the lucid control of suffering. The ferocity of these machineries of injustice will be destroyed again – I am certain of it – by our imagination, or by the renewed spiritual Luddism of our children. (G12 Rebibbia – 3/4/5 May)

Folio 31

The electoral campaign is under way. Marco P. comes to see me.

He is organizing the conference and tells me that he plans to suggest that the radicals should not field candidates for the election. I sign up. I've known Marco since forever. From the days of the UNURI student union. Then, one time, I met him by chance in the street, in Saint Germain, under the statue of Diderot, and passed him a suitcase from the Algerian *réseau*. He certainly wasn't non-violent in those days!

There's a kind of generational brotherhood between us. I admire some aspects of his politics; I am, epidermically but no less strongly, fascinated. Negatively attracted by the superficiality of his approach to problems. Big projects backed by tiny forces generate, if not the comical, then certainly an irreverent paradox. Gulliver and the Lilliputians. I enjoy listening to him. It's almost impossible to get a word in edgeways. He is very alert and tries to achieve a kind of interlocutory 'feeling' in conversation (so-called; yet it is true that, miraculously, it really is always a discussion, even when he's the only one talking). His is a Humean personality – he does not believe in the objectivity of physical and political relations except on the basis of the construction of a dialogic 'belief'; on the basis of a kind of trusting self-abandonment of his interlocutor to the power of his own imagination. He continually creates soft scenarios, making his interlocutor feel comfortably at home, and then he uses that relative ease of feelings to get his own way. Is this seduction? Sometimes he becomes a cat, in the sense that he exercises an extreme tactility of approach, of initiative, moving forward cautiously, but being ready to react instantaneously. His weak point is culture: he ventures there readily, but with an uncharacteristic timidity.

It is the only point on which he seems to seek indulgence. Otherwise he asks for commitment. He is only completely frank when he is analysing networks of political relations – then he becomes lucid and downright cynical. And you still have the sense of a very violent ambivalence. Not subtle but hard. Necessary in that environment of wolves where he has decided to conduct his battles – but this is an environment to which he also belongs, with a reformism that is structurally homogeneous with the constitutional conditions he accepts. This scares me. I can't see clearly how our political relationship can be organized. The only way I can resist his style of constructing ethics of sentiment is by applying humour and thinking of their philosophical destiny – between Hume and Berkeley: between faith in appearance as effectuality and the demystification of appearance as illusion – a real stereotype of critical thinking. I strongly reject his hard way of living the system, though. I talk about this with the comrades. They give me strength, they tell me to press on. However, Marco P. is plainly determined to push the line of electoral abstentionism. What does that mean for me? A glimmer of freedom all of a sudden extinguished? There is ambiguity here. (G12 Rebibbia – 8 May)

Folio 32

Today it's Gianni S. in court. Day thirty. 'I was tempted to become a *pentito* – in other words to make false confessions – just so as to get out of prison.'

Gianni has been inside for three and a half years. At the back of the court, and then in front of our cage, his whole family passes: brothers, sisters, nephews and nieces – one big Veneto working-class family. Gianni has absolutely nothing to do with this whole infamous story. Nothing, absolutely nothing. Not only has he been accused under a series of pretexts right from the start – but now he is being accused by a whole series of *pentiti* who come out of a particular area. It's terrible. It is pure infamy. A life has been shattered. Eaten away by a state's determination to destroy, a state which does not respect the liberty, the simple liberty, of the working class to revolt. In Gianni's case I have no difficulty in calling his treatment fascist. Purely and completely fascist. Meanwhile, in Milan, Corrado A. is on the attack. With carefully chosen words he says explicitly that 'Rosso' was never an armed organization. This position on the real nature of 'Rosso' was also evident in the outcome of the recently concluded trial in Bologna. So what are the Milan judges going to do now? Barbone has received his payment in the form of having his girlfriend released from prison, and with the promise that he himself will be freed and given a passport and all the security he wants – after the horrible crime of the killing of Tobagi; and the sole intention of all this was to prove that 'Rosso' was indeed an armed organization. This Judas, this slanderer, this agent provocateur, this fattened pig . . .

I imagine that the speech made by Corrado A. was serious, lucid and sincere. But how can one have any faith that the courts – which are the sworn enemies of the truth, organized around the small amount of power that repression grants them, and vengeful into the bargain – are capable of accepting this call to truth? I watch as Gianni is cross-examined by the court. The more obvious the juridical error becomes, the harder it is for them to extract themselves from it. Faced with the obviousness of his innocence, the judge seems to take fright. The machine has rendered him a slave. Leaving aside these executioners, the ones who are before me as I write (in the last trial they conducted, they handed out forty life sentences) – let us imagine other judges in this situation, judges actually concerned to arrive at some form of truth. How would they deal with Gianni? How could they breathe the truth of his affirmations, when they have been constructed to be pneumatic and impermeable to the outside? Gianni's anger in his self-defence is precise, concrete and pugnacious. No, there is no possibility of speaking truth here. Gianni, you are good and honest – but that just makes it all the worse for you! Enough, enough! (G12 Rebibbia – 9 May)

Folio 33

Before he goes up to take his turn in court, Emilio tells me: 'Toni, do you remember that day in '68, in front of that little factory in Padova – Peraro, wasn't it? That's where the party – but also our destiny – began. The police were there. We wanted to get through to the picketing workers. The police told us: "Stay where you are – you can't cross this point." And I crossed the police line, for the first time, with a clear awareness that I was taking a step that was irrevocable. I was tense, but I was happy to have done it. They gave way. That day, when I went through the police line, I was taken by an irresistible certainty, a certainty about the truth, a belief in the way things were going. So,' Emilio continued, 'today it's the same. I want freedom.

Once the cross-examination is over I shall start a hunger strike to highlight the problem of preventive detention. OK?'

OK, Emilio, I agree. No point in telling you that today's situation is not of the kind where such an act of mass illegality can bring about a new law; and, equally, there is no point in telling you that, on the contrary, the illegality of power extinguishes souls and hopes. No point in telling you that we are alone. That's the way you're made. You are so beautiful, the way your eyes shine when you present your testimony. A formidable animal made for struggle – and particularly when you shift from the landscapes of generality and emerge in all your singularity. In the adventure of your own life experience – a frank and solitary voice. I am tied to you by a thousand memories – what can I tell you? Sometimes we keep death close because we consider it the only source of life. On this basis, with this charge of energy, this morning you went up for your day on the stand. Severino, the court president, does not understand you – or perhaps he understands you but prefers not to. He is troubled by you and fears your power. It's a classic: your power points you up as the one responsible, in the horrifying game which these damned people are pursuing, in their theoretical schema which requires a continuity. Once again innocence is turned on its head. But innocent in relation to what? We are not innocent, we are guilty – of the truth. And yet, once again, innocence is turned on its head – because they refuse to accept the empiricism of truth and the verifiability or otherwise of the charges, the value of the law. True innocence, our innocence – innocence turned on its head, guiltiness of truth, for them. That's the way this underhand mechanism of justice works. Unless . . . unless you can succeed in overturning it, by attacking its pillars – and succeed in demonstrating its hypocrisy, and the infamous, shameful Machiavellianism of the judges, their identification with the idea of punishment, repression and deceitfulness. They are pushed out of the cave in which they live, in which the shadows of illusion construct their logic. They are pushed into the sunlight, so as to be blinded by the light. Today French Marano in Milan told the story of the killing of Tobagi and of the cruelty of Barbone. 'It took a couple of seconds.' And then Barbone, the pig, shoots again. 'Justice' – the verb – that's what they said. And you, Justice, as a noun, are you sure that you are not also a band of small-time killers? Faced with Emilio, faced with his proud defence of the truth, Justice, are you sure that you are any different from Barbone, and that your hands are not holding the same gun that killed Tobagi's quest for the truth? (G12 Rebibbia – 10 May)

Folio 34

Emilio continues his defence. A very powerful vindication of his essence as a subversive being, and then again – on the so-called facts – [one made] with sufficient uprightness, with the disenchantment of truth. Today, after three hearings (we are already into the thirty-third day – this trial seems never-ending), he finishes. He announces his hunger strike in protest against preventive imprisonment. It is a very dramatic moment. We talk. Emilio says: 'My course of action is individual. I feel it necessary to put my life on the line in order to assert the truths of this trial. I am moving forward on a terrain which must lead outwards from the truth of the trial, from the problem of my own innocence, and must extend out to the whole problem of unjust laws and repressive policies. Against preventive imprisonment and for a political solution to the Years of Lead.' There is something barbaric in what Emilio feels he is being forced into. Emilio's heroism and resistance are a practical fact. He is not satisfied with pride in our intelligence, which sustains many of us. I don't know how I can share in these decisions of his beyond a certain limit – and I feel guilty about this. Maybe Emilio is right with the physicality of the path he has chosen, with the bodily kind of witnessing he is offering. Tomorrow they will take him to the cells, that's for sure. He will have to multiply the strength of his testimony. Hunger is hard. To go on hunger strike is to eat yourself. He has to do it; we have to win. Then I become aware of the illusion of will into which I have been drawn, and I begin silently to weep. My cell comrades notice me crying and, as is our custom, they say nothing. (G12 Rebibbia – 12 May)

Folio 35

The thirty-fourth day of the trial. Silvana is defending herself like an animal at bay over the killing of Saronio. She doesn't care about any of the rest of it. But the vile slander of having kidnapped her own dear friend, a young man whom she had caressed and loved – no, not that. Those who are accusing her are animals, as are the state and its functionaries, who want to load this infamy onto her. (I am re-reading Spinoza: 'The aim of the state, I say, is not that of converting into animals men who are gifted with reason . . .') In this Saronio affair there is something at stake which is more than just the question of her innocence (and ours) – it is also the question of the institution of the killer-*pentito*. Here in Rome that means the role played by Fioroni. In Milan, in the Tobagi affair, it means Barbone. What is at issue is the barbarity of a state which has to generate infamy in order to condemn. In order to attack its adversaries politically, it has to hit them morally. The process becomes political through these meta-physical contortions of the prosecution. Today the judges amused themselves by putting on the clothing (finally, they will say among themselves) of common morality. But they are not credible after these days of purely political examination of Luciano, Chicco and Marione ('I am not concerned with politics but with the law . . .'). Today these high priests of common ethicity strike me as hypocritical bishops at the court of some king. Silvana reacts with that Lombard sense of innocence and sincerity which must also have characterized those tortured at the Colonna Infame [Column of Infamy]. In her generosity she creates a lot of confusion. Her enormous humanity excuses her. And yet her humanity remains crushed by this impos-sible scenario, by the machinery that upholds this scenario. Monfe is even stronger. He responds with matching violence, interspersing truth, an impassioned truth, into a long series of denials. With Silvana and Monfe you actually taste the flavour of their innocence, a true innocence, in the face of these massively serious accusations. You feel their sincerity. And at the same time, never more so than now, you feel the pointlessness of it all, the premeditation of the staging of this trial, which is designed to annihilate their souls. The tragedy appears to leave no way out. Today we have reached the thirty-fifth day of the trial. Alongside this tragedy in the courtroom, other tragedies are developing. Arrigo and Schroff – both in isolation cells, both stagger-ing under the weight of accusations coming from the new *pentiti*, and shattered by the betrayal and falsification of friendships. A new abyss opens up. Always within the happy confines of democratic legality! And then there is Emilio, who continues his hunger strike – in isola-tion, like a tiger in a cage; a function of annihilation, of destruction. The picture is complete, perfect in its total cruelty. The trial appears for what it is – a hugely powerful and inert machine of destruction, of provocation, of outrage, of isolation, of falsity, of death. An enor-mous body, flaccid and cold, which is tipped over on top of you. Only with superhuman strength can you resist it and not be instantly suf-focated – the asphyxiating, fetid, gas-like breath of the Dragon. We are resisting. And we are learning better to know the object of our loathing. They deserve it. Silvana, Monfe, I hope that you manage to continue your resistance, until some force – I don't know what, I don't know which – manages to extend to you the hand of peace that you desire. Giving you what you deserve. A bit of respect, please, for these great, generous comrades. (G12 Rebibbia – 18–19 March)

Folio 36

It is hard to arrive at an overall view of the trial up until this point. But I need to do it. In a few days it will be my turn on the stand. And by then I have to get things clear in my mind – because the trial, and the elections, and my possible eventual election, are beginning to come so close together that the one thing is having an effect on the other. (The elections are getting close, and it's one big mess. The Radical Party conference has decided to push for abstention. I suppose I was expecting this. I'm telling myself, without any great disillusionment and with a certain irony, 'Bye-bye freedom!' And then Rossana, Alberto and Jaro came to see me – and what were they proposing? That I should put myself up as a candidate for the Democrazia Popolare (DP). I could only smile at the thought, and then I felt a bit of shame for the irresponsible love that these very dear comrades bear me. But then Gianfranco Sp. arrived with a lawyer, to get me to sign the formal papers to stand as a candidate for the radicals. How the radicals are able, on the one hand, to proclaim electoral abstention, and on the other to organize electoral lists is one of the mysteries of politics. Marco P., whom I have been seeing these past few days, is like a tightrope walker. The problem is that I find it hard to gauge the elasticity of the rope he is walking. I am still a bit taken aback by this first bruising experience of a relationship with Parliament as an institution.) With justice as an institution, on the other hand, things are unfortunately a lot clearer. Thus far we have not been able to give positive weight to our testimony of the truth. We need to bear this in mind and recognize it with clarity. The machine, and its time, are powerful, infinitely more powerful than us. The time of the machine grinds our history and our present time. Our alternatives, vital, political and intellectual, are destroyed when they come into contact with the machinery of the trial. They are assimilated destructively to its dialectic. The time of the trial annuls historical time, and we are not managing to break its sequence. We are aware of this, but we are unable to do anything about it. Without wanting to exaggerate, and with a certain bonhomie, I actually think that my whole theoretical history is in crisis: between the refusal of work and the theory of the self-valorization of time, the force of the political alternative is not succeeding in making itself heard. It is not managing to check this massive, infernal, inertial mechanism we have before us. It may be dead, but it is enormous. I am having doubts about my own intelligence. Very soon (immediately in fact) big things are awaiting me. I must give strength to hope. I must succeed in this. These days of trial activity are terrible. They are doing the duty that is imposed on them by the machine. (Spinoza: 'The aim of the state, I say, is not to turn people from reasonable beings into [. . .] automats.') We have to do more than simply our duty to be honest: we have to transform hope into strength. This is revolution time. (G12 Rebibbia – 22 May)

Folio 37

Today it was my turn. On the witness stand. Tragic solitude. The theatre has arrived at its first big show. Jam-packed today. But we don't start. A *coup de théâtre*. They won't let me speak. Instead they begin by reading statements – on and on, without a break, except for the occasional wrangle between the president and the Public Prosecutor. I don't listen. I hear a babble of words – words flying around, a kind of garbled gibberish, *sinnlos*. A semi-rituality in the reading. Nobody listens. A continuous murmuring in court. I look around. A change of perspective brings friends closer. Rossana and Massimo – something different from our embalmed presence in this cage. With a chilling sensation I realize the absurdity of the situation. I am a political prisoner in a democratic state. Why deny this state the qualification of democratic? No, really, one cannot – this is a democratic state, democratic in its rituals. The problem is that democracy is not – with this constitution, with this political class – it is neither liberty nor justice. Good old Marx was right. Democratic prison and democratic political trials – democratic exploitation. While the reading of my interrogation statements seems to go on forever, without anybody taking a blind bit of notice, the shame of this democracy leaps before my eyes. I concentrate on the concept – how much suffering it takes to demonstrate the falsity and the dishonour of this democratic mystification. The witness stand in the court is uncomfortable. I have brought with me a fat file of documents, a red file. I put it next to the witness stand and lean on it. I dream of liberty. No, that's not true – I dream of resistance. That's not true either. I don't dream, I never dreamt. Instead I sink into my tiredness and into my hurt dignity. The ritual of the reading is becoming unbearable. They take turns to read, and they read faster and faster, so that it becomes increasingly incomprehensible. It would be laughable if it were not so monstrous,

such an infamy. They suffocate you through this ritual. And I sink further. At a certain moment I awake with a start: I ask myself, like every time when a man wants the truth, I ask myself: why? Why this tedious ritual? At the same time, watching them and listening to the monotonous drone of meaningless voices which, as they read, make a nothingness of the suffering, the struggles and the tragedies enclosed within those statements – at the same time a weird little thought comes into my head. Namely that I am justice. And for the first time since they put me into prison, without any doubt, without any spiritual effort and without any particular thought process to accompany the sensation, I feel in its entirety the pleasure of a past that has been rich in life and struggles, and the joy of being here to defend it. I feel that what I have theorized and done was just. And still is just. And will continue to be just. The machine does not frighten me. The examination about to happen – and their slanders and vulgarity and brutality – well, all that is their stuff. Stuff of the machine. My role here, in my rediscovered rawness of life and in my simple pride in my own history, will be that of a saboteur. Through a declaration of truth. I have the sense of having pulled on my balaclava . . .
(G12 Rebibbia – 24 May)

2

Self-Defence in Court

25 May to 8 July 1983: Folios 38–57

Folio 38

The thirty-eighth day of the trial. The reading of the verbals continues. Maybe Santiapichi is doing this so as to reduce the tension
that has crept into things, in the run-up to my court appearance and
in relation to the electoral events in which I am involved. He is also
doing it in order not to to reintroduce the Moro affair into the 7
April trial – that would make the whole thing just too comical. Then,
suddenly, he changes tack. After exchanging words with the public
prosecutor he asks: 'Can you tell me something about yourself personally?' So the examination has now started. I am accused of insurrection. He lets me talk. I say:

> I am an intellectual. I have always lived in contact with a reality of
> which I have always tried to understand the contradictions and the rev-
> olutionary tendencies. Now I am before the judges to answer a charge
> of armed insurrection against the powers of the state. This accusation
> honours me. Paradoxically. In other words, not because I was working
> for some kind of impossible insurrection, but because I lived, inter-
> preted and developed an event which was already a given. Probably
> I am here before this court because nobody wants to take account of
> that reality, of that insurrection which the working class had brought
> about and carried out. The events of '68 were the only insurrection that
> I have known. People's spirits changed in those days, those months,
> those years. You do not wish to accept this truth. As for myself, I have
> devoted my life to developing the political analysis and the strategy that
> derived from that reality. Today you are judging me on this account;
> and it is precisely on this account that I consider myself to be innocent.
> You accuse me of an event which had already consolidated itself in the

spirit of many generations – a revolution in being, of which we should all feel proud. I have tried – I shall always try – to close the gap that has been created between the transformation in people's consciousness and the possibility of political expression. I have worked at factory gates and in working-class neighbourhoods, I have taught the critique of the bourgeois world in the universities. Certainly, that I have done – and I shall continue to do it: to give political form to the great transformation under way. A transformation that sees thousands and thousands of workers, students and women rebelling against the traditional cruelty of the roles assigned to them in society – and finding joy in their rebellion and in the act of building a new sense of community. When we first started, this was not a feeling that was limited to just a few people: the desire for revolution was hegemonic. And gradually this desire began to expand, and was fed by experiences of community and movement. The students went to the factories – and then, from the factories, following and overturning the growing capitalist socialization of work, the movement crossed over into the social. An insurrectional politics – but it was something more: a politics of transformation; the question was to understand what had happened in the consciousness of the masses in the course of those movements which rendered the revolt circulatory, progressive and expansive. That great transformation was the key to the development and the antagonisms of social consciousness today. You accuse me of having been an 'evil teacher'; certainly, from your point of view you are right. I taught that revolution is not only possible but also necessary, because people's consciousnesses had already changed. Gentlemen, this epochal transformation cannot simply be erased from history. Your arrogance is born of a lack of historical understanding and of a deficit of intellect. Insurrection there certainly was. And now we can only continue to work on that terrain. By insurrection I mean the great and sudden transformation of people's consciousness, that happy hour in which a new time triumphs. Now there are only two possibilities: either to repress this transformation, consolidating the existing mode of production with a violence equal to the depth of the transformation, or to empower the revolutionary strength of the immense productive social proletariat. The first path is simply non-viable – even you must recognize the impossibility of moving against something that has become so solidly sedimented in people's consciousnesses: repression can only fleetingly affect ontology, it can never annihilate it. In Porto Marghera, Milan and Turin I lived this situation: a revolution in action, a political scenario transforming itself into a horizon of war. Then I saw generation after generation conquering, in full awareness, the pleasure of being active protagonists of this transformation. You have tried to create a desert out of this field of hope – and you call this desert social peace, legality and justice. For a short – very short – time, this might be an option. But do not delude yourselves. The insurrection continues on its way, working on reality. It is now the only seed of any hope – a hope which, albeit poor, is also often very rich. It is the basic groundwork of science. The very first collective experiences of communism are not reversible. It may very well happen that there are betrayals, both individual and collective, and the transformative structures may encounter obstacles which for the moment are insuperable. However, do not think that this will lead to a defeat sufficiently profound as to annul the transformation which has taken place. The history of struggles has produced the ontology of the new need for communism, and this social subject now produces history. Thus this trial of ours is no more than a caricature of justice – it denies the reality of social transformation – only this transformation, only the revolution in people's consciousnesses and its capacity to be a substantial, real and proper force of the proletariat can today bring about legality and justice. We are in the midst of a clash between forces which are opposed and irreconcilable. We do not understand you, and there is no understanding between you and us. You accuse me of insurrection; you make me responsible for a transformation in being which you feel to be threatening because it is bearing down on you. No – not from above . . . Rather, it digs. It digs in the consciousness of every one of us, and of your children also . . . All you can expect from the future is the revenge of this transformation of spirits. You are right to fear history. It does not legitimate you, it destroys you. (G12 Rebibbia – 2 May)

Folio 39

You accuse me of having taken part in discussions about armed struggle with Feltrinelli, with Curcio, and with many others. It is true. But this admission on my part is not a recognition of guilt. Guilt about what? There were vanguards who had tasted the flavour of transformation, and of power. They represented more or less traditional ideologies, which were attempting to interpret the desire for revolution – and there were, above all, mass movements which had no intention of giving away the power they had won, but wanted to organize it. Now many paths were opened up in this great debate. Not necessarily complementary. Often contradictory, and often in opposition to each other. In real class struggle division is necessary. My discussion with the forces of armed struggle was always conceived of in terms of division. Political division in order to build and win a correct mass tactics. For myself and my comrades mass tactics has always meant the critical and practical recognition of the truth of the needs and the reality of struggle. This truth is what divided us from the terrorist movement. You, on the other hand, are here to verify the assumptions of the prosecution case: that social subversion and terrorism are one and the same thing. This dreadful equivalence is the main driving force of a repression designed to strike not so much at terrorism, but at the movement – a putrid hypothesis and a swamp for intelligent thinking. Here the truth is replaced by a muscular project made up of police machinations and the fabrications peddled by paid *pentiti*. It is a disgrace. No, this is not the way it really was; the history of that time was not what you want it to be. The revolution is based on the human, and the passions of the human are many-fold. The fundamental element consisted in the opposing ideas in the conception of the party – between those who wanted it to be made by guns and those who thought that the masses were capable of liberating themselves. You know which front I was fighting on. You know how hard the battle was between these two political lines. And you know about the defeat into which the militarist and terrorist line drove us. Extremism played the game of reaction and repression. The long historical memory, which at that time was still alive within the movement, was of no use to us in warding off the peril. You know all this; but you have turned the truth into an instrument of mystification. You flatten everything, as your way of straitjacketing everything and destroying it. But if practical cynicism may sometimes pay, sadism of the intellect is *always* made to pay. These unfit judges are thirsty in their throats, and they only want to drink lies. You, my judges, you don't want to see the truth, because you will be blinded by its light. We throw this truth before you, the truth of a mass movement which has internalized the revolution and is experimenting with the first forms of communist life. Ah, is my good judge changing the subject? I too have muscles to reply with. Muscles with teeth, and I do not accept the farcical accusations of the prosecution. The years of 1973 and 1974 were times in which the retreat of the trade union movement, the fear among the institutional forces of the working class that we were about to face a Chile-style coup, and the opportunism of the Historic Compromise, all appeared as a threat. Both of them, hand in hand: the repression and the restructuring of the Works Councils. This was the first great setback to the class struggle. But it also marked a first new apparition of singular and diverse movements on the social terrain. Can all of this really be reduced to a plot organized by a handful of people, to a hopeless bunch of incapables? Do you not know what the masses are? Do you hear the underground noise of their movement? Do you smell the scent of their hopes? Certainly, I did see people trying out their first experiences of armed struggle. They were mistakenly expecting the first critical transition of a ten-year revolutionary movement to translate into a continuous upward linearity of behaviours. They were wrong. Ideology was eating into their brains and gave their determination the quality of madness. Rejecting all that – as my comrades and I did – was certainly not a service rendered to the state. It was a lucid and different perspective on revolution. Yes, certainly, we were reckoning to topple the Palace. But there was a profound difference. So profound that only people who actually lived it can appreciate all its subtleties. I would not expect similar sophistication of detail to enter into the reading of judges. You are not capable of it. No – only the masses are subtle, muscular and intelligent. How solid they are! Like Gothic porticos of cathedrals, infinite fantastical forms, a design unified by the desire of producing a new world: and you judges, you pass through those doors (this masterpiece of art of the masses) in the emptiness of your rituals and the absurdity of your dogma. No to the terrorism of fanatical small groups, and no to the sadism of state justice. *Signor presidente*, I am not expecting you to understand me. You have been telling the journalists that communication in court has been difficult because of differences of language. Not a bit of it! There are differences – absolute and insuperable – but they are differences of spirit. Defence is an impossibility. All that is possible is to declare the truth of the matter, with absolute lack of illusion. (G12 Rebibbia – 26 May)

Folio 40

Outside, the wind of the elections is blowing. I am very tired. Pannella's see-sawing between electoral abstentionism and voting for Negri is beginning to irritate me. Maybe they are right, maybe they know the iron laws of propaganda and are using paradox as a winning weapon. But basically most of their tactics are based on nothing more than weakness and the fear that they won't even get a quorum vote – so they are preparing an alibi for themselves. Marco P. assures me that, if they get a quota, my candidacy is assured. We shall see. I am very tired. These games may be intelligent – astute might be a better word – but they tire me. I am not a circus animal. I don't like doing tricks. A closed horizon suffocates me, but one which is arbitrarily open gives me asthma. I prefer to risk things out in the open, cleanly. The problem is that I am not managing to resolve the problem of the relationship between the trial and the elections. These elections are a great publicity opportunity for the 7 April case – the electoral campaign, although only at its start, is already posing the big themes of preventive imprisonment, of a political resolution for the Years of Lead, and all the rest. Now we need to be capable of puncturing the trial within these electoral times. The comrades are not necessarily sensitive to all this. The trial is a tortuous, knotty interweaving of many things – basically there is no single logical thread which might be grasped and then used to resolve its complexity. Maybe in fact the only viable tactic is to do the opposite – prevent things from unravelling, pull the knot ever tighter, retrace its dimensions, complicate it. And then, in the electoral campaign – as it develops, and if eventually I get elected – suddenly to cut the knot with one fell blow. The technique of the Gordian knot. We are not capable of that, though – we are unprepared. The comrades are full of reservations. And Pannella's see-sawings do not help. Only *Il Manifesto* and Rossana are moving effectually, despite all the difficulties which I can imagine being put in their way by the pro-Communist Party tendency. But they too are moving extremely ambiguously. Remember, Toni – if you get out, you owe a lot to everybody, but also to nobody. Everyone will be wanting you as their puppet, everyone will want you for themselves, not as a person, but as a means . . . Don't trust anybody. The 7 April battle is ours and nobody else's. But we have to find a way of reframing the trial in political terms, and of reframing the elections in terms of our trial. And at the same time it is necessary to develop a powerful self-defence, based on a broad discussion of the role of the state and of the magistracy, and of everything that follows from it. This is what I think, and in recent days I have written a few letters on the subject. But I doubt that, in the present state of things, this will succeed. I have the impression that I may perhaps end up being elected – but on the basis of an angry vote of protest and refusal. Not of a positive programme. That's Marco P.'s playground: his propaganda about abstaining in the elections is really a message to the media inviting people to vote for the Radicals. But the media are poverty-stricken and cynical. The call remains hollow, and this protest and refusal does not translate into programme and political organization. As a result, our trial is the only thing that offers a chance of pushing things in a political direction. It is the only point where I believe we have the possibility of intervening. Our self-defence, in addition to asserting and claiming the contents of the movement, must also be programmatic of movement. The weather is hot in these days. I am literally prostrated by the tasks that await me. I see no value in my getting out of prison, if this does not constitute a new political proposition. I am fully conscious of the negative dialectic of the situation and of the unravelling, even among my friends, of any unitary, positive horizon of proposition. The electoral bloc and the 'lobby' which they have formed have interests of different kinds. I am having no success in bringing them together into a discourse about hope. What is to be done? The only thing which is in my power (and one should not bother with things that are in the power of others) is to try to restore political dignity to the trial. I have this feeling of trying to get out of prison, pulling myself out, pulling myself up by my braces. I have such a desire to be free, to do cartwheels on the grass. It's been four years since I last set foot on grass, I've almost forgotten what it feels like. But this election campaign that I'm involved in, why is it not a flower of the field, a conspiracy of nature for liberation? Why is it that – if all goes well – this liberation of mine has to grow in these cracks, in these smatterings of soil, in the cement of this prison? All my friends seem to be scared of the positions I am putting in the trial and of my faith in revolution. This electoral bloc is no more than a bloc of contradictions and reservations. I didn't deserve this last challenge. But will it be the last? Will I gain my freedom? And then what's going to happen? I am tired. Days of prison and lying low. I am filled with uncertainties. I don't dream at night; the comrades tell me that I toss and turn in my sleep. I wake early in the morning and I daydream in the warmth of these spring days. I see again the strength and the joy of the movement, and people's faces fired with collective enthusiasm. In the trial I would like to find a way of expressing this, and a way of winning freedom by cutting decisively through their cheap trickery, their half-hearted supports and their vulgar insinuations. I don't want them to give me freedom – I want to take it. (G12 Rebibbia – 27/28/29/30 May)

Folio 41

The fortieth and forty-first days of hearings. My examination at the hands of the court continues. The line I am arguing is more or less as follows:

> You want to prove the existence of an organization which – by a stroke of genius (for the first time in this trial, because policemen are not noted for strokes of genius) – you have decided to call the 'O'. A powerful and adaptable structure, a mafia of the revolution, a Holy Spirit of the struggles. A maxi-organization of minimal dimensions. A Bolshevik party of the 1960s and 1970s. Capable of directing everything. Capable of bending everything to the unity of its insurrectional project. Well, all that is false. And it is precisely this falsity that offers you the possibility of attributing everything to this organization – the worst crimes as well as the smallest ones, the organization, the movement as a whole. If this 'O' had actually existed, you would have needed to provide material evidence of its crimes. But, when things are invented and falsified, obviously there is no evidence. So that takes us into the field of 'moral responsibility'. The only thing that results from your judicial fantasies is repression. What you are claiming is false. Such a conspiracy-oriented

organization never existed. There never existed a P38 to sit alongside your P2. You project your methods, your sickness, onto our health, onto our irreducible yearning for life. More than liars, you are in fact mystifiers. You reduce a political reality (which, because we live in a democracy, you cannot strike at) to a mystified reality, which the fascist laws so dear to your heart enable you to persecute. You are right – there really did exist an element which was irreducible and opposed to a republican constitution – a constitution that had been traduced to the point of becoming an amalgam of reactionary forces. Most of all, there really did exist a refusal to accept things as they were, and a rebellion, and a rejection of all this hypocrisy. If you have even a shred of respect for truth left in you, and if – as you claim – you are impartial judges, allow me to tell you what *really* happened.

They look at each other. They know that I want to impose on them that very simple, elementary thing which is a telling of events in chronological order. An abacus of time and events. Of rights, and not simply of punishments. With the determination of pig farmers who carry their animals screaming to the abattoir, they are unable to accept it. It is on the basis of a flattening of time and events, and of the negation of differences and evolutions and separations, that this infamous concoction known as the 'O' is constructed. Things which ten years ago were lawful are now branded as brigadism and terrorism. The prosecution case is based on nothing more than this 'it turned into'. And now they impose 'present' sets of repression and 'present' readings of our actions. As functionaries, Santiapichi and Abbate are too diligent – the forward bastions of reaction – to allow themselves to forget it. They reject my arguments. What I am experiencing here is an internal pain. I am no longer moving in the area of truth, but find myself forced into a game of defence, faced as I am with a hard-line schema of mystification and hatred. This is Russian roulette.

Gentlemen, you cannot do this. This is the fourth transformation of the theorem that I am witnessing. The first version said that I was the head of the Red Brigades and the killer of Moro – you even recognized me in via Fani, with sworn witnesses and an identity parade. However, despite your provocations, that collapsed. Then – *in secundis* – you invented a truth that was testified to by those gruesome murderers, the likes of Fioroni and Casirati. Then Gentili, Tarsitano and the PCI manipulated the provocation. May shame fall upon them and may the kiss of those bastards poison their blood. The third time, you moved to organize the judicial *putsch* in Milan, using Barbone. A magistrate who was young and inexperienced sanctioned the operation. He was unable to control the stormy passions of vendetta, and was caught up in a collective paranoia which only ignorance of class struggle and ignorance of the law could permit. So Barbone was let off for the killing of Tobagi, our defender. Then you rewarded him by setting his woman free and by promising him freedom so long as he agreed to invent the existence of an 'O' in Milan. Today you have arrived at the fourth transformation of the theorem – the most evil of all, because now you have given up actually trying to prove anything, but you are still determined to push ahead politically, to fulfil the undertaking you made to your corporation. In this trial, all you are seeking to do is to create suspicion. You are seeking to create a material scapegoat. A scapegoat which is not even useful for the future of Italy's poor democracy, but is merely functional to the survival of your self-standing corporation as judges. Too many mistakes, too much hatred, too much ignorance. This cannot be permitted. This game is too brutal. And yet I am obliged to accept it within the terms in which you impose it: either everything is true, or everything is a lie. This has been the frame of this trial during the past few days. All right, then . . . let's say that I built an 'O'. It was not illegal, it was definitely not, and you cannot strike it down with a law that purports to be democratic. The choice is yours now, between democracy and corporative infamy. (G12 Rebibbia – 31 May–1 June)

Folio 42

Outside things are beginning to move. A big campaign is being mounted in my name, organized by old comrades, but more particularly by people who have simply had enough of the injustices of this state. I have the impression that the train of my freedom is beginning to move – with some difficulty at first, because it's an old train, a steam train in fact, which chuffs and slips on the tracks and is pulling too much weight, has too many carriages, and is just at the start of its efforts – the same as equality, in fact. (But the new technologies, what values have they produced?) Quite a few people have come to see me in recent days – Félix came, and Gisela too, dear comrades who represent the international experience of communist life. They fill me with hope; they tell me of positive signs. In Germany the Greens are drawing up a conference document to support my candidacy – or so Gisela tells me. Félix tells me about Latin America and the great spread of movements for democracy, happiness and revolution. It is not enough for me that my train simply moves forward – it is the Finland train; what needs to be set in motion is this tactical passage, proud and forward-looking, this message for universality. I look around and I understand the dimensions of this extraordinary adventure of reason. By chance, through the stupidity of the powers of repression, I find myself playing a role which, by myself, I would never have succeeded in taking on. This is their weakness – the fact that they have to build up their enemy. This, of course, until the moment when they decide to kill him. OVRA comes to mind. But then they risk transforming the killed person into a hero. Today, despite these grey presentiments, I am in good humour. I sense that *they* are the ones caught in the shit of their own contradictions – not me. We shall see. But I see no reason for doubts about the extraordinary adventure that I am living. A breaking of bureaucratic legitimacy. If I end up being elected to Parliament, it will be a big break. Of course there is no way they'll allow me to get away with it – they won't leave me free for long. But it will be a clash between two legitimacies – between party-political and democratic legitimacy, between bureaucratic and charismatic legitimacy. In either event it will be a defeat for them – or rather a wound, something to touch them where it hurts. So today I am in good humour. At last. The Finland train is on its way. It has begun its journey. As I look out of the window I see contradictory landscapes, green trees and sterile tundra. But contradiction is the key to life. In a few days I shall be back in court again, facing the deathly inertia of the prosecution and defending myself from its icy kiss. I find that I care less and less about it. I am gambling on freedom, not on the trial. Perspectives are beginning to change. I can look the judges in the eye, perhaps – holding the arrogance of their gaze and destroying it with irony. I shall be able to exorcize the death which their wrinkles and their facial tics extend to me, with an understated smile and a metaphysical irony. I think of love, for sure. I want to make children on the Finland train, in the precariousness of that future life, within the sweetness of a gentle breath – even if it is only a moment – of freedom, in a destiny which is an adventure and a reclaiming of life. Sometimes they accuse me of undervaluing the collective meaning of our experience of struggle and community – but what is more powerfully symbolic than risking one's life to the utter limit, within a living hope? Go, Finland train, go . . . That which is singular is collective. Only the desire for communism destroys passivity and solitude. (G12 Rebibbia – 2/3/4/5 June)

Folio 43

I find myself this evening writing up five days of court examination – from Monday to Friday, from 6 June to 10 June, continuously, without a break, day after day. And I have a psycho-somatic reaction: a terrible toothache. I am thinking about these days of incredible tension. Things have come to a crunch over the question of dissociation. These people associate the term with some kind of evil intent. That's why they keep pressing that particular button: 'So', they say, 'you tell us that you don't agree with terrorism. So now tell us some people's names, and tell us everything you know about terrorism. Otherwise we shall think that your behaviour is opportunistic and simply designed to reduce your sentence.' They will never understand. Is it better to leave them to boil in their own greasy broth? No. I counter them point by point. I try to launch a discussion. Who knows if they understood anything I was saying. In reality what I would like to say is the following:

> For me, dissociation does not mean withdrawing from something, but arriving at a point where my actions are in accord with my thoughts. For me dissociation has meant above all dissociating myself from what you judges wanted me to be. A breaking of the image you have constructed and imposed on me and my comrades and on the movement. Dissociation is not a betrayal of terrorism (impossible for me). Rather it is a claiming, it is an attack on your theorems and on your stupid and odious schemes of criminalization. I hate terrorism because I love life – because in my view that terrorism bears the same symbolic and homicidal image of life as you judges have. *Signor presidente*, with Savasta you found yourself on the same symbolic common ground as you say you have found yourself (or perhaps you actually have – I did not check on this) with the general span of common criminality. With this latter you have something in common culturally, by sharing the same bourgeois sense of decorum; with Savasta, by sharing the same view of power. You are on an equal footing with one as well as with the other, in a dialectic of similarities. Punishment has to be a restoration – repaying the harm done, mediating it through the law, dialectically, within a whole set of homologous values. It does not surprise me that you like Hegel. His anger, the incommunicability of language, you discover all this when you come face to face with difference. Then you go into tilt! Then your wrinkles become set into your face. The very *physique du rôle* changes – it functions only in a homogeneity of values: money and power. Revolution is a bulldog snapping at your leg, and the movement is a toad in your belly. Good sense does not understand. But good sense today is depraved, it is tied to the meanings of power – of a power and

of a state that are degraded and corrupt. This court represents them. Under this representation, good sense goes crazy and authority falls into decadence. As my Spinoza says:

> For if the ruler of the state runs drunk or naked with harlots through the streets, acts on the stage, openly violates or holds in contempt those laws that he himself has enacted, it is no more possible for him to preserve the dignity of sovereignty than for something to be or not be at the same time. [Spinoza, *Political Treatise*, translated by Samuel Shirley (Indianapolis: Hackett Publishing Company 2002), Chapter 4, p. 697]

Has not this metaphysical paradox been challenged, perhaps? As regards the problem of dissociation, here for sure the virginity of truth has been violated. There, *signor presidente*, I watch as you read these words – who knows, maybe tomorrow or the day after tomorrow a cell search here in prison will carry off this notebook and give you the privilege of being its only reader – I watch you reading it, smiling arrogantly as you read. I am firm in my opinion that there are no limits to the idiot complacency of the present ruling class. But at least let us set aside vulgarity of the intellect, and let us seek the pleasure of reason.

Let us try to find a common language, in order to communicate – even if it is only to supplicate. In short: not with the dirty eroticism characteristic of the sexual habits of the discreet bourgeoisie – but with a desire that embodies love, removes the clothing from reality and hunts out the truth. Try to come close to those infinite points (since they are infinite and widely spread, it should be possible to catch one or two of them) on which desires of life and desires for renewal separate themselves from the vices of your world. And try to understand the love and fullness of the needs for innovation that pulse within revolt. Dissociation . . . for heaven's sake, you too should dissociate yourself – from the intrigue in which you have become enmeshed.

Probably you might even find it satisfying. You and I are divided by life and death – my search for identity is life; your requirement that I repent and become a spy is death. I don't know what power it is that imposes this on you, but it is, for sure, a power that keeps company with prostitutes. Good night, *signor presidente*.

Obviously that kind of talk is never going to be allowed. This evening, however, thinking back over the court examinations of the past week, this is the only way of summing up the whole business that I can find. The serious stuff, about dissociation, I already wrote some time ago, from inside the special prison, in conditions so fearsome that I really don't want to recall them: I paid too high a price for them down there . . . close to death. But there is no point in repeating them to the president of this court with his gross insensibility, which is so functional to the project of power. (G12 Rebibbia – 6/7/8/9/10 June)

PS It is worth recalling instead my article 'Terrorism? *Nein, danke!*' published in *Il Manifesto* on 23 March 1981.

Terrorism? *Nein, danke!*

Since the events of Trani many comrades have told me that we – my comrades and I – were right to dissociate ourselves from the Red Brigades initiative in this struggle and in the D'Urso case. But these same comrades add that: (a) this dissociation was an *individual* operation, which does not address the problem of the other thousands of comrades in prison; (b) this dissociation does not produce political effects capable of going beyond itself, and therefore it runs the risk of not opening perspectives; (c) this dissociation is an *ambiguous* operation because, both in its form and in its method, it can be instrumentalized by power.

Criticisms and reservations of this kind are not only coming from prison. The condemnation of the Red Brigades' behaviour at Trani is almost unanimous in prisons, or at least represents the majority view. Criticism is also coming, particularly harshly, from outside the prison, from quarters where solidarity with the comrades in prison demands a *unified* approach, and, first of all, over and above any criticism, it demands a focused attack on the nature of the repression. Since, in the events of Trani, power has revealed a bestial face, going beyond all limits, it's on this that the whole debate has to focus. It is very doubtful that a similar attitude will be taken by the comrades in prison, even though some of them may appreciate our motives. Myself in particular. In the circumstances in which the dissociation has taken place, I personally believe that I must have run the full gamut of the problems and emotions which communist militants would have experienced in the 1930s, in dissociating themselves from Stalinism and from blackmail arguments about unity. What I mean here is the emotions and problems – obviously this has nothing to do with Stalin. What people need to appreciate here is the fact, felt by many comrades and particularly by those outside prison, of the seriousness of dissociating oneself from the struggle while it is actually under way, while people are still under enemy fire, while people are still in pain from the wounds received – whereas the first task is to resist, and unity is taken as the supreme value – so that, in a classical sense, being scabs is an ontological fact, and not something ideological or abstract.

Why do I claim dissociation?

So, why do I claim dissociation? Why do I reject the accusations of those outside prison? Why do I insist on listening, answering, and persuading my comrades in prison along the line that the – effective – limits of simple dissociation can be overcome and are organizable in a general direction of liberation? I do so for a number of fundamental reasons, which I permit myself to submit for discussion herewith.

1. Because working-class and proletarian struggles, in their mass aspect, are far from being suppressed or on the decline in Italy and Europe. The armed line of class struggle, in the unilaterality of its discourse and in the acceleration of its project, has not only been effectively defeated, but also logically discarded by a movement of struggles which does not see necessity and rigour of consequences in armed struggle. *Terrorismus? Nein, danke.* Certainly there do exist war-orientated residues in the movement as a whole, but by now they are wholly extraneous to the dynamic of political reproduction of the present generations and to the expansion of the communist movement. From this point of view, the Red Brigades initiative will continue to be what it was at Trani: purely and simply an instrumentalization of a real movement of protest, a continuous, murderous overdetermination of the movements of struggle. Today, in organizing the struggle, we have to exclude from the outset the possibility of the Red Brigades or other 'combatant communist organizations' (OCC) involving themselves in the struggle. *To exclude overdetermination is a precondition of struggle*. Political assassination is, today, an assassination of the struggles. The autonomous reproduction of the communist movement excludes this distortion spontaneously: the distortion needs to be excluded consciously and politically.

To destroy the image of civil war

2. The image of civil war was not imposed by the Red Brigades or by the other 'OCC' but was constructed and used exclusively, solely and unilaterally by power. In exchange for a death or two – of people who were soon replaced, anyway – power constructed the general conditions of a recession of the struggles, a reduction of political spaces, and a weakening of the strength of the class movement. What was horrible to see was the support offered by the forces of the 'Left' to power's project. Never has it been so clear that the destruction of the ideology, image and scenario of civil war is a fundamental precondition for a reopening of class struggle and for the reconquering of political spaces. The strength of the proletarian movement is ready to deploy itself into the expression of a political programme. *The struggle is political*. Who, in the classics and in the history of the working-class movement, has ever upheld the fable

that – given conditions such as those that apply in Italy – withdrawal from armed struggle, and therefore the resumption of political struggle, is a betrayal or a desertion? Only fanatics or imbeciles, like those people from API in Trani prison, who are particularly resourceful in the instrumental mystification of theory and history, can sustain this – or perhaps, even worse, believe it. Proletarian political struggle has to destroy the image of war. It has to chase back, into a black and terrible past, the feeling of desperation, the frenzy of murder, the obtuseness of combatant logic. Today political struggle comes to occupy pride of place, being, once again, fully tied to the mass struggle, to its possibilities and its powerful efficacity. Today mass political struggle is a means made possible by the growth of the new class composition and made mandatory by the force of its material needs. Subjective behaviours and the drive towards centralization need to be mediated within the levels of political class recomposition. The mediation is not imposed by the enemy, but by the development of the communist programme. Today it is opportunist, infantile, stupid and suicidal for anyone to refuse the mediation geared to the mass practice of the programme. Immediatism of objectives is nostalgic and now belongs only to the state-effected simulation of civil war.

The isolation of the prison struggle within the prison walls

3. The centrality of the problem of the prisons (and of the 3,000 political prisoners) cannot be instrumentalized – as happened in the campaign over D'Urso – and subordinated to the construction of the 'OCC', let alone to the victory of one political line over others. This line of approach is destructive in all its aspects. It presents moments of such an instrumental coinvolvement as to appear to be in contradiction with the minimal principles of revolutionary ethics. Anyone who instrumentalizes the mass struggle and the proletariat's desire for freedom in this way is not much different, in their ethics, from the opposite ethics presented by *pentitismo*. Combatant immediatism, in prison, joins desperation to instrumentalization. Its watchword is 'let Sampson die together with all the Philistines', or *'après moi le déluge'*. It is quite another thing to articulate politically, within the masses, the sacrosanct watchwords of 'no to the culture of life imprisonment', 'no to prison segregation', 'no to annihilation'. Prison – and prison for political prisoners at this particular moment – is a central problem, and of such social and historical dimensions that it cannot be, I'm not saying solved, but even discussed outside of a mass political line, and struggles, and general political solutions. This is certainly not the moment to introduce juridical questions (depenalization, amnesty): this is something that we can begin to address only once there has been a resumption of a mass political campaign. But

the negotiations on the question of prison are central only in theory, as long as that question remains isolated, as long as it does not become part of all the campaigns of the movement, as long as it is not intrinsic to all the struggles. We do not need 'solidarity committees'; what we need is rather to carry the discussion of the prison question into all the situations of struggle. The fact that the struggle on prisons is confined to the prison and identified with the combatant line of the 'OCC' has only one result: from power, reactions in the manner of Attica and Stammheim; from proletarian prisoners, a vertical and unresolvable rupture. To avoid both these outcomes is a duty for all the comrades, but above all it is the task of the political struggle for liberation. To succeed in articulating the mass problem of liberation across the entire fabric of political confrontation is today the only method of securing the centrality of the problem of the prisons (in effective terms, and not rhetorically) and of restoring a perspective of hope. And not only for the people in prison: because in fact these 3,000 vanguards thrown into prison, the consolidation of the practice of mass police arrests, and the infamy of juridical innovations (from the repressive laws to the use of *pentiti*) constitute, at a wider level, a continuous threat to the struggles and needs of the masses.

Rebuilding the conditions of political struggle

But perhaps I need to express more forcefully the points outlined here. Not because I, together with other comrades, am a protagonist in the 7 April case, but for reasons that I shall explain below, it is my belief that we need to focus our attention on the events of the spring of '79. What has really happened between then and now? This: the political struggle inside the movement has been crushed by a stupid and insane initiative from the magistracy and from power. The wealth of political alternatives has been removed; as a result of the destruction of the whole political fabric, the Red Brigades have been left in the position of representing the movement globally, and this played into the hands of the state, with its decision to enact a simulacrum of civil war. To what end? And what have been the effects? Two years of reciprocal killings and the introduction of barbarism into political debate have shown what the aim had been: to bring about a state of emergency which, while showing the necessity, the opportuneness and the possibility of destroying terrorism, at the same time destroyed the guarantees of democracy, the spaces of struggle, the decade-long continuity of the proletarian struggle. Has power succeeded in achieving this? Today we can reply that it has not. There is still resistance – albeit often in the form of absenteeism, estrangement, lack of involvement. And today new struggles, which carry with them the freshness of the new generations, are exploding everywhere and breaking up the spurious coherence of the big trade union and party-political corporations. But we (and they) must recognize that the price paid in the past two years has been enormous. Were it not for the total elimination of any critical dialectics in the movement, many lives would have been saved. The insanity of the campaigns of annihilation, the absurdity of the reciprocal killings could very probably have been avoided. The delirious circle of repression and reprisal, of terrorism and repression, could have been interrupted. Today we have to say, with maximum clarity, that the problem of terrorism can be solved only politically – politically both by and within the movement – and that therefore we have to rebuild the conditions of political struggle. Nobody is so deluded as to think that he can wipe out the 7 April case and, with it, two years in the history of repression. Nobody imagines that he can cancel out the materiality of these years and the new problems they have opened. What is clear is that we have to interrupt the murderous process which has brought us all to this point. Is there anybody out there who still thinks that they are going to win? The millenarianism of the theoreticians of catastrophe does not interest us. As for the labour movement, is it not also coming to terms with the defeat that has come about through the flattening of politics and the simultaneous terroristic crushing of the movement? But similar questions could be posed also in regard to other productive and intellectual strata: nobody has anything to gain from the prolongation of this situation.

Who can destroy terrorism?

Terrorism has to be defeated. This, however, is possible only through political means, which nobody possesses through traditional delegation, even if he claims them from the point of view of political representation or of his institutional functions. The only way to defeat terrorism is by intervening in the mechanisms of its reproduction and by being politically legitimated to do so. And we are only legitimated in this sense when we speak from within the class movement, in its interests, and through the plurality of its organizations, within the specificity of its culture. There are many comrades – particularly comrades who are now in prison – who want to move in this direction. Is there a possibility of success? Who knows? What is certain is that the traditional workers' movement, and the other forces – mainly cultural and religious – who are moving towards a political resolution of the problem of terrorism (but is it not the problem of the movement itself?), will not succeed unless they are able to break with a discourse which, even when it is not running into the sands with pious calls for the abolition of the death penalty, nevertheless ends up being impotent when (as has happened) it tries to deal with the problem at the level of civil rights [*garantismo*] (in the period of discussions about reforming the constitution) – unless it lets itself be dazzled by the revelations of some *pentito* or other. And so things go on, and the situation gets worse, and the simulacrum of civil war becomes a monster which lives and destroys, not only human lives but also the possibilities of struggle.

A terrain of communist hope

It is for all these reasons that:

(a) I reject the accusation that dissociation from the Red Brigades and the 'OCC' is an individual operation. It is not, because it expresses fundamental needs of the movement and the necessity of doing politics and of living within the mass movement. Everything always begins in individual terms. Or at least this is the way we have always done things during the past fifteen years.

(b) I reject the accusation that explicit dissociation from terrorism is a minimal operation. Far from it. It represents the beginning of a political project which has the task of representing, once again, the cultural and social identity of the movement. These are its perspectives: to make a record of the history of the struggles, with the intention of giving it both a political representation and an operative representation. Breaking definitively with terrorism and with all the militaristic deviations of the movement – on the basis of a strong critique, which, historically, has already occurred at mass level (albeit until now only in spontaneous form).

(c) I reject the accusation that this dissociation, this project and this struggle are ambiguous. For communists, doing politics has never meant accrediting the present state of things. The problem is quite other: it is one of not getting fetishistic about the critique of arms, and of not diverting social struggles onto a horizon which, in place of liberation, substitutes the hysteria of its simulacrum, which often becomes crudely identified with a (highly ambiguous) conception of the seizure of power.

Reopening a terrain of communist hope today means taking the path of dissociation and turning that dissociation into a programme for the victory of the mass struggle, in the plurality of its organizations and needs, and in the wealth of its desires.

Folio 44

So the trial has been postponed until next Tuesday. Three days of rest. Oh the pain of this trial, this weariness transformed into a sore. (Speaking of which, Mrs Thatcher has won – a big victory – confirmation of a Europe-wide shift to the Right, which is solid and enduring.)

Turbulent events on the outside. Intervention by the magistrates against the Socialist Party (in Savona), and against the Christian Democrats (in the south). A strange climate. Heavy. The corporations and the parties are glaring at each other like dogs, and sometimes they bark and bite. Italian democracy is ulcerated by the state of emergency. Meanwhile there has been a television 'blackout' as regards the trial – obviously they're scared of providing me with electoral propaganda. In postmodernity chaos and functionality lie under the same blanket, and when necessary they swap roles. I don't know where to put my head – it seems to me that my head is already rolling in this apology for a Jacobin trial. Prepare the basket, my friend. I shouldn't take things too much to heart – I try to console myself – if I don't understand much, people on the outside understand even less. Maybe not even keeping this diary is worth the effort. It's hard to document things that are incomprehensible. Or, putting it differently, to extract some light, even if only from afar – probably only metaphysical undertakings could succeed, by detaching themselves from the concrete, in giving it to us. But how can I put my trust in metaphysical imagination? The wound burns. The spectacle of the trial – and of the election – are certainly postmodern, being played out completely on the equivalence of the images in circulation. On the other hand, is my own individual condition something different from this spectacle in which I am caught up? During these years I have been snatched away from reality, from the continuity of a dialogue and of a collective building process. Only the collective moment gives you the possibility of understanding yourself. And, instead, here I am wandering wide of the mark, in a circuit of things that don't make sense, and I don't understand how this unease of mine – when it is not (as it often is) pain – and this disorientation can be overcome.

Maybe they are only mine, internal and solitary, an inevitable effect of the misery in which I am living and of the extreme crisis I am perceiving among the comrades – what is certain, though, is that it stuns me, and that all this is also the reflection of what I have around me, of what I see on the outside, of the disorientation of a disconcerted world. In the personal libraries of my colleagues in prison there are many books on postmodernism. Does this represent an attempt at understanding and deepening – or is it a drug? The wound burns and recalls me to reality. This is the critique of postmodernity:

a philosophy, a conception of the world which does not know pain – and therefore an illusion.

And yet, I ask myself, can our humanity be changed by that whirl of signifieds which go towards non-sense? Why is the totality, required by man to understand the particular, given back to us as insignificant? How are we to reverse this situation? In other times humanity suffered similar lacerations. In the 1600s, for instance, my main field of study – that epoch of formidable inventions and fanatical pyre-burnings, the Baroque. Between the Baroque and the postmodern there is not much difference – the insignificance of the former was in intensity, that of the latter in extension; the former emptied out the soul with an evanescent use of the sensible; the latter empties out the world with a totalitarian use of the image. Between baroque culture and the postmodern public I do not see a difference, except, precisely, the formal difference between intensity and extension. Non-meaning repeats itself. But my wound burns.

And it is here that my (initially timid, and then increasingly conscious) protest lifts off. Is it purely illusory? It could be. I imagine a new and unique language for Babel – a language which permits us to reach the heavens – but this is a transcendental deception, driven towards an abstract recomposition of the divisions of the world. I imagine an ethics for Sodom – it is an illusion that risks becoming a moralistic obscenity. I imagine a simple metaphysics, able to reorient the world – but no, not even this works – do you know the boredom and indifference which would attend its teaching? In the search for the one and the universal there is little space for protest. It seems to me that, paradoxically, I nourish the desires of a small-time Balkan dictator: language, ethics, metaphysics, all dominated by my power. (At root, why should the One not be defined as a kind of power? Is that not what it is among the mystics?) No, this postmodern aspect of the trial and of the election run the risk of filling with infamy even the protest and the reflection on liberation. So what else is there for me to do, except throw pieces of my flesh, of my passion? What can I do, other than exhibit my own wound?

There is no reflection on liberation, there is only the immediacy of the passion and the protest. Either we succeed in saying this, both in the trial and in the election, or we succeed in saying nothing. I think of a hydraulic system through which my pain might run – between prison, the trial and the outside, the world and its life. The total disenchantment of my heroism does not, I believe, remove its meaning. Only my indecency overcomes the senselessness of it all. In this forest, in this labyrinth, only the exasperation of a global witnessing can repair the insult and the wound in the soul. Postmodernity is injustice, because its perception has no place for pain. But on the basis of pain and protest we can rebuild the world. (G12 Rebibbia – 11/12/13 June)

Folio 45

Signor presidente, and gentlemen of the civil parties, I would say that these last three days in court have been horrible – certainly for me, and possibly also for you. Absurdity has jumped to the fore. Your professionality and your corporative duty (namely to lend credibility to the political provocation of the 7 April trial) have been placed under serious stress.

Everyone has been defending their own positions, nobody has been attacking. I have not succeeded in attacking the paltriness of your allegations, and you have not succeeded in rendering them credible. At this point we are all caught up in the falsity of the situation. We are moving on shifting sands, those of a bellicose cruelty, which today we all regard with suspicion. You persist in repeating a set of allegations that has fallen apart, attempting to revive it in new forms. But here absurdity rules. You are not charging me with stealing peanuts, but with a series of murders. The way in which you are conducting these proceedings is shameful. It is obvious that you do not believe in them. But not believing in them does not change reality: murders are the kind of crimes of which you have to find me guilty in order to render credible the only thing of which you are convinced – namely that I am an irreducible subversive. I cannot risk lending credibility to these killings with which you are charging me, and which I did not commit, by mounting a passionate defence – in other words by accepting the rules of the game, so to speak. An absurd and slippery reality, and the trial is going nowhere. We are in the shit. What do you intend to do? How have we ended up in this blind alley? Why are we all so cowardly? *Signor presidente*, the fact is that I could easily break your ban on discussions of politics – all I need to do would be to talk politics. To push the court proceedings to their limit, to present, within the absurdity of the political trial, the facts of the case as they concern me, bringing together the political and the criminal. But what would be the point of my explaining how the movement functioned, in its infinite articulations and its indefinite possibilities? Your job is to prevent history from being reconstructed. The materials of lived experience can feature as an ensemble and as a unity only under the form of the accusation. A claiming of that history is impossible. *Signor presidente*, it seems that this claiming of history is what most frightens you and the court. In other words the possibility that in this trial there might emerge the only clean thing that can exist – a history. I am speaking precisely of that: *historia rerum gestarum, Geschichte*, and so on. Relax. That claim, that history, are rendered impossible by the very nature of the machine. However, I am trying to be subtle and convincing. In short, I am asking you this: why this blockage of awareness? What good does it serve? You are judging a general picture – insurrection – with a vulgar attention to which the general picture does not align itself. The real frightens you. The claiming of that history terrifies you. Why? It would not change anything at the level of the trial itself. Our sentences are laid down in advance. If you happen to fail in your task, the machine will easily make up for the loss. So why this blockage? Why this reproduction of historical confusion as the condition of your repressive resolve? I don't want to play this game – but neither have I managed to break it. I am ashamed to admit it, after all the high-profile arguments about defence and about claiming of the movement. Gentlemen of the court, the fact is that you have succeeded in putting yourselves in line with a set of totalitarian accusations. What you have decided is the Gulag – the Gulag for me and my comrades. Your acceptance of these accusations consists in flattening out everything, in bringing into some kind of a present dreamworld a past that was historically complex and full of life. You are attempting to squash into a single prosecution the lives of thousands and thousands of comrades. What I can't get over, and what is destroying me, is the dreamworld condition of the accusations and of the argumentation in court. I find no way of resisting them. I find myself bogged down in them. I am suffocating. But truth has to win. Despite the force and violence with which you organize the abstract void of the prosecution case, it does not have much space – the impossibility of your translating it into concrete evidence becomes immediately apparent. And all this drives me to rebellion. I have to control myself on this witness stand. But not to the point of not expressing to you my concept. This is not a trial, it is a fraud, a charade. But you are unable to accept the truth. And yet I say it, and I repeat it again. I have killed nobody. I confront in myself this fact of being accused as guilty of murder. I confront the real swelling up, my upsurge of anger, as a kind of immediate allergic response. I consider the appalling nature of this monstrous condition. But I do not tremble even for a moment, not one single moment. The heaviness of the accusation barely touches me. I find myself unable to reply to you, gentlemen. I cannot reply. All I can do is tell the truth. But listen to this: this trial is a phantasm of iniquity. Stop it! It is running rampant through our country, bent on destruction! (G12 Rebibbia – 14–16 June)

Folio 46

Very tired. I take a rest from the trial. I work on drawing up appeals and preparing election materials. The prospect of my freedom is growing. But it is a dry hope. I find that I can't unify the imaginary, which arises out of the concrete reality of these days, with the great hope I am living. I can't manage to free myself from the immediacy of the trial and from its squalid, dreary reality. I'm left on my own, a masturbator, in this situation. (Outside there is pandemonium in the organs of the state: a *blitz* against the Camorra, and the question of Tortora's imprisonment. The impression is one of uncontrollable madness.) This is not succeeding in its project to become a diary. Too little time, and too much tiredness. I can't even manage to provide myself with a notebook, a logbook for the journey. And anyway the tension is too high to permit a simple documentation.

What is to be done? Maybe the only way to save this work is to focus our gaze on what is immediately at hand. People – it is the people who will pull me out of prison – that's what I am thinking this evening, precisely in the immediacy. So what then? I have to throw my dead body into what remains of this trial. Can't you hear it, Toni – can't we all hear it – this powerful signal of hope that is coming from outside? Let us play it. But how? In the only productive way that is open to us, of course – and this is what life has taught me. By building. Building life against death, freedom against repression. There is a moment, and it is this one, in which the entire meaning of existence is put on the line. A very powerful pleasure in revolution – this is the origin of our current woes. And at the same time the sole origin of all our hope. So we work on rebuilding tensions and expectations: of finding some way of surviving between the imbroglio of the trial and the call for freedom that people are putting up. Then let us go down the path of claiming our history. What were we? We were the hope and honour of many generations. We were the totally deployed subjectivity of the revolutionary movement. It is difficult to relive a passion that existed in the past, but which will also come again in the future. I see faces which are pale and tense with fear, in the sweat that comes from fear, awaiting this reappearance. No, our trials are not a sign of defeat. They are powerful symptoms of the future. I get a buzzing in my ears when I think of all this – I am in unison with hundreds of thousands of people. With that 'second society' that is so full of desires. The dialectics of this trial disgusts me. My intellectual anti-dialectical passion reacts against it. I believe that, despite everything, I have behaved well. I have not renegued on anybody. I should claim my past more powerfully. This is how I see things today. Push to the limits. Revolution. What is it? It is to be together, it is to build the conditions for freedom. Here there is an enormous programme, which the masses are disposed to put into play as an element in the creation of a new society. Why do I need to repeat its objectives? Every major struggle displays them as elements that are irreversibly present. I have written and talked about this, possibly even to excess, drawing from the movement what the movement itself was producing. Now we can add, in the hope of revolution, a recompense for our sufferings. Enough of these black legal robes, enough of this ill-famed justice. I believe that my judges have understood this too. I am tired. And yet never too tired to carry forward our revolutionary utopia, taking it a step further than what in reality we have been capable of fulfilling. A step forward. Many steps forward. The process of defending myself in the trial has enabled me to place this further step before a huge public opinion. Claiming our history. They are trying us for our hunger for freedom, for our thirst for justice. You, my friend, who are walking along the road, oblivious of us and of everything – prisons and movement – are you with us, friend? Truth and justice are not merely the abstract high-sounding terms that too many people imagine them to be – they are not money, abstract equivalence of ideology. No, they are hope. Not a dried-out hope but a life-filled hope. My bad mood of today is passing. I look forward with enormous hope. But all this will be worth nothing unless we also manage to make our claim – I want to move more determinedly on this terrain. I am proud of the movement, of its reality, of its capacity for imagining. We have to overturn the emptiness of the dual image of the trial and of the parliamentary elections. Hope. An affirmation of all that has happened. The gutter rats of the media and the wolves of the political parties have robbed us of that unique innovative mass experience which was working-class and proletarian autonomy.

I claim all of this. With serenity, with the humility of someone who knows that this overturning was an established fact in the consciousness of a multitude of comrades. So let us go forward with courage and with occasional small portions of heroism. (G12 Rebibbia – 17/18/19 June)

Folio 47

Today the trial blew out. The lawyers are angry. They have gone on strike. The judges, the corporation of arrogance, have been treating them in the same way that they treat us. They'll be striking for the whole week. Only Tarsitano, the PCI's man, was not on strike – he was there, like a crocodile, his jaws gaping – the provincial idiot – a toothpick with the function of a pole keeping his jaws eternally open. But he and his party bosses will find their own ways of getting what they want, through those sectors of the judicial corporation with which they are associated. From Perugia, another arrest warrant has been issued for me: they say that, six or seven years ago, I organized a prison escape in Perugia, and that I organized a prison riot to facilitate the escape. They're claiming that I put a handgun into a football and threw it over the wall. And that I left getaway cars all ready outside. An impressive operation, no doubt about it. If it were true, it might even be amusing. Pity that the person who is claiming all this is one of their murderous *pentiti*. Is there anything they would not concoct, to avoid life imprisonment? What I find particularly striking – today the judge arrived from Perugia, in a vain attempt to interrogate me – is the fact that they are starting these manoeuvres right before the elections. Against the Socialist Party in Savona, against the Christian democrats in the south, against the Camorra (in other words, against all parties, but in favour of some) in Naples. And then against my comrades and me here in Rome – from Perugia. This is obviously a counterattack. An attempt to overload the situation, to raise the stakes in terms of spectacle. I already had an intimation that the newspapers were preparing some such operation, and a few days ago I had a first hint of new criminal proceedings. Today the warrant sits before me, accompanied by the slimy face of one of their hit-squad judges. He is very angry when I inform him that, in the absence of my lawyer (who is on strike), I am not able to reply to his charges. Maybe he thinks that strikes are still illegal, like in the good old days. I am angry, too, as I look at him, I think – I don't understand why the fact that he passed the examination to become a magistrate and now earns a fat salary gives him the right to get so personal with me. Then I chuckle to myself – in fact I laugh in his face – as he gets all worked up, and I reflect on the fact that his first name is Wladimir. As in Vladimir Ilych? Was that the intention of his father – who, for sure, must have been some old communist? The ironies of fate. Instead of growing up to become a guardian of freedom and communism, he is possessed by his function. A baleful situation. I look at him with a certain sympathy now. I wonder, are we in a phase of a new offensive now, one supported by the PCI central office, to uphold the fabrications of the 7 April case and to conjure up new charges in the election period? I have the impression that this is the way things are going.

We'll have to wait and see if this is how it turns out. What is certain is that the whole affair is dragging on and on. It's like some endlessly self-reproducing amoeba. The ferocity of the counterattack. Precisely at this moment, when it seems that my candidacy is bringing about new political possibilities. The ferocity of an institutional attack against an experience of struggles, which were intent on changing the institutions through the institutions. But this is too much! What do they want? Did they feel, maybe, themselves to be heroes, being shot at and killed? Why? Why do they not accept the symbol of peace-making that my presence in the elections represents? The fact is that the mixing in of politics with the trial proceedings – that unnatural coupling which was wanted from the start, by the PCI, by Gallucci, by Calogero – is now reproducing itself never-endingly. The ferocity is located in the subjective political valence, which preserves the continuity of this relationship. I am obliged to hold onto it, even though I denounce it. And they are obliged to reproduce it, even though they are its prisoners. I have the impression that the issue of a correct re-founding of the relationship between the political and the juridical – in other words, the breaking of the imbalances created by the political functioning of the magistracy – are problems which affect everybody. Enough of this net in which we are all caught! However, it makes me very tired to be endlessly driven onwards by a constitutional mechanism which is utterly corrupt. Breaking these dynamics is going to take a lot of political planning. Claiming constitutional justice instead of these depravations of the political spirit demands a lot of strength. We have neither the one nor the other – for the moment, I resist by means of anger. But not without hope. (G12 Rebibbia – 20 June)

Folio 48

The trial is postponed yet again. The lawyers' strike continues.

There's a huge amount of tension. Mine, and also that of the comrades. I have a long talk in prison with Don Nicola. He is accused of things to do with the 'ndrangheta. We have been friends for a while now. He is an exquisite person. He nurtures a nostalgia for the old Calabrian system of justice, and he hates the bands of young men who have destroyed that ethics. As for the justice of the state, with which he has had a lot to do, he sees it for what it is: a settling of accounts between gangs; a corruption, abstraction and alienation of the real relations of justice, which people live and produce. I enjoy talking with him. I like the formality of a relationship, even one of friendship, which is hard to arrive at in prison. We address each other in the plural, '*voi*'. I ask him what he thinks of this new volley of warrants, which have been dumped on me during election week. After the Perugia ones I am sure that others will arrive shortly. 'Vendetta,' he replies. 'But don't you think that it might be counter-productive?' I say. 'Professor,' he replies, 'you do not know these men of power. Power gives them pleasure. One man might like women, and another the oranges in his garden – but these people like power. Power is a rent. They say that it's not like that, but here it's now just the same as in America. When I realized this, that a tax could be put on power, just as you put a tax on someone who has too fat an income, I was happy. That's what I do to him – because power is wealth.' Again I reply: 'But these little provincial judges who are persecuting me today, right in the middle of the election period, I hardly think that they are earning or gaining from it.' He replies: 'Professor, you, who profess to be a teacher of men, understand very little about people. Excuse me, professor, I wouldn't want to offend you . . . that's the furthest thing from my mind. But you do not know them. After four years of prison and of persecution, have you not yet realized that justice is a small but arrogant power? These microbes are vain-glorious, green with envy. They like the power they have, and they want to see it grow. All you need to find out is who pays them – believe me, not with money or chickens (or maybe also with money and chickens, but they are only half men if they are content with that . . .). Paying them means giving them power, and prestige, or maybe sometimes even the chance to recover honour. One time there was a judge whose wife had been sleeping with another man. So that the village didn't talk about it, he sold his soul. You don't know how much shit there is in people's minds, professor, if you will excuse the expression. It is for that reason that I like you . . . You can't be bought because you don't have shit in your heart. But them, they are all the same. Slip them a bribe and you'll discover the nature of their souls. The minute you let them sniff power, they become like bull mastiffs. They will do anything and everything if you show them a bit of money. There is only one law: buy this one, because for sure someone else has bought the other one. You professor . . . there is nothing that is going to lift a life sentence off your head, because they're building their power at your expense – and every extra year you do in prison is a treasure for them, a gift. So relax – you're a good man, but you're just out of luck.' 'Don Nicola,' I say. 'How much longer do you think this can go on? I have had enough of it.' 'It will go on for ever. Justice is dead.' Justice is dead. Don Nicola confronts me with this atavistic sensation that I have experienced before. But justice today is worse than dead. It has become a servant. A slave to masters who are sadistic and mad.

'So,' says Don Nicola, 'don't go thinking that things are any different from how they've always been. Justice has died of old age. This eternal repetition of itself as a copy of power without the understanding of life. What has died is its internal law. But you, you will shortly be free. I have told the lads to vote for you. You be thinking about life and youth. Get yourself a young wife, and find yourself the warmest sun. The only justice is that of desiring beautiful things for everyone. One time I saw a shepherd up on a mountain. He told me: "Watch out for them, for the judges, for the *carabinieri*, for the bosses, they carry on killing your sheep like under the law of Cain. The only justice is the vendetta that is born of love." Do it. Get yourself a young woman.'

I am sitting here waiting for new warrants to arrive – I wait for them with the kicking desperation of a hunted animal. I can't be wise about all this. Nor can I take on board entirely the teachings of Don Nicola. But I love the man. (G12 Rebibbia – 21 June)

Folio 49

In the afternoon they summon me to make an electoral tape-recording. They take me to the prison governor's office. They put me down at a tape recorder, and they sit in front of me – the governor, the deputy governor, a couple of uniformed officers and the sound technician. A small bare room. To whom am I speaking? The tape will go out to the radio and TV. I can't imagine . . . What I have sitting in front of me is just prison officials. I speak to them – the rest of what I say escapes me, carried away by the tape. The situation is hallucinatory. I didn't expect it. Now they tell me that I have to hurry up. They show me the phone message from the ministry. Twenty minutes. What the hell am I supposed to say to these gentlemen, and to this machine? Now it is evening and I am in my cell, and I have no idea what I recorded. However, I can say what I would have wanted to say. Why do I want to get elected and get out of prison? Because I am a revolutionary. I speak to you as man to man. I believed in justice, and now I find myself faced with this persecution. Now I place my reliance on the community of prisoners, on its powers of resistance. I want to get out of here in order to be able to tell people everything that the community of prison has taught me, and the hope of revolution which it has renewed. I want to lay claim to the truth and values of revolution, which these comrades have lived – and to attack and abolish, or at any rate transform, the laws, the pre-judgements and the political agendas that keep us locked up in here. I look each of my comrades in the eye as I continue my discourse – in my mind's eye, I mean. Concretely, in reality, what I have here is the faces (fairly kindly, as it happens, given the nature of the occasion) of the prison screws. But here I'm straying from my argument. I want to act as a spokesperson, as a megaphone. Imagining the faces of the comrades gives me the strength to speak in this surreal situation. What would you say, Paolo P., if you were in my position? I think you would say that the revolution has been the great possibility of change – of an internal change, which develops densely between the infinite possibilities of the world – so that liberty becomes collective, within great mass dimensions. For the first time, in this relationship between the individual and collectivity, we have seen a fundamental role being played by the body, by the physicality of that liberation. Isn't that so, Luciano? And you, Tino, you would add that this hap-piness does not remove rigour and commitment, but encourages them and multiplies them in a concrete hope. I continue talking to the machine. I have an impetuous desire to speak of revolution. To repeat the aristocratic contempt that Francone has for the old world, and the very powerfully aggressive intellectual candour of Paolo V. Then a desperate recall to the truth which destroys all mystification – now I hear the breathing of Monfe and Arrigo and Schroffen. Then comes the shrill intrusion of an irony that breaks and destroys all cynicism – that's Lucio next to me. But perhaps desperation itself can become irony, ironical resistance, implacable serenity? But no, Marione and Emilio, you must not permit serenity to cancel out anger. Now I hear again the proletarian resistance of Oreste Str., as hard as it is intelligent, and, once again, the prophetic indigna-tion of Chicco, as spiky as it is generous. I talk into the machine: what I want to say is that revolution is love and irony, sobriety and abundance of passions, desperation of internal renewal, intelligence and utopia. Facing me I have deaf faces. I continue talking into the machine: to so many people, while I think and hope that the micro-cosm of prison corresponds to all other microcosms. Little by little I convince myself of this. Who can tell me that this is not the telling of a truth? It is a concert – yes, my dear prison guards, you who are listening to me in perplexity – it is beautiful music. It is not me that is playing it. We are saying it, many of us, in order to make ourselves understood to equally many. I admit that it is a strange symphony – but a symphony it is nonetheless. I launch these appeals to the world outside, a world I love. I wish they could be stones hurled against the windows of power. And in fact they are. The electoral campaign is a huge sounding board for our battle. This accumulation of injustices can be shown for what it is. The faces I have before me blanch, or blush, and sometimes they show a hint of humour. I continue – now a healthy excitation is getting to me. Now I really am talking with the people, and with the comrades outside. I overcome the impediment of the machine, and my psychological resistance to expressing myself in this bizarre little room. There's no longer any point in my talking about the past and the injustices suffered, of the struggles and the closure which the 7 April case has forced on them, criminalizing them. There's no longer any point in singing the song of the present and of our dignity. So let us speak of the future. It really is like a concert. I find myself listening to it even as I'm playing it. Look, a door is opening onto the future. There is a sense of expectation. We all know what its themes are, and we await their development. The future is made by us. We have it already prefigured in our minds, and the instruments are performing it. I talk into the machine about the future – paradoxes of democracy and of machinery. I speak slowly – then more loudly – and then passion takes over. For one comrade I say shit to the bosses, for another, I speak of liberating desire and of the joy of communism; for another, I speak of our justice and hope; for another, I stress their cruelty and the horror of their ideology. Let us change all this by going to the roots of things: by transforming people. We, here in prison, are people who have been transformed. It has cost us, but that is what we are. The revolution has taken place within us, and it is the constant of our existence. I have a habit of beginning to raise my voice, keeping it right on the subject, when I am coming to the end of a lesson or a speech. Here, in that moment, I was calm: I waited to allow our collective hope to speak out coolly. (G12 Rebibbia – 22 June)

Folio 50

A new arrest warrant has arrived for me – from Padova, from Calogero. Likewise for other comrades in Rebibbia. And then it appears that Augusto, Achille and others have been re-arrested. It is unbelievable. After four and a half years, again and again. Four days before the elections. This story really is absurd – and irresistible. By now I have accumulated something like five trials. We're ruined [*rovinati*], as they say in prison language. How is this unbelievable story ever going to come to an end? There is no way of getting out of this death-bearing machine. My body reacts by developing a raging toothache. Fortunately they haven't locked us in the cells, or deprived us of visits, as usually happens when new warrants are issued. I feel a terrible rage inside me. This is a monstrosity of cruelty and violence. This is the kind of moment when your claiming of your revolutionary choices rises in your gorge with a huge force. Knowing your enemy, and feeling his blows as they fall on your bones, you verify the truth of the analysis which has led you – and which leads me once again – to say that the only option is to destroy him. It is shameful, this opacity, this obduracy, this inertia which kicks into operation once the initial persecutory impulse is out of the way. As of today, with this warrant, my preventive imprisonment begins all over again. A further eleven years. As of today, my personal future is back to being what it was on the first day of our imprisonment. All the battles, the hopes, the demands, the legal defences and the self-criticism – all this is simply swept away. The machine sniggers to itself. Its gruesome separateness from life triumphs over my life. And yet I have to resist, I have to know how to handle this. Freedom is close, I can feel it. Like the joy of a successful act of rebellion. Of an act of knowing the truth which arrives at its object. I throw myself into my bunk. I chat with Oreste Str. – friendly and good-humoured he reminds me of a few very obvious points about justice, prison and trials. His bonhomie puts me into a better mood. There's nothing on TV. My toothache begins to wear off. I start to doze and my mind begins to wander. Desires and images of revenge, which I have not experienced for a long time, drift into my state of half wakefulness. Our capacities for self-control should not be overstated. I wake up and start to write. What an anger, and what an exhaustion! I feel as if I am falling, falling, falling – into a huge ravine. I experience the return of a childhood nightmare – a bomb that was dropping on me out of the sky, and getting closer and closer. I try to stop this movement, which is making me giddy. Into my mind comes Zeno's paradox of the immobility of the arrow, the paradox of my body in its rushing, of the bomb in its falling. This is how I manage to conquer that insensibility to pain which I am describing here. Yes, it is no longer a matter of concern to me. Maybe the metaphysical miracle of having plucked myself out of this dreadful gravitational force, which is dragging me towards the ravine . . . What I am left with is my anger; a very powerful anger. I hold it up and project it forcefully against this cowardly justice. I cannot accept them destroying me in my inner being. I want freedom. (G12 Rebibbia – 23 June)

Folio 51

And it's still not over! Today the judges from Ancona arrived, to interrogate me over the killing of Alceste Campanile. A terrible *choc*. I find it hard to bear the weight of these infamies which are being piled onto me, one after the other. It is clearly deliberate, the plan which these judges are running – this is the third warrant they have served on me in this pre-electoral week! Heinous charges, designed to have equally heinous fallout effects. No, enough! The vulgarity of the political use of the courts! An overbearing dynamic, intent on destruction. The comrades are standing by me. The evident iniquity of this persecution is beginning to get to everyone. The TV is on my back. They broadcast with gay abandon every bit of slanderous news. But, I ask myself, will these people never have enough of it? My situation has become a caricature of the injustice of the court system. Eternal preventive detention, which is nevertheless made additionally eternal by this continuous shower of warrants, which arrive in bunches. A hatred against me which has become a mechanism of enlarged reproduction of the injustice of the court system. An ongoing reproduction of the overweening power of the judges and of the repressive teleology of this regime. No, enough! I look around myself and I see the horror which this machine produces. This is its sole function – to spread horror in order to preserve a ruling class and a regime of injustice, and also to eliminate democracy. What scares me is the banality and the extreme stickiness of this mechanism. In the days when I was a professor of state doctrine I used to teach that, in the relationship between the state and its subjects, the former has the advantage – that of being able to survive even in the absence of consensus, on passivity, on negativity, whereas the subjects have only one possibility: that of activating themselves, whether in democracy or in revolution. What I did not imagine, even when I was teaching as a professor, was how powerful and brutal the mechanisms of passivity could be. Today I am experiencing them at first hand. This discovery, the outcome of my years in prison, is a small one, but even so it serves to repay me intellectually for much of the suffering. That said, the project is to destroy this passivity and to drain violently the swamp of power. 'In the Swamp' – that could be the title for many of the scientific and political discoveries made in these years. A swamp whose stench and corrosive nature I have experienced in person, but which also corresponds to a regime – to an internalized crisis, to a passivity of subjects that seems to be unresolvable. In this little swamp only homologous elements operate – it is an imploding ecological disaster. The judges are the maximal reproducers of putrefaction the maximal agents of the rot in this immobile state of nature. 'Getting out of the Swamp' – I think that's the only slogan possible today. A word for my comrades: don't make fun of me. I am not talking of means and forces, and I am not talking of politics in quotation marks. I am talking about moral resistance, which is the necessary basis of all political reconstruction. We're talking ecology here. I hope that people's sense of smell will develop, or rather will be restored, both in us and in our fellow citizens. So this is not a moralism; it is my own moral protest. The anger which grips me when I face the machine of repression is the same as the disgust I experience with the regime. Often tiredness undermines the protest. But the hope of overturning this state of things must never be allowed to fail. Our prison stands in the middle of a swamp of civilization – and not only as regards the justice system. It is growing and spreading. Today I refused to answer the judges from Ancona. I explained to them that my lawyer was not here (he is still on strike) and that I reserved my right to reply. They are obviously not aware of the vileness of their action. One of them, the procurator, was wearing a Rotary badge: a fish grown fat in the swamp. The instructing judge had a yellow face – malaria from the swamp. There was also one of the lawyers representing the civil parties, equally full of bile. No, gentlemen, I am not coming down with you into this swamp. I prefer my life in prison. I prefer the freedom I am waiting for, which has dropped from the skies so unexpectedly, and so catastrophically for you . . . this opportunity given to me by the elections, so that I can continue fighting. I have too much anger still in my body. And now, after these latest warrants, I also have a terrible bitterness. Sometimes I still have the reactions of a professor. I cannot believe – or only with bitterness can I accept – that your democracy really is such a stinking pit. (G12 Rebibbia – 24 June)

Folio 52

I voted in the early afternoon. It would have been bad luck to vote for myself, so I voted for Vincino as my preference. All the others voted for me, all the comrades, political and non-political prisoners alike. There's a festive mood today. We had an excellent meal. The comrades keep calling to me from the other courtyards, or from the cells, wishing me good luck. The physicality of freedom is beyond question here in prison – and also the extent to which it is an inalienable good. This is the reason why they are voting for me – for my freedom, which in itself would be enough to repay their vote. In no sense are they expecting an electoral programme from me. They are voting for an escape. As for the programme, I am getting down to work, and what little I can do I shall do. They know that. Gradually, from the struggles in San Vittore to the Rebibbia delegation, and then increasingly – passing via the activities of the political prisoners and via the generalization of the contents of the document written by 'the 51' [*autonomia* prisoners] – a new movement of prisoners has developed over the last few years. I think about this, I think about the things that need to be done. The truth is that I really cannot concentrate at the moment – I am very tense and emotional. This waiting is horrible . . . such a wait . . . For how long? Just until tomorrow evening. Probably we'll have the results of the exit polls by tomorrow afternoon. That's good. Hope is young and strong. The movement in the prisons certainly has no relation to my election. I have been very careful not to superimpose the two questions – I have received many public political positions of support even from people inside the prisons, but it would have been better if they hadn't. It was not good for the two levels to get mixed up. So today I am in waiting mode. Freedom does not scare me – I don't feel myself to be so far away from the world. I don't understand how all this is going to end, but the main thing is to get out, to stick my feet out, to break the asphalt, and to begin to walk on grass again. And supposing I fail to get elected? In that doubt I see an enormous danger. The Radicals have conducted an insane election campaign. It was in their style, but really it was a demented approach. Buffonery *alla* Bertoldo. It stirred people up, then it moved the proposal for abstention, and then it directed people to an alternative vote. Their game has been far too sophisticated. But we shall see. What is certain is that, if I fail, they will make me pay dearly for this escape attempt. They will never forgive me. They would never forgive themselves for having been scared that I might get away with it. Anyway, we shall see. I just have to wait. Until tomorrow afternoon. They tell me that the comrades on the outside have been pushing themselves to the limit on all this. I find that easy to believe. If it were possible to establish an ongoing relationship between prison and society, the problem of the prisons could be today an element in rekindling the struggle and in reawakening the consciousness of the whole of our society. This prison world is like a filter for the whole of society, and when I go out into society I should – briefly but efficaciously – represent its hopes. That will be the moment to take up the issue of struggles in prison by forming a relay [*relais*] of communication, of proposals, of initiatives. But we shall see, we shall see . . . A very nervous wait, between now and tomorrow. (G12 Rebibbia – 26 June)

Folio 53

Hard to find the words to describe today. I've hardly stopped crying. From joy. My election is guaranteed. I am practically free. I cry – for what I have lost, and for what I have gained. It feels like I have eaten up the whole of my humanity in these years of imprisonment – but it also feels like I have regained it. I'm crying for the whole affair, but at the same time I'm as happy as a kid. I kiss all the comrades whom I manage to see. From the spyholes in the cell doors people shout comments, shouts, screams of joy. The election is for sure. The Radicals have certainly got more than the number of votes needed – in fact the whole thing has been an electoral success. But a day like today deserves to be written out in detail, because it's been so full of ups and downs – almost an example of everyday life in prison. And, what's more, an example of the conflicts and the tensions, the whole stage-setting, of these past years. So let's do that – let's tell the story of today.

The weather is dry this morning. All this waiting is beginning to get to me. I eat breakfast and I write letters. But they are letters that I shall not send – just exercises, to pass the time. I go down into the passage-way. The usual good-humoured backchat, the usual well meant jokes. Then they summon me. A magistrate! Who is this magistrate, who wants to see me? It is exactly 3.00 p.m., and any minute now the big TV news programme is about to start, examining and commenting on the results of the election. In an hour at most, we'll have the results of the first exit polls, from which it will be clear whether I'm a free man or not. A magistrate! I have to go down. No choice. Otherwise they come and take you down by force – this is prison, after all. They don't tell me who it is – they never tell you – and the guards don't know anyway. I go down, furious that they're going to make me miss the TV results. I go down and into the examination room, and behind the desk I see a young man and a male secretary sitting at a typewriter. Suddenly, lo and behold, from the other side of the room, hidden as you first enter the room, out pops Calogero.

He reaches out for me so that I shake his hand. I am turned to stone. It so happens that I am unable to shake his hand, but it is only for this reason – because I am completely thrown by the fact of seeing him there. My inability is entirely due to the fact that I've been thrown by the moment. So he gets upset and says: 'So you won't shake my hand?' It's like he's whipping me. A flood of insults rises to my lips and I want to jump all over him. I manage to recover my cool. However, I look at him with eyes which, I think, are not dominated, and with a look of hatred. He avoids my gaze and sits himself on the other side of the desk. He has aged. Now he's fat and sweaty. His eyes switch here and there, obviously embarrassed. A big difference from the Calogero whom I saw – just once – two or three days after my arrest – four years, four and a half years ago! In those days he was completely on the ball, smoking cigarettes one after the other, halfway between a front-line judge and a detective, plainly seeing himself in the role of some genius San Francisco cop. I watch him intensely. He is yellow, just as I remember him. But four years ago, he looked half Chinese; now a flabby Mongol look has taken over. His eyes dance in an irregular rhythm and seem to be out of his control. 'Why should I shake your hand?' I eventually reply. In actual fact, I realize it immediately, after having thought for long years about his contorted and weird half humanity, after having imagined it: the truth is that he needs me. Just as a parasite needs a body from which to suck its blood. Like a sadistic lover, rejected.

And he is suffering from my rejection. 'All right, if that's the way it is . . .' he says. At this point I can no longer keep my mouth under restraint. I can do it, now I am controlling myself internally. I've got over my surprise, and also my desire to throttle him. I can go over the top without going over the top. I come out with a flood of insults.

He listens and does not know how to react. His colleague intervenes. He tells me to calm down, but he doesn't even dare to threaten me with legal consequences for the insults which, by now, are flowing from my lips. Now it is Calogero's turn to be turned to stone. Obviously, in the mystified projection of his dehumanized consciousness, he had seen our encounter as a historical moment – two protagonists meeting in the field – a kind of honourable accommodation between our two respective truths, in mutual respect. Honour under arms! He probably imagined this encounter as it might have been seen on TV, and for him it probably was as if we were actually on TV. Maybe he would have confessed this desire to some prostitute he was frequenting. 'My lawyer is not here,' I said. 'Can we get this over quickly. I have to go back up to see the exit polls.' 'But I have come here to explain to you how I have reshaped the prosecution case,' he stutters . . . 'To show you how I have studied the thing,' he hisses. I ask him, now icy-cold and furious – how dare he come here and say such things. I ask him if he thinks that his hypotheses are worth four and a half years in prison. I tell him to go and stick his theorem and his modifications . . . His colleague intervenes again – he is no longer a judge of the republic, poor thing, but a pacifier: 'Keep calm,' he begs.

The *carabiniere* on the typewriter watches in terror. I want to go back up. They'll already be giving the exit polls. But why, I ask myself, does this wretch have to come and demand to see me right now, after four and a half years? Is this one final act of sadism? Probably I have already been elected – so maybe he wanted to deprive me even of the pleasure of finding out about my freedom through the TV election programme. In any event, he is now feeling the cock up his arse, and he can't continue with his natural sadism. He withdraws into himself every time I look his way, this yellow simulacrum of injustice – like worms, he has an amazing ability to make himself small. I think of the cruel games played by country children, doing nasty things to worms and snails.

'I refuse to be examined by you – and I call for your resignation from your post and your withdrawal from this case against me, since you have taken public positions and spoken publicly to my detriment.' My very words, plus various other insults, which I imagine are also in the transcript of our encounter. He reacts. 'I have always spoken through court proceedings.' Obviously he has gone mad. He forgets the interviews – many of them – with the newspapers and the TV. He has gone crazy. But that doesn't stop him. He stammers justifications. By now his colleague has gathered his wits, and he issues me with an official warning.

It comes easily to reply calmly now, avoiding the insults. However, I address both of them in the informal '*tu*' ['you']. 'But stop this,' I say – to the one and to the other. 'Who exactly do you think you are?' With a bit of luck, this will finish them off. At last I can go back up. I am very tired, but this time they are not going to be able to lay a hand on me. I go up the stairs – a huge long journey, right through Rebibbia, on the inside . . . never has it seemed so long.

I look closely at the door frames, at the corners, at the windows, at the grilles of the gates and at the bars, as if I'm seeing them for the last time. I arrive in the wing, and from the first peephole I hear a shout: 'It looks like we've done it! Bravo, Toni!' This is confirmed from the other spyholes. Luciano waves across and tells me that we've done it. I go into my cell. We've done it – I see it, from the first results. I feel faint, like some feeble teenager carried away with amorous fancies. I don't remember what happened after that. I ate supper in Luciano's cell, and I wept, for the first time since I came into prison. (G12 Rebibbia – 27 June)

Folio 54

People send me flowers. The guards allow them in. Avalanches of telegrams – I want to reply to all of them. The news arrives that the voting figure is somewhere up around 50,000 – incredible. I have been elected in the three constituencies where I put myself forward – Rome, Naples and Milan. This is a huge political fact. I don't know when I shall get out of prison, but it will be soon. A few moments of aggressiveness towards me from some of the comrades, but never moments of animosity. What we have here is joy mixed with hope – and, for some of them, also a feeling of envy, which is entirely understandable. The things that I keep promising to do are mounting up – shall I ever manage to do them all? On Wednesday 1 July there is the hearing – what to do? There are two counterposing arguments – one, that I should keep a medium-to-low profile in my speech to the court, and not go too far in personalizing the event (and the trial) we are living; the other says that I should make a strong intervention, calling for all the 7 April defendants to be released. I don't think this second line is correct. We need more intelligence. First we have to draw up an overall strategy. I argue that at the moment we simply do not have the time to do this. A few people get angry. I hear an accusation which I often hear when I insist on reason against the immediacy of needs: people accuse me of a lack of generosity. With great freshness of spirit, I sense the trap that lies behind this accusation. I am happy to concede both the value and the force of this slight lack of (and most certainly not absence of) generosity. How else would it have been possible to modify the internal climate of the prisons, and to make politics even in situations where desperation was seizing you by the throat? How would it have been possible to transform the refusal into contestation and to articulate a revolutionary strategy, both inside and outside the trial, with a realistic tactics? I am always ready to wait for anyone at the last station – and precisely at the Finland station – and I count on having the courage to arrive there. And, concerning the occasions when I raised my arms in a sign of momentary tiredness (when I look at myself, I realize that my gesture resembles the raised arms of one of those scissor-corkscrews when you open a new bottle): the astuteness becomes humanity, while generosity, on the other hand, becomes stupid when the struggle is getting tough. But these are not the main problems today. The handling of my exit from prison must be a major, solid, political act. A project for justice must be prefigured in that event. In the determination we have to be able to see the universal. Exiting from the sensation of paradox. Laying the basis for future work. In the confusion and emotion of these days I am very much keeping my feet on the ground. I have won. But how are we going to make this victory productive? Up until now, our heroism has struggled against the implacable machine – now the time of life has broken the repressive intrigue of the trial. How shall we now bring out into the open this collective hope for liberation, at this point of intersection between the times of exploitation and the times of life? How are we to organize the work on this? I want to be clear-headed – the happiness is catching at my throat . . . the new things that need to be done are disorienting me in the globality in which they present themselves – a political problem, and at the same time so very, very many individual concrete problems of justice that need to be dealt with. I need some time to think. But, anyway, it is done. The first step has been taken. A flower, a beautiful flower, has suddenly appeared through the concrete of this damned prison. (G12 Rebibbia – 28–30 June)

Folio 55

Trial again today. The fifty-first day – and this is the final day of this phase. The trial will start again on 26 September. Just to be clear: either I'll be there, or I won't. I took this decision today, sitting in court, as I listened to the learned and malevolent speeches of all the supporting actors in this ignoble farce of justice. But let's take things one at a time. We arrive in the courtroom, there's a commotion, with a load of photographers and a lot of public. From the back, applause and cheering – for the first time, a big sound of happiness comes across this desert, and the spotlights somehow become more humane, and the highly sophisticated systems of internal control react hysterically. Their temple of idiocy has finally been profaned. I find it hard to hold back the tears, and I keep blowing my nose. This is perhaps the last day I'll be in this cage – at least for the moment . . . we'll see about that later. Enter the court, in the midst of all this fracas. I am called up. I ask for the trial to be suspended, as is my right, since the vote of the people has lifted me out of these judicial proceedings. I say this clumsily, rapidly, which is what happens when I get emotional. All I want at this moment is to go somewhere far, far away. A long way from everything. I wish I could just collapse into myself. When I win, I get little pleasure out of the fact of winning. Instead there come crowding into my mind memories of the wretchedness and injustice of still being here, up on the stand, in the dock. Suddenly I feel an incredible sensation of disgust. I want to vomit. I go back into the cage. The president has accepted that the proceedings have to be suspended. As I go down through the tunnels that lead back to the cage, I hear shouting from the courtroom. Marini, the procurator, has started speaking. Coming up from the basement, I hear him making wild and provocative statements – he is bringing new *pentiti* against me – Savasta, Libera and Marocco. He is multiplying the shame of their lying accusations – accusing me of murders, accusing me of political vulgarity – with an impassioned rhetoric and with the voice of an inquisitor. By the time I get into the cage, all the comrades are on their feet and reacting violently to his accusations. The defendants who are not in the cage are also protesting noisily from behind the screens. The public has started shouting again. A tremendous din, you can't hear a thing. In the journalists' section of the court I see Rossana ranting at the public prosecutor. The comrades say we should walk out. The *carabinieri* open the cage door, and we go down to the cells. I understand nothing of what has happened – but I feel the immense warmth of the comrades. It seems to me that suddenly, as if by magic, we have re-found ourselves in one of those working-class struggles of years ago – a music resonating on feelings of a joyous great aggressiveness in the face of this barefaced injustice. Meantime the hearing has been suspended – the lawyers come down into the cells and ask us to come up again. They tell me that Marini has been shut up by the president himself. 'But why didn't you say anything?' we ask. 'Wasn't that what we had agreed?' They don't reply. With lawyers, distinguishing the sense of opportuneness from opportunism, or from cowardice, is a problem of high mathematics, with margins tending to zero. Marini has stopped, and the court re-enters. Emilio goes into the dock. He calls for us all to be released. The president says nothing in reply – and when Emilio starts getting to the point he tells him to shut up. Then, having silenced Emilio, he starts talking himself, and outlines for the various parties the problem of the eventual suspension of the trial. They all have something to say on the matter – the civil parties, the various state lawyers, and finally, once again, the Public Prosecutor. They wrangle over the correct forms and procedures. Once again the hearing is suspended. Finally Giuliano steps up to have his say. 'This story of yours,' he says, in other words the story of this trial, is a dirty story . . . The way the proceedings have been doubled up is also dirty, what with the various different cases and bunches of new warrants, and the way the procurator has made deliberate use of this period of the elections. Enough, enough! Do whatever you like, just as you have always done. Stir the shit with the stirring-spoon of the law, if that's what you have to do. But my client has to be freed immediately.

His denunciation is powerful, and the invective is efficacious. The court withdraws. They go into consultation for three or four hours. I imagine that they will have eaten and drunk well in that period. They will also have consulted all their friends and political protectors. That much seems obvious. Then comes the decision to suspend the proceedings. Until 26 September. We go back to prison. Very tired. I think: when the stickiness of the trial is a mechanical fact, then that is just the way it is. However, when, as happened today, the prosecution transmutes the stickiness into deliberate provocation, then it is hatred. Political hatred pure and simple. So it is true, what I had thought and projected ever since that first day of our imprisonment: you won't get out of here by juridical means. This is only possible through political means. Four years of my life it has cost me. In relation to the political dimensions and effects of my rebellion, this is not a lot. But in relation to justice – the justice of a state of right [*stato di diritto*] which we appreciated and wanted to preserve – it is too much, too much. (G12 Rebibbia – 1 July)

Folio 56

I am waiting to be freed. (I find it hard to imagine the world outside. Flashes of a life lived. What is it going to be like? I get clear images of particular people and places in my mind's eye. Strangely, mostly I remember Paris – my last weeks of freedom. What is it going to be like? They tell me that prices have gone up a lot. But people aren't dressing so very differently from five years ago. And what has happened in politics? What can you grasp with the new gaze of a man fresh out of prison? Very violent visual flashes . . .) I need to get out of here quickly. But, before the judges will let me out, they set up 'bicycles' – that's what they call it, in prison, when they create deliberate pretexts and obstacles to give you the runaround. Pedal, pedal – the pretexts, the difficulties, the deliberate obstructiveness . . . once they are set in motion, it's like being forced to do a cycling marathon. But I really don't think they'll be able to block my freedom. Basically I'm already free. This must be because I am thinking and thinking – with my comrades and within myself – without straining myself in doing so, but with a huge feeling of exhaustion as soon as I finish – thinking and thinking about what needs to be done. For some time now we have been on the path to reconciliation. Now, with the strength of the vote behind us, we need to take some big steps forward. For how long will they leave me free? How will these dogs succeed in putting me back behind bars? I am optimistic – perhaps not on the basis of any reality, but in my head, with my mind, which is so wearied by projects; I am optimistic, profoundly so. Optimism of reason. The road we have travelled has been long. From dissociation as the reconfirmation of our non-terrorist identity, to the campaign for a political solution. And then also our handling of this trial, always on the attack, against the loathesome practices of *pentitismo* and against their emergency laws. Optimism of the intellect: we cannot not win. From what I have heard, there is a deep crisis inside the PCI on the problem of repression. However, the only way we can get out of this situation is by putting ourselves forward again as a political force. Pessimism of the will: in other words, our enlightenment thinking [*illuminismo*] meets with opposition from forces which do not want, and which cannot handle, a radical modification of the political horizon. The constants of the scenario are in place for a long time – a modification in the materiality of the political framework is almost impossible to obtain through proposals which aim to win over the components of that political framework. Unless some radical political change [*catastrofe*] occurs. Italy needs a new Resistance. In part, that is what the 1970s represented – but the defeat has been very hard-hitting. How are we to get over it, how can we bring the comrades out of prison and reintroduce a spirit of radical political change? That world out there, which I shall shortly be entering, is dominated by war. Corporations at each other's throats. Rot and corruption of political power. And a magistracy incapable of controlling a society in violent crisis. Pessimism of the will, extreme realism and extreme attentiveness. And yet, simultaneously, there is this enlightened, reason-based hope for radical change. Is it my fault if, today, the only way in which reason can sink this empty representation of the political is through radical political change? Is it my fault if this world, which I am re-entering, is marked by an insane and absolute lack of meaning, and is a body of the most absolute contingency? Petrified in the repetition of itself? Of its rituals and stupidity? As I step out, I am strengthened by two considerations. The first derives from my knowledge of what we were in prison: the only force (because this is precisely what we have become) which, cancelling out the negative effects of a historical memory which cast us out of political struggle, has succeeded in making its way back into it, and in producing new subjects of social war against the un-removability of a regime of repression, against a constitution that had been killed. And we did all that from prison. So that brings me to the second consideration: from prison to society. The vote which has carried me into Parliament. This was a vote given by people who recognized, in prison, the symbol of the society we are, of the crisis we are living. There are very many of them. I am referring to the estimated number of voters. It seems that the total number of people who voted for me throughout Italy was about 500,000. So perhaps it is possible, with a bit of optimism of the intellect and extreme attention to our initiatives, to set in place a *relais*, a multiplicative relationship between the struggle for truth, which the comrades are developing in prison, and political struggle in society. Against their infinite reproductions of prison. They – the enemy – have sought to establish a social peace organized on the model of prison. They – the enemy – have introduced radical change in the lives of individuals, and of society as a whole. Our response, too, has to be made on the basis of radical change, on the arc which extends between prison and society. However, we should not underestimate the difficulties of the intellect. The ineptitude and the vulgarity, the ponderous ritualism and the priestly stupidity of the political class we have before us, all this creates cruelty and violence. It is an obscene spectacle. I shall find myself up against forces that are decisively and strenuously fascist. And today, given the way the world is going, it seems that the only alternative to fascism is opportunism. Don't trust anyone, the comrades tell me. They know that I shall do this – I shall address my words to everybody, even to the enemy, without placing my trust in anybody. Except in the comrades, and in all those whom I love and who love me, and in all those who have been living, outside of prison, the same prison that I have been living on the inside. So let's get ready. What awaits me is fearsome. I have to be capable of combining hope with strength. (G12 Rebibbia – 2–7 July)

Folio 57

I am out. After another day of interminable waiting, all of a sudden . . . I hardly had time to say goodbye to the comrades . . . they let me out all in a rush . . . pushed me out. There was a car in the prison courtyard, with a senator on board and a very skilled driver, and we went out through a side gate. We headed for the countryside, moving very fast. Going down roads that I had only seen from the windows of the armoured vans they used for transporting us. The violence of the image seen only through steel grilles now diffuses into another image, of nature – the image of this rich and splendid Roman summer. The colours of nature fill my gaze. The oncoming dusk is really beauti-ful. I'll never look at the sky again – for too many years in prison all I could look at was the sky. Now I look at this earth, this grass that changes at every step. My foot savours the sensation of walking on grass. After four years of cement, this is another life – and the muscles communicate it to you, right up to your head, in the tenderness of the contact with the earth. I hug Paola, with love – and astonished that we don't have the usual prison bench between us. Anna, my daugh-ter, hasn't come – she has exams this week. I walk with Francesco, my son, chatting. I phone my relations in Venice and Padova. I look out Doni and Sylvie, my friends – I don't find them but I am think-ing of them. Then Tommaso, Rossana and Luigi F. arrive, and I am able to express my gratitude to them. None of us can get over our amazement. Pasquale and Claudia are my hosts, and they are emo-tional about this moment. With them, as with everyone else, I have difficulties of language. Talking on the outside, with free people, is like talking a foreign language. You think in your own language, and you have to translate. There's a swimming pool in the park – I feel like jumping in fully clothed. I take a quiet swim. Then I drink a fair quantity of whiskey, after four and a half years of going without. It still tastes good. The strangeness and the difficulty of communication are still with me. I pinch myself – this freedom is real. The night is full of stars. Now everyone has gone. I'm writing, letting off steam a bit. Tomorrow . . .

Marco P. arrived in the afternoon, and we worked on a kind of programme. But that's the last thing on my mind. The physical-ity of freedom is the only feeling I have – a dream come true. This physicality, I swear, conquered through prison . . . this sensation of reconquering the body . . . it's like being a child again – a sensation which comes after you've passed through the total dispossession of your body through prison and torture, on top of the fact that life before prison, and becoming adults, had, unbeknownst to ourselves, forced us to reduce the body's presence to the point of mystification . . . this physicality will now stay with me forever. If there is such a thing as baptism, for me, this evening is it. If there is a trinity of body and reason and life, this evening I have finally understood it. I get flashes of the unhappiness of the past. The faces of the comrades parade before me like ghosts. I shake hands with the ghosts, and I reject with horror the unhappiness. As I write I am sitting out in the open, under a lamp. Silence. You don't even hear the monotonous chirruping of the crickets, which made me hate the summer nights in Rebibbia – the sounds of a nature that was unattainable. Now everything is perfect. Tomorrow . . . the struggle will begin again. I feel strong and able to sustain it. I think it is probably very late. I have no desire to sleep. Now I lie on the grass, smelling it and stroking it. Never have I felt the passion for justice so strongly as in this quietness, as if I am immersed in a compact silence. And anger for everything that has happened, for the comrades who are still in prison, for the injustices suffered – all this is very close at hand. In this complete serenity of being, the time of life, of rebellion and of transformation is very dear to me. In the arc of this day it stood poised between different worlds, between contradictory sensations, through to the certainty of having it in my hand. A point of real knowledge, against the intrigues of power. I stretch out on damp grass in the night air. (Rome – 8 July)

3

In Parliament

9 July to 18 September 1983: Folios 58–98

Folio 58

Morning. I went to bed very late – drunk with freedom – but I woke early and started to write. So many things were going through my mind last night. I was mentally preparing the press conference that I shall be giving shortly. But, above all, I imagined the world I was just about to enter. I note that I shall now be able to pursue in more complex forms my analysis of the institution – which, up until now, I have only looked at from within the confines of the trial: Parliament, just like the court, is one face of the institution; but, compared with the court, it is more of an open space. Furthermore, whereas the trial experience was wholly swallowed up into the institution and antagonistic elements could only appear as heroism, here I already have the possibility of referring to other things: to alterity, to the diversity of the social forces in relation to the institution. It is fundamental to understand – and I need to put all my cognitive enthusiasm into this: previously the logic of prosecution and defence was locked into the confines of the courtroom; now, by contrast, I can live it externally, magnifying and endlessly discovering its antagonistic dimensions. In the trial, the contradiction of the institution can only unfold in an opaque space; now, in the free life I am beginning to live, I can make that contradiction transparent – if I take as my reference point these things which are 'different' from the institution and from the rotten politics that dwell within it. Transparency: of love and solidarity – the fresh force of people who are against this wretched world. Together with many other people we shall succeed in reconquering the meaning of transformation and democracy . . .

Everyone is asleep – I can't sleep. I am writing on the balcony, on the Lido. I have the San Marco lagoon in front of me, in all its beauty. The island of San Lazaro – a wonder of wonders – I can almost touch it if I reach out a finger. The enchantment of the night, and its bodily, humid transparency. What a day! This morning Marco P. had me doing the triumphant rounds of Montecitorio. I know Montecitorio well. I've known it for years, since the '50s and '60s, when I came to visit friends who were party secretaries and Members of Parliament, and to study. I allow Marco the satisfaction of thinking, in his triumphalism, that I am amazed by all of this. The good savage at the court of Madrid. Then we go in a big procession from Montecitorio to Piazza Argentina. With *paparazzi* running after us. Rossana does everything in her power not to be photographed together with Marco, and Marco does everything he can to get a group photo. Then the press conference – a hellish heat. Is it always going to be as hot as this in the institutions? Idiotic questions from the journalists, except those from the foreign press. Everyone is looking at me as if I were some kind of weird animal. What does it feel like to be out after four and a half years of more or less special penitentiary? They are amazed to see a man before them. They can't work out whether he is an intelligent criminal or an innocent cretin: all their questions are directed to finding the answers to that question. Thanks. The crush is impressive. The photographers add a couple of hundredweight of extra frazzling heat to the temperature of the day. I have to smile and put up with various of Marco P.'s customary incredible idiocies about Marxism – but, for the rest, he is behaving well and he is obviously comfortable in this role. I, on the other hand, only feel comfortable when I spot a couple of friends in the crowd. I wink at them and pass them little notes about meeting up. Mauro G. is among them – I know him since the early '50s, and I love him – we have in common glories and pains. He is now a symbol of that incredible continuity of revolutionary history, which constitutes us – almost a sign that our prison-imposed separation from all the others is at an end. Finished, finished. The idiotic, rapid fire of questions from the journalists continues. (Speaking of which – examine more closely the bestial character of the ignorance and arrogance of this corporation; resume discussion, not only of the corporation itself – which is brutal and cheap, but perhaps better than others – but of the journalists: ask them one by one who pays them, what is the balance between business and corruption, etc., etc.) I don't care. It's party time, I should be happy, and indeed I am. We continue. But it is beginning to get boring. Marco is on top form. More so than a peacock. Why? Anyway, I feel the need for a bit of novelty. At a certain point, the

Radical senator pulls me into a corner and tells me: the secret services want to protect you. Well, that's an entertaining novelty! They can go to hell. At lunch with Rossana we find the time for a free-ranging interview. Very emotional. I love you, Rossana. I don't care that your old-style communism is grafted onto the institutions, I don't care about that doglike Togliattianism of yours. Often you go beyond all this – and I love the fervent way in which your intelligence is conjugated with your communism. We eat well – and then we rush to the airport. The *paparazzi* hard on our heels again. At Fiumicino I meet Giulio E. and we embrace. A plane for Venice. Oh, what a splendid sky! How many times in prison did I follow from the prison corridors the vapour trails of high-flying aircraft!

An almost hysterical emotionality – a nervousness that affects my whole body – I am like a young animal released from the cage in which it had been caught. These are the dimensions of your freedom – the dimensions of the sky – don't forget it. Venezia, and a motor taxi to the Lido. From Tessera we do the canal between Murano and Fondamenta Nuove, between Arsenale and Vignole. And right there, out on the waters, Paola starts crying – no, not crying . . . yelling and weeping her happiness and all the accumulated pain. Evening is about to fall: the colours and shades between the sea and the sky are those of the bosom of the great mother. Paola's scream is that of birth, of entering, of returning to life.

On the terrace at the Lido I embrace my relations. With great emotion. From this terrace, you can see for miles. I am already restless. On the first evening I see, one by one, the comrades whom I left behind in prison. But imagination and revolutionary hope have to go further. On this terrace, on this evening, I am going crazy. Everything is pulling me out, pushing me beyond, towards that line of the marine horizon that is always light-filled and always infinite. (Rome/Venice – 9 July)

Folio 59

Padova. I go to visit my mother's grave in the cemetery. She died while I was in prison. I pour a bit of earth onto her grave, letting it slip between my fingers. The earth is dry, but my hand caresses it. I think of your smile, Aldina, my old young mother. I cry like a baby, without trying to restrain myself. My son, Francesco, 16 years of age, holds my arm tightly. Hope: of my freedom, of revolution, of community – how many sad and deep thoughts in this tender metaphysics of filial piety – how much of those desires and those imaginings did you nourish – sweetest mother, Lucretian figure – *alma Venus*. (Outside the cemetery a photographer tries to get a shot of me: I would have killed him, if it was worth the effort.) Then Milan. Once again, I set foot in that much loved and damnable city. It is Sunday evening when I arrive. The city is empty. I think about the metropolitan sidewalks which I love, and about these internal horizons, which are unknown to outsiders and jealously guarded by those who hold them. My metropolis. I conquered you in the times of revolutionary movement, from Pirelli and Alfa down to the city's network of canals. I know you in your decades-long dynamics of unsuppressible movement for liberation and in your charming, permanent but by no means predictable capacity for transformation – and also of repression. What a strange complexion you have, my Milan, at once working-class and bourgeois, virgin and whore. The few remaining comrades in town come to visit me – from what I was told, several thousand have left, to go either into prison, or into exile, or into their private lives, which often involve drugs. And they are so many. In our quick chats they reveal aspects of what has been happening here, of the frequent, harsh and deep reality of repression. It is no longer the city that I left behind me, they tell me. I react: 'Do you remember revolution?' But, most of all, have we forgotten that formidable growth of metropolitan science which we saw developing in this theatre of action? And what about the quantity of knowledge accumulated? Good for you, they reply: at best, Milan is the capital of intellectual black labour. We shall see. Meanwhile I am doing non-stop interviews. I try to make myself one with the tiredness of the people I encounter, to destroy myself through work. It is obvious that I'm feeling a sense of guilt about having come out of prison alone, without my comrades. I begin to compensate for this sense of guilt by giving myself a bout of impossibly strenuous work. I sleep in snatches, I don't make love. I work like a machine. My children, Francesco and Anna, look at me as you would at a monster. Am I beginning to live reality as if it were a prison? I have been out for two days now, and the only way I can relax is by working. Immediately, as of now, for the freedom of everyone. From 1971, since the time when I transferred myself definitively, Milan has been the centre of the world for me – both that of analysis and that of political practice. Milano: *experientia sive praxis*. This is where I should be moving ahead. If only Rome would let me work from here. But it won't happen, of this I am certain. In that institutional shithouse which is Rome they will throttle me. I continue talking and talking with the few comrades still left in the city. I am a survivor, and they are people who escaped with their lives. Not much comes of it. All I understand is that the wound left by repression is so deep that it will not heal soon. Only a radical political change [*una catastrofe politica*] can set in motion these great and cherished forces. But I cannot allow myself yet to play the card of wisdom. A long job, a subtle project, Milan as the centre of the world, as the crystal of contradictions, of the crisis, of the possibility of reaction, of innovation: this has been and continues to be the correct working hypothesis. And yet I cannot permit myself to follow the correct hypothesis. I have to continue working like a lunatic, swimming in the shit of Rome. First of all to get the comrades out by whatever means – before becoming wise.

This evening Piazza Vetra is sweaty instead of dry – standing aside from the love I bear it. Tomorrow to Rome, to begin a work that I detest. Farewell wonderful damnable Milan. (Padova – Milan – 10–11 July)

Folio 60

I enter the Parliament Chamber. The radicals, my colleagues, do not – as usual, for some strange tactical reason. They tell me that the leader of the Christian Democrat group has called on the Speaker not to let me in. The Radicals protest and make a racket, but they don't enter the Chamber. They like their little jokes, these colleagues. For myself, when there's uproar I'm in my element. I don't think there's too much to worry me here. I enter the Chamber with the comrades of Democrazia Proletaria (DP) – all of them great people. As soon as we sit down – the house is full for the opening of Parliament – as soon as we get ourselves seated on the benches on the far Left, on the 'mountain' – from the right they start shouting: 'Murderer – Out!' The people around me reply by chanting rhymes – in my view, the band of imbeciles in front of us don't deserve the sometimes over-passionate responses of Mario C. and Guido P. The comedy repeats itself. Theatre and bourgeois Parliament are pretty much made of the same stuff – in what sense do their histories cross? (Diderot – the paradox of the theatre, the extremization of types, the imitation of the market – study this topic.) And the trial? I amuse myself by replacing the heads of these ugly monsters jumping around in front of me. I replace Almirante's head with that of Santiapichi, Abbatangelo's with that of Calogero, and so on. That way I feel at home, and the comedy becomes a scene that embraces the totality of the institutional experiences I find myself living through. However, the uproar shows no signs of abating. In the time-honoured rituals of *commedia* the characters line up. The fascists make as if they are about to cross the floor – 'Just let me get at him . . .!' – What a pantomime. The leader of the house, poor Scalfaro, who is old and therefore possibly mindful of the Constitution, reminds the halfwits that a member of Parliament is a representative of all the people – and that they should not get too angry with the people, since the people don't understand much, and they have elected Negri, and in addition to Negri all the rest of this rabble, constituting it into an indivisible sovereignty. (Scalfaro – Musil – Count Leinsdorf.) The cynical heads of Santiapichi and Calogero nod, and gradually calm returns. (I think the final entertaining call was 'Murderer, I'll kill you . . .!'.) Then the new Speaker of Parliament is elected – Jotti gets the job. She goes to sit in the Speaker's chair. I watch her – she's used to this kind of thing – she sits with her body rigidly firm and she always moves both arms at the same time, as if she is conducting some kind of ritual from her perch. But there's nothing sacred here, only degradation and indecency. Conjuring up a worthy ending to this parliamentary session, which began with the insults of the fascists, the Speaker thinks it appropriate to move the immediate reading of requests to initiate proceedings for the arrest of the honourable Member of Parliament Antonio Negri. Her intervention restores order and the house calms down at the announcement that a quick surgical excision will work to cure the 'Negri sickness'. Not just quick, but immediate. Miraculous efficacity! It's time to get this over with – the priestess is sweating. I think of her old teachers – maybe in some senses revolutionaries, sometimes antifascists, and certainly with a well-founded sense of the sacred: Gemelli and Togliatti must be spinning in their graves. Today, in the lobby and in the antechambers, I met a lot of people of my own generation, now members of Parliament for the first time. Lula, Gianni F., and many others. A new generation of parliamentarians. Will they be able to represent the country as it really is, in all its dynamism? I really wonder. Giacomo M., the great southern gentleman, the socialist – the only one who shows recognizable signs of sincerity in what he does for the proletariat – he seems to me infinitely more real as a person.

For the rest of them, the formalism of the relationship is interwoven with the nervousness of functionaries who have just been promoted – emotions may well up, but they are dominated by a dry instrumentality of reason. Of the generation of '68 I find Franco R. and Franco P. to be different from the average run of MPs, and more enjoyable to be with. For the rest, at this first contact all I experience is a bitter feeling of pointlessness. The rustle of gowns and robes. Cliques, sometimes secret, sometimes blatant. The long march through the institutions . . . memories of ideological perversions, which now I see before me as perversion in action.

No, my dear Scalfaro, unfortunately you are not right – what you say is that they may all be a parcel of rogues, but here we have sovereignty and legitimacy of power. But your view is simply stupid. Here the rustle and the murmurings drown everything – every now and then a Radical shouts something, like the sound of a motor scooter stuck in sand. In the evening I dine with old friends, in Trastevere. God, how wonderful Rome would be without Rebibbia and without Montecitorio. (Rome – 12 July)

Folio 61

Obviously I should not allow myself to be carried away by these initial sensations. It is certainly the case that they emerge from a theoretical terrain that I have been cultivating for the past twenty years – but what do they mean? I could be wrong. I am aware of at least two elements which need to qualify my feelings. The first is self-critical. Basically I would never have ended up in Parliament, were it not for the fact that the mechanism of needs–organization–struggles–counter-power – on which, in linear fashion and incorrectly, we organized for many years – has functioned. The second element is simply theoretical: the function of representation which Parliament embodies has always been an abstraction, but now it is very much strengthened, in postmodernity, by the circularity of the world of information and by the importance of the symbolic. Certainly Parliament no longer 'represents' anything in the proper sense of the word, but it is a fundamental component in the structure of the politically symbolic. In Parliament you represent nobody – but you have the kind of power that used to accrue in the *ancien régime* from the fact of having married into the royal family. An insertion into the *medium* of the age. That antechamber, that rustling – and the end of representation and the hegemony of the symbolic – carry you directly to the images and the reality of absolutism. This is how I see things: I have comrades whom I must get out of prison, so I have to do everything that can be done, for as long as it remains possible – or rather for the very short time that is left to me – in order to deal with the problem of getting them free. I have to play this new symbolic game of palace politics. The only way they – my comrades –

are going to get out will be through *lettres de cachet*, like the aristocrats of olden times. Is that really the depth to which politics has sunk? I would say so. From what I read in the *Mémoires* of Saint-Simon, the political life conducted through the bedrooms and antechambers of the King of France was far more rich, important, creative and efficacious than that produced by the bedrooms and antechambers of our present rulers. So I have to play to its limit the symbolic breakpoint that my election represents, not so much because it is a real break-point as because it is an efficacious kind of symbolism. I have to accept the games of the press and media – knowing their poverty and detesting the vulgarity of their operators. Interviews, interviews, interviews . . . It feels like Liza Minelli's 'money, money, money . . .': I enter into this whole dirty market, voluntarily taking on the function of symbol – and also all the effort and work this involves. I am well aware that this is likely to destroy me, but I have very little time – after that I shall have to leave – who knows where and for how long. Without any nostalgia for this Parliament – but with a huge nostalgia for my comrades. And with how much anger. So let us pay it all – entirely and immediately – the price of this market. And so saying I put myself in the hands of the journalists. Who are they? Some of them are sympathetic scroungers, others are police spies, the scum of the OVRA, representatives of Santiapichi on a mission, Montanelli's rats . . . The few good and brave journalists find it hard to get out of the shadows. Anyway, I put myself into their hands, because the world of the media is stronger than their imbecility. '*Cheese, cheese* . . .' Smile, my old carcase. (Rome – 13–14 July)

Folio 62

During these days I have been in Milan. It is very hot. That fine heat of Milan – in the evening it feels good, and life is a joy. I rediscover easy friendships and deep affections. I spend a day at Radio Popolare, doing a phone-in that seems to go on for ever. Another day I spend at Rete Cinque in Segrate, being interviewed by Bocca, whom finally I get to meet, and who strikes me as a bit dull. These are hard days. Interviews and yet more interviews. Hard days. Maybe it would make sense for me to start thinking about myself, rather than being simply an extension of prison. My personal discourse, constructed during my years of imprisonment, I find it hard to get it out into the open. I don't have the time. On the other hand, this week I have been seeing my children again, and I try to understand the differences produced by the years of separation – I find again an enthusiasm for getting to know them. And I find new attachments – a web spun by myself, it's true – but also a web of great love, of desires fed during what has been a very long dream. What will be the passage from this wretched reality of mine to the dimensions of a dream that will be real and solid and productive? Where will such a passage be possible, in the confusion and tumult of feelings that the separation – this too long separation – has brought about? Every decision I take in this tangled web can cause unhappiness to someone. Move carefully, Toni, carefully. But when time is short, prudence is like homeopathic medicine – it will do the patient good, but it won't produce quick results. It is true, however, that I have to find an equilibrium in this bordello that I'm having to endure. I've not even been out all week, and all my personal problems – of getting back in touch with the world in terms of emotions (at the level of life) and in terms of knowledge (at the level of politics) are not only unresolved, but are not even classified. My life is political, of that I have little doubt. However, I fear the suppression of life in favour of politics as if it were a sin against the Holy Ghost. That's what prison is, and the division is imposed by the bosses. Is it maybe the case that, at a certain point, in this moment, I am reproducing, masochistically, the same indifference to values, albeit in the opposite sense to that of the bosses? There is no doubt that my life is political, but the problem of politics in my life remains unresolved. By accepting to move within the spaces of the symbolic, I am destroying many possibilities of praxis. Politics is human only when it is rooted and when it grows with passion. There is no *Beruf* without passion, and there is no vocation without a unity of being. I pose this problem to the comrades whom I see. Embarrassedly they reply that having posed themselves these questions has meant withdrawing from politics into the personal. They are alarmed, to tell the truth, to see me moving – almost participating – in this world-without-soul which I now inhabit. They ask me if I want to continue being a Member of Parliament. I tell them yes, for as long as I am allowed – but maybe in a month, or even less, I shall be obliged to escape. Then I add that this is not the problem – whether I stay or whether I have to leave. The problem is that of rebuilding the relationship between politcs and life. The problem is how to demolish the truth of the *pentiti* and of the people who have withdrawn from politics, for whom life is betrayal – or rather it is a programme of eradication of the political, of the collective, of the common. The fact remains that my problem – that of life and of its full and creative coherence with politics – is completely open. Within this loneliness, within this invading desperation of mine, only the thought of my comrades and the recent experience of prison create a continuity between life and politics. But in a little while Rebibbia will remain a transcendence, an indisputable value of suffering, something to kneel to in the absence of a political dialogue. Outside they offer you nothing. Nothing. It is easy to recognize it – but, for a person coming out after more than four years of prison, it is tragic. Literally. I have to throw myself into the symbolic – its efficacy is no smaller than its precariousness. In the evening Piazza Vetra is very pleasant. I walk, I walk a lot. (By the way, I have a sizeable escort. They have provided this for my own protection, they say – but from whom and from what? In my opinion they are doing it in order to prevent my escape. The escort is beginning to annoy me.) This condition of liberation, and the work I have to do, and the frantic activism that all this requires, certainly do not help me to resolve my personal problems. OK. I shall address them after I have emerged from this brothel, from this condition of being an active extension of prison. In effect I am only out on licence – I must never forget that. People outside, in the streets, greet me and kiss me. And, just as I accept this immediacy of affection, the question of what my life is today imposes itself on me afresh: the fact that this work I am doing may not be determined by duty, but rather a projection of the pleasure of liberty, of the rediscovery of life! I shall give my all. But I am sure of not being able to resolve the problem. Then there's the question of flight . . . of escaping . . . and then . . . and then . . . (Milan – 15–18 July)

Folio 63

The problem of my re-imprisonment has come to the fore again. So let us examine the situation. I have returned to Rome, to this world of rustling parliamentary robes and murmuring corporative noises. They want to put me back into prison. Fine, let's get it over with quickly. I have no chance to think about life, or to study and work on the new movement, on its powerful and destructive revival. And yet all the preconditions are there. There's no time – I have to hurry. The only thing I can do is to play my new role – this strange 'medium' that I represent, which has no need to be performed, since it is immediate. To put irreversibly onto the agenda the urgency of breaking with the laws imposed during the Years of Lead – the urgency of putting an end to the state of emergency. To play the conditions for a revival. Two possibilities immediately strike me –

the first is that of the prison movement. I go to G12 in Rebibbiba, to say hello to the comrades, and then, most particularly, to G11, to judge the will for struggle and transformation that these tremendous comrades, the ordinary prisoners, are expressing. I have the impression that a very strong movement is in the making – a movement which has learned from the past experiences of defeat and can now express itself with great political lucidity. Then I go to Rebibbia's women's wing. I see Fiora, with the incredible emotion of a brother – and then the comrades of the 'homogeneous zone', with the affection of a father. *Forza!* I feel that we can do it. The disaster of the non-negotiability of the armed struggle is now behind us. Without provocations, without hysteria, we can now begin the big struggle of all the prisoners – from within prisons, with strength. The second possibility derives from the fact of being present in that zone where the institutional panorama is in crisis. I go to Naples. A formidable group of comrades. They have understood everything, with the alertness of people who grew up in the midst of a problem so radical as to become unsolvable, and in a highly dramatic social situation. Their alertness is the tense expectation, almost atmospheric, of somebody living on the edge of a volcano. Here, at this level, within these 'enclaves' of the political and social crisis, the irreversibility of the courses taken by the struggle and by the needs that the struggle has consolidated can be built and imposed upon the institutional forces themselves. They tell me: in no sense are we willing to pay for a deepening of the crisis, or for its solution in static terms. We are willing to take part, with our struggles, in the selection of the values of a new development of liberty. It is incredible how close these proletarians of the crisis are, in my view, to the movement in the prisons. Prison is a social paradigm of repression in the crisis: a paradigm which has to be destroyed. They tell me about the latest police blitz in Naples – hundreds of people arrested – and about the insane mistakes made by the magistrates, and the dozens of mistaken-identity arrests. They describe the brutality of the police . . . These comrades need to express themselves at the national level. Now, and quickly. However, the only thing which is moving forward quickly is the question of my re-imprisonment. The media are pushing for it relentlessly. Everyone I meet – friends, new friends, complete strangers – tell me 'Escape, Toni, get away at once'. Then they fall silent. I have to work fast, really fast. I am tired. But never mind. Must hurry. One single objective is to be achieved: to render irreversible the launching of a solution for the Years of Lead and for the problem of preventive imprisonment. It is little, very little – but even if only one comrade was able to get out of prison, out of this whole business and all this work, I would be satisfied. The rest comes later, when I'll have done my get-away. Today, in this month that remains, it is not possible to do more. (Rome/Naples – 19–21 July)

Folio 64

Padova – it's three in the morning. I think I started my phone-in at Radio Gamma at about ten last night. It has continued until now. I am very tired. Not so much because of the phone-in as because of the charge of love and affection that I have felt among people, among friends and comrades. A love which, for me, means responsibility, and which overloads me. A joining together of affection and joy which could become new movement – but there is no time. Let us consolidate immediately what is irreversible. And yet I am slightly frightened about this project. Precisely this evening, in the discussion on the phone-in, I had a clear sensation that an irreversibility of behaviours, if it is not conjoined with an articulated strategic discourse, can become an ossified fetish. The resistance also accumulates negative stuff: bad feelings, lack of imagination, repetition – a kind of obligation towards repetition, forced on us by the memory of a movement which was great, yes, but has now become rigid. This reactionary phenomenon shows itself in stereotypical language and in a poverty of analytical reference points. So what we are getting is a kind of second-hand heroism – the heroism of solidarity pure and simple. I find it hard to see the strength of this continuism – and anyway, if it has strength, it is only a bureaucratic strength; within itself it shows definite symptoms of cancellation of potential and progressive exhaustion. A stunting of growth. If things were indeed this way, it would be a disaster. I try to widen the discussion, to advance provocative suggestions and proposals for the building of a new movement – one capable of recalibrating its forces in the light of the changed conditions. My impression is that people understand what I am saying – but they are dominated by a fear of not being able to control consequences – almost an expectation of counter-productive side-effects. If state repression has been successful in bringing about such a deep and negative expectation, we have to admit that they have done well. We need to break this condition of substantial passivity. How? What is the radical political change that will make this possible? (Padova – 22 July)

Folio 65

This morning I went on a parliamentary visit to the Due Palazzi prison in Padova. They didn't want to let me in – I had to wait outside for an hour, with the other visitors, under a ferocious sun. This pointless cruelty is run-of-the-mill normality for the prisoners' families when they visit – and it's such an offence to them, and to the prisoners, and to good sense. The prison is modern, a bit like Rebibbia. I see a lot of comrades, and particularly the ones whom I had already seen before in prison: Achille, Augusto, Marzio – and then Ettore, Libero and so on. The latest blitzes have resulted in new and old comrades being locked up, in this absurd witch hunt, which is continually fed by the fanatical repressive passion of Calogero. Fanaticism . . . It's really not worth framing it in terms of higher values of political and moral rhetoric – that way you'd end up giving value to the personality of this fanatic, giving him a kind of dark grandeur. No – let us look at this fanaticism from the viewpoint of the disasters it has provoked and of the suffering it continues to generate – then there really are no excuses. I feel powerfully the offence that has been dealt to these imprisoned comrades. May your soul finish in hell, you madman Calogero! I go to see the ordinary prisoners. Here too I have a clear sensation of a deep and wise desire for struggle and transformation. The prison movement is picking up again, with force. I propose to the comrades that it needs to be supported and fed with political purposiveness and with a sense of impending deadline – against preventive detention and for a way out of the Years of Lead. Living and visiting prisons, I come to believe increasingly that prison now represents a slice of society, and that this slice of society gathers articulated signs of the great transformations that are under way: the criminality of the administration indicates the end of political representation and the triumph of corporatism; the crimes of violence show the decline of solidarity which accompanies this process; and the many economic crimes should probably be related to the imbalance between the chaotic and diffuse desire to produce, and the command and productive hierarchy of a capitalism which is now both mature and atrophied. Today prison gathers only autonomy – political autonomy, and autonomy of appropriation and demanding, and finally the new entrepreneurial autonomy. In the chaos of our society, the violence of the institution has now become a form of repression against social innovation. Repression is blind: and this blindness criminalizes everything that is innovative and new. What is offered to us is an extreme limit – the institutional perversion and its stupidity are horrible to behold. I ask myself how we are going to be able to get out of all this. The pain that I find in the prisons is tangible, and the solidarity of the comrades contains a symbolism of rebirth, rebellion and transformation which is offered to you open-handedly. How can we get out of all this? I think I know the answer. But I cannot do it – I know that this general meaningfulness of prison should be developed in society as a whole, and the revolt against prison should be understood as an element of social reorganization. However, I cannot move on this terrain because I have no time. In a little while either I shall have to leave or I shall return to prison. I would feel re-imprisonment as a mockery – but what would it be to leave the country? All my family, and the comrades in Due Palazzi, political and ordinary prisoners alike, are asking me apprehensively whether I plan to go or stay. '*Vattene, Toni, vattene.*' 'Leave, Toni, go . . .!' My unease is related to the absurd alternatives which are being offered to me – the diabolical mechanism of the 'either–or'. If you go back to prison you can do politics; but, if you choose exile (because obviously this is what we are talking about), you won't do politics any more. The comrades exclude this alternative. I am uneasy about it – I don't understand the basis of it – or rather I am beginning to think that its bases are only in the nature of a blackmail. So then what? I have to move with caution, trying by every means possible to remain in Italy. Then, if they don't want me, I shall leave. But before accepting this unanimous advice to leave immediately – which is coming from family members, from the prisons, from all those who love me (and it is singularly expressed in different forms, from the loving '*vattene*' of people who no longer want to endure the experience of prison, to the political '*vattene*' of people who know that the development of political initiative cannot be shaped and calibrated on the day-to-day requirements of defending ourselves in the trial) . . . Anyway, before accepting this unanimous advice, I have to do everything possible, and above all measure myself against the world of prison. 'Escape,' they're telling me, 'escape.' The individualism which sometimes underlies this prompting is infinitely more important than the moralism which underlies the suggestion that I should accept judgement and sentence. Why? Perhaps the times really have changed, and the richness and liberty of the individual person, creating spaces among the ideological illusions, are once again gaining a potency in the communist project. 'Escape, escape,' the comrades in Due Palazzi keep telling me, almost to the point of tedium. (Padova – 23 July)

Folio 66

This week I'm living my days between Milan, Venice and Rome. I am enjoying the 'Negri case' – I try to act it out. It brings to mind a story my grandmother used to tell me, about a man building a haystack. A peasant had correctly constructed a haystack, building from the bottom up, but then he overloaded it with hay, so that it ended up a bit of a mess, and the hay in the bottom part began to rot. So what does the silly peasant do? He starts digging out the rotten hay underneath, and the whole stack tips over on top of him. That's how I see the magistrate in the 7 April case. He built the 7 April case from the bottom upwards, in other words from the need to put an end to local disorders. But then he overloaded it, and the whole thing became top-heavy and tipped over on his head. The same is as true for the magistrate as it was for the silly peasant. At this point, enter the corporations – the magistracy and the politicians – who cannot permit the stupidity of the peasant to be seen, because it would reflect badly on the whole corporation. So what happens then? Grandma said that, in order to prevent further problems of rot and infection, you have to burn the haystack. And that is exactly the impression I have. This is what is happening. They are preparing the fuses. What is emerging victorious is the old peasant agrarian ideology of the corporation. They want to burn everything – and make sure the fire falls onto us. The 'Negri case' is the symbol of the perversion of Italian peasantry, that is for sure, and also of its ferocious fables – but above all of this magistracy, of this disproportionately large power of regulation in a state deregulated, in a state which is gothic. To defend their prestige they are ready to do absolutely anything. It would be so simple, so clean-cut, just to wipe the slate and forget it, but this is not possible – it would only be possible for people who are not Levantine in character and dirty in their complexions. I feel downright racist in their regard. But when all is said and done the fault is also mine, for the way in which I have behaved. I resist, I hold my ground, I produce a dissociation which is a definition of identity and not a *pentimento*, I get myself elected as a member of Parliament, and in the trial I react by claiming my existence – but, Toni, don't you realize that this insane priesthood which is the Italian magistracy – an uninterrupted continuity of monarchy, fascism and capitalism – cannot be granted dignity and honour? Only submission: I kiss the toe of your slipper, o Grand Vizier, and I crave pardon. That's how it's done. Italy, Italy, shame upon you! Only a Grosz could do justice to the faces I see around me – or a Buñuel, in the cinema. The 'Negri case' is an arrogant obstinacy, the caricatural continuity of the rule of bureaucracy – this is why there is nothing to be done other than to resist. Oppose it with another rationality, another way of life. It would be so easy for them to say: 'The *pentiti*? They are a bunch of rogues, and we've made them confess what we wanted them to confess, so now let them keep quiet with their lies, and not project their massive slanders . . . And the emergency laws? These were simply a necessary means that we had to use for a while, but now it's over, finished . . . let's get back to legality . . .' But instead . . . Maybe if we had a monarch, whose virtue was honour and to whom obedience was due on the charismatic basis of a truth that is seen as absolute – ah, if only I had a monarch and the arbitrariness of his judgement to judge me! The bureaucrat can't do this – his so-called virtue is coherence. But it's not even that! Here in Italy, in the crisis, the bureaucracy's loyalty to itself is no more than a political defence of its own separateness, of an independence which does not participate in the dialectic of society and of the state but simply pursues a line of self-reproduction. The magistrates of the Nazi regime, in the horror of their function, respected a sworn value: obedience to the law, in the *Obrigkeitsstaat*. They were dogs, but they were obedient. Here they are no less dogs just because they have not yet decided to build Gulags and concentration camps (remember that they have constructed the special prisons, and Article 90, and Voghera, and death cells – and they have no values, and are crazy with power. This perversion has to be fought and destroyed. I don't know how I shall come through this 'Negri case'. Apart from anything else, the whole thing is so absurd – my image is so distant, in this horizon dominated by the media. No matter how things turn out, they will operate on a distant horizon and I shall only be able to live them as science fiction. But what is certain is that, whatever happens, I shall continue to struggle against the possibility of further 'Negri cases' – in other words against this irrational and cruel figure of the magistracy and of repression. I don't want to do it as an avenger or as an executioner – no, that really is not my mission – only political struggle can change this world of ours – but at the same time I cannot remain silent about my disgust with these animals – they are repellent, clandestine, and infected, both for society and for civilization as a whole. (Milan – 26 July)

Folio 67

More perversion – that of the political class. Here in Rome I have no way of avoiding contact with them. People tend to see me as a cynic – but here I find myself being a moralist. Even cynicism has its limits; and in Sade, at this limit, you read the highest of poetry. But not with these people! Here poetry really does not exist any longer, not even as a resolution of their evil. The perversion of the system is simply vulgar. Why continue talking of crisis and objectivate a reality which in fact is subjectively unrecoverable? A perversion that is functional. I continue with a crazy rhythm of interviews – I feel that we are at the outer limits of imbroglio and defamation. This is a rule from which journalists – a breed of person even more despicable than that of magistrates and politicians of the big parties, if such a thing is possible – cannot deviate. Malignity. On the other hand, today I received an article by Karl Heinz Roth. Worse than Calogero! – what's got into him? Today I have no wish to get angry – it is just amusing to see how a German autonomist can be so wrongheaded! But this does mean that I'm on my own. The game of politics – in the perversion that is its nature – does not accept strong impulses towards breakthroughs. Not from the Right, for reasons that are obvious; not from the Left, for less obvious and sometimes banal motives – resentment, envy and the like (it would be instructive to write a little handbook of the vulgar passions of the Left). I'm on my own. Bitterly I have to admit it. I have to hurry. Sometimes I'm so tired that I could almost wish that they would speed up the business of my re-arrest – I am alone, and they are making me more and more alone. At this point I'm expecting even my closest friends to start distancing themselves. I have to fight a lone battle, between myself and people who shower me with opinions. From the Right, they tell me that I am morally responsible for Italy's terrorism, hence I should go back to prison. From the Left, they tell me that, because I have dissociated myself from terrorism, I am a traitor deserving to be killed. And from the centre I have to deal with people who want to use me politically. I cannot fight this battle on so many fronts on my own. So what then? Let us hope that it comes soon, this battle on my own personal terrain, where I can demonstrate powerfully that I am outside of that generalized perversion – alone, yes, but still alive. All the time I argue with myself about the political and cultural value of escape – conceived of as sabotage, as an act of absenteeism. Today this is the only communist possibility of bearing theoretical witness. Why didn't you do it immediately, Toni? Because the perversion of the enemy has to be revealed right down to its bare essentials. The only key which can permit us to pass through the perversion of the political and judicial system and system of the media is, therefore, that of a passion-driven alterity, of a confidence in ourselves which is founded on justice, which is continuous and always on the alert. Each of them has to hate me not only because their bosses have told them to, but also because they feel my contempt. That contempt is my denunciation of their perversion – it is honour against vulgarity, it is collective love against their individual concern for their jobs. I am certain that they are winning – I have no illusion about that. But I am serene in my lucidity and contempt for them. I say no to the game of politics, that is, to the game of constructing vulgar homologies and common interests, a general will and a common interest – a game whose law is to draw you into their camp. No, really, I do not go along with this perversion. I try it sometimes, but I simply cannot do it. I am Spinozan by nature, and I think that God is on earth and that our life is constitutive of ever-increasing humanity. And them? No. *Ultimi barbarorum*. (Rome – 28 July)

Folio 68

The escort is beginning to drive me crazy – I have told them clearly that I can't stand it any longer, and that I don't feel myself to be under threat from anybody. But they still carry on. Paola often goes berserk with them. We are followed, monitored, blocked – with an attitude half of control and half of complicity. I've had enough of it. However, the whole thing can be amusing sometimes, even comical. Like tonight . . .

Today I was in Naples for a series of TV interviews. There were no trains, because the lines had been blocked by a protest of the unemployed, so we had to hire a car. In the evening, returning from Naples, we stopped in at Formia to say hello to a group of comrades. Really nice. Agostino took us all for a meal up in the mountains, behind Formia. Wild, fearsome places. Counting the escort we had four or five cars, because they had two following us. At a certain point we got lost up in the mountains, down tiny roads that would have been inaccessible to anyone but lunatics like ourselves. We started the most incredible manoeuvres with our cars, and got ourselves thoroughly lost down the little lanes. When we finally got to meet up at the restaurant, our guards were looking so scared and despondent that we almost took a notion to buy them dinner! Anyway, back to reality . . . A day like today brings me back to the pleasures of life and struggle. On the one hand the crisis and the perversion of the system, and on the other this enormous wealth of proletarian society – in Naples I meet many comrades who are still managing to remain active, like living fishes in this swamp of misery, corruption and criminality; and they are managing to keep hope alive. Always an inch, just an inch, above the level of desperation which this damned power has distributed – they are drugged on hope. And in Formia I find a group of comrades in whom the tendencies of the old marginalized proletariat and those of the new, educated and abstract proletariat have constructed a new universe of revolutionary values. The material, irreversible fact – the solid knot – of these behaviours has always fascinated me – and here you feel it as a solid force. And here, yes, through these given behaviours, you can read again, outside of any sectarian and small-group fantasies, a memory of class struggle which cannot be erased.

This seems to me like a small experience of recomposition along historical axes (in the revival of all the stories of struggle and revolution that have been lived), and along social axes at the same time (in the recompacting of different sensibilities and different sectors of the proletariat). A small and symbolic experience. Taking a stand against the obscenity of this system and the perversion of power. There are many of these groups of comrades, and, as such, they need to be discovered and put back into contact with each other. They remind me of the best moments in the building of the autonomy movement in the north during the 1970s – and then my thoughts run to all the experiences of the autonomy movement, strong and diffuse, which, albeit solely at the social level, have consolidated themselves in all the countries of developed capitalism. I never forget this strong social dualism – but when, in the night, in the long discussions which precede this dawn that begins to show itself before me, I find myself looking at it, in the interpretation the proletarian protagonist makes of it, then once again I begin to think that it will be possible to make the transition from the social to the political and to dream of this radical political change in the class consciousness of the people. What is a class? Certainly not the aggregate of typical proletarians that Engels describes, beloved of so many fusty nostalgic comrades. No, I prefer the slogan of Flora Tristan: 'constituting the working class'. And then, why forget our good old teacher Marx, where he said that the working class is revolutionary, otherwise it is nothing. Here, once again, on these mountains, I too feel myself high on hope.

PS Today, before leaving for Naples, I held a press conference where I presented the proposal for a bill on the reduction of preventive detention, as prepared by the comrades. (Naples/Formia – 29 July)

Folio 69

Today is my fiftieth birthday. A turning point? A trifle. These days I am living life with a great desperation – this life which could be so rich and fine. Ten years ago, 1 August 1973, was the starting point of this whole story of the *autonomia* movement – a big supper, with a hundred comrades present. I look at my life now, the life of a shipwrecked sailor washed up on an island, released from the waves and the perversity of the trial, but at the same time I see my space getting smaller and life becoming impoverished in the most extreme tension. I have decided that I shall make my escape, and shall get out and retain my freedom – but I am preparing nothing to that end. I feel that to set about preparing things would weaken the strength of my struggles in the here and now. And yet, in this very difficult situation, I am living – and I cannot avoid recognizing it – a kind of suicide. Unconsciously, long, drawn-out. With words I have the same poverty as I have in the face of the object to be described – a certain repugnancy to say them. I have to live this life even on the edge of death, and I must not admit that death is near. But why is it that destiny invites me to choose between life and death? Sometimes I think of having a sickness, a terminal illness, as a moment of rest, as a melody which resolves for you the drama of thought, and then everything finishes gently. Life and its desperation would have just one final spasm, as everything came to an end. But, when all is said and done, this just represents a new desire for suicide. Sometimes, when we're arguing and shouting, Paola tells me: 'When you were in prison, and when it seemed there was absolutely nothing that could be done, your mother used to tell me "Cheer up, Paola, at least he hasn't committed suicide!"' That was the great fear of my mother, and the great tension in me during these fifty years of mine. Paola reproaches me for accepting this state of affairs, for not preparing my escape. It is true – in some ways this living of mine, now, seems like a strange mixture of struggle and testimony and rupture, and at the same time of unwillingness to act and acceptance of fate. But it's not really like that. I try to explain to Paola that this rhythm of life, this way of its proceeding – in which even desperation and heroism some-times turn out to be empty masks – can be broken. The linear logic of life and its nullifying rhythm reach a threshold where even destiny imposes on you an alternative. This is how my fifty years of life have been – always right to the limit, to understand, to struggle, to organ-ize moments of love. And now I am faced with the invasive presence of death and power. Struggling to the utmost limit. And then, at that limit, a jolt of hope and a re-beginning. Paola reacts by telling me that I'm crazy and that this is completely irrational. Irrational, I answer – and what is rationality, except that tragic and horrible figure which is seeking my death? That figure which calls itself law, or that nebulous machine which usurps the name of the will of the people? No, I shall not prepare my escape – I want to live it right to the limit, without ambiguity, this situation of struggle on the edge of a possible death. I shall escape – believe me, Paola – and it will be on that margin, after having savoured to the limit their perversion, and after having enjoyed their death-bearing machinations. It will happen, this escape of mine, like an act of hope, like a moment of destiny. You have to construct inside yourself an impulse of struggle and of knowledge that thrusts you to live in a way that is irresistible. So don't get scared, my dear Paola, if death is our companion, if suicide coexists alongside the desire to live. It is we who have to decide between life and death – it is life that decides, the decision is made by its immediate truth. If that's not the way it is, then there is no value in either living or dying. (Milan – 1 August)

Folio 70

Now we're coming to the heart of the debate about the authorization to proceed and my eventual re-imprisonment. A big battle. Everyone realizes that the problem is not only about me; it is also the problem of giving a strong sign, an indication, for finding ways to break out of the Years of Lead. Maybe I'm wrong, but it seems to me that it is precisely because this sign does not want to be given, precisely for this reason, that they will decide to put me back into prison. A moment of great nervousness. I continue with developing contacts and relationships, and also with the slow work in Parliament, to block possible prejudicial decisions. Infinite problems. Growing tiredness. Rossana is back from her holiday, which was very short. I am very fond of her. I really would like to manage to stay out of prison and to work on the things she is suggesting to me – an inquiry into class recomposition in the north, and the restructuring of industry and the explosion of this huge and innovative tertiary sector. An apology for Rossana. Her optimism is boundless, and sometimes it even rubs off onto me. She loves me like you'd love a kid. I go to Rebibbia and manage a brief meeting with the comrades. The first problem is that of the conference on alternative forms to imprisonment, planned for September.
We have to manage to put the maximum amount of meat on

the fire, over the whole range of problems that have been opened up – and I have to do it in the shortest possible time, insofar as it involves me. I go to G9 to see the fascists in prison. Good people – the problem is how to give weight to their voice, as part of the prison movement. This question of unity is fundamental. All this happened a couple of days ago, if I'm not mistaken. In Rome it is unbelievably hot, unbearably so. And what have I been doing since then? Ah yes – a three-hour phone-in on the Radical Party's TV channel. Some of them insulting me, some of them happy, but definitely a noticeable ebbing of the initial tension. Then endless arguments with the police escort – we almost came to blows. Paola drove into them with her car. This whole business is turning grotesque. Meanwhile, in the debate in the special committee, the Liberal Party spokesman, who is arguing for my re-imprisonment, has caught measles. So on this side too things are pretty weird. And they are refusing to give me a parliamentary passport – not actually refusing it, but bouncing me around from office to office. Here the grotesque is taking on an aspect of Andreottian malevolence. Then, yesterday, there was a meeting in the Giunta, to decide on my case. Summary justice? I wait in the antechamber.

The usual rabble of journalists. The whole thing is postponed until September. Halfway through September there will be a vote in Parliament. I've gained a month. Good. At last I am in Milan, at home. Enormous tiredness. I am shattered by a situation which is terrible, and the tasks I have set myself seem too much for me.

PS As regards the fascists in prison, I am continually clashing with those on the Left who refuse even to talk about them, both in prison and – above all – outside. They say that they're criminals. No less than those who arrived in prison from the Left, I reply. They tell me that they are confused, that their ideology is shit. I reply that it seems to me not much different from that of a lot of people on the Left – and that in fact sometimes I find bits of lively thinking among them. And finally they tell me that these violent fascists are often instruments of the state.

This is the only argument that gets to me. Spontaneously my mind says: with all the problems that we already have, why do we need to concern ourselves with them? Let them be looked after by those, often within the state, who used these people as tools of provocation. But this too is a false argument – yes, maybe these lads were instrumentalized (and how about those of the Left, were they not?), but they are perfectly responsible. They are not of the Right – maybe at some time they have been subjected to the ideologies of the Right, but their motives do not lean to the Right. We really would have to look at the history of these past few years through the eyes of a Valiani or – and this amounts to the same thing – through the eyes of the secret services engaged in imperialist destabilization, in order to fail to understand that these so-called (one-time) fascists are simply a product of the blocked system of Italian politics. They have nothing more to do with Almirante and with the right than my comrades do. Furthermore, they are deeply involved in the prison movement, they have lived the experiences of liberation that prison imposes, and they have to be brought back into the political debate – fully and completely. I'm not sure how to go about this. I am certain that *Il Manifesto* will respond negatively when I ask for their documents to be published. Never mind, I shall keep pressing for it. I like those lads – behind them lies the whole history of the Italian provinces and its malaise, and the working-class neighbourhoods of Rome and their antagonisms. In them there is a hope for renewal, albeit badly interpreted. But who interprets things properly these days? As far as I am concerned, fascism is disgusting – but why be so blind as to call these lads fascist, and not the movers and shakers of the Historic Compromise? (Rome/Milan – 2–5 August)

Folio 71

I talk with Paolo. Intelligent and cold, as ever. No, not cold, but dispassionate – capable of abstracting himself and keeping himself at a distance from the immediate. He has a good way of interpreting what has happened to his generation, between movement and repression. *Horror vacui* is the phrase he uses to define what he feels – the wind of emptiness. A wind which blows things all over the place. The wind is empty, and so is its meaning. Starting from the enormous collective experience which the spirit of the 1970s had created in Milan and other cities of the north – an experience of community and constitution, an experience which, very naïvely and yet correctly, we called communism. The experience of fullness – followed by the horror of emptiness. It is incredible, this collective subjectivity of suffering. The 1970s were the opposite, with their saturation with joy with alternative life experiences, with community. But today? Fear, the horrors of everyday life, loneliness. I read the 'Summer Notes' published by Censis: Italy's social decomposition, it complains, has come about in the absence of any significant initiative (at this point I would like to add 'except for the repression' – why is it that Di Rita forgets these terrible events, which are so deeply etched into the collective consciousness?) – in the absence of any significant initiative coming from power: that's how the Censis talks. The flabbiness of power. Society is terribly segmented, it says – it calls for a resumption of the entrepreneurial autonomy of the social in relation to the political. You make me laugh – do you really not see the desert you have created? However, there is at least no hypocrisy here – the Censis people are not claiming that the desert is a garden. But in their mind's eye they desire the garden, and they have not measured the impressive material depth of the drought of life. This is a classic situation, once characteristic of priests, and now of the policemen of thought – to destroy life and then lament the ontological deficit which is the outcome of their actions. They moan about how everything is adrift. But this is a result of the drifting of the movement, of the repression of its creativity, of its ending in the *horror vacui*. What desperation, what wretchedness there is in all this.

How can you think that an act of political will can alter this ontological destruction of life? The autonomy of a creative politics which is proposed here is impossible, just as the autonomy that permitted the repression of our movement was shameful. They tell me that one of my worst enemies, in Padova – in that agglomerate of evil that passes under the name of a university – is today looking back regretfully to the 1970s. They are still running late with their crises, these irresponsible young men – they should get themselves up to date, for God's sake, so that they can feel at first hand the malaise and the horror, for real!

Today they are running around in the labyrinth – all of us go round in a labyrinth – and we have to exhaust all the possibilities (shall we have the courage for it?) of the labyrinth. Of this will, which becomes cowardly every time it loses contact with reason. Of this cowardly will of theirs – of all the intellectuals who have surrendered to repression because they lacked the serenity of reason. Failing in their task, which is to fight to make sure that reason stays always serene and constructive. But Paolo is insistent: he is not interested in polemics with the intellectuals. He lives the tragedy of the repression, of the movement being adrift, of the emptiness. And yet it is only on the desperation of will, on this presence of death and imprisonment, which sits on our shoulders like a monkey – it is only from this intensity of pessimism of the will, of the contact with desperation and repression – it is only from here that we can reconquer serenity. Labyrinth, *horror vacui* . . . Will is projected onto this unresolvable screen. Break it, Paolo.

Reason is the overturning [*catastrofe*] of the world in which we live. The expression of a generation needs to be reconquered through the exercise of reason – what we are setting up here is an enormous concert, which reason can produce to the limits of the collective moment. We have lived it, Paolo, that collective moment. Your desperation is the desperation of abandonment. No, what is done cannot be undone. *Factum infectum fieri nequit* – the principle of every civilization. Today defeated Mongols, tomorrow Genghis Khan triumphant. Don't be scared of the labyrinth – it is not one of reason but one of the will – an obstacle and not a limit. (Milan – 6 August)

Folio 72

Yesterday evening, a major scene with the escort. Paola stopped the car in a dark corner of a small street – and then reversed straight into the police car that was following us. I got out and started hammering on the car with my fists – like we used to do against scabs crossing picket lines – and then they followed us to the police station, where I put in an official complaint because they hadn't given me their particulars. Ridiculous but effective. It will certainly prove useful. I don't want the escort following us any more, for one simple reason – I have to start thinking about my escape, and having the police always on my tail, and in such numbers, inevitably makes it more difficult. It's not impossible, because anyway, like any policemen, the worst they can be is irritating. So I am getting rid of an irritation, nothing more than that. And in a state which pretends to have a clean face (in order to hide its dirty face), you can make things easy by putting on a show of indignation. What a performance! So many people are telling me not to go back to prison. Almost everyone, in fact. Except Rossana and Marco P. Who knows what they have in mind for me . . .? Most of all, this is the word I'm getting from lawyers, in other words from people who know what's going on in this trial – the frame-up and the machinations. I spent the day in Gressoney – at the house of Marcello G.; Gressoney is extremely beautiful. Already last week I was there to visit this extraordinary lawyer and friend. I would appoint him minister of justice. It seems that his friends don't want him in that position. Why? Perhaps because, unlike most politicians with high hopes, who end up becoming Levantines, he is a Levantine who became political in order to loosen the knots of injustice. An injustice which he experiences in simple terms, as a partisan and as an antifascist. Simple, but within such a quantity of doctrine – that is the fundamental thing. Not that his brain is not still Levantine – in this he is like all the rest of the teachers of Italian law – but, in the drama of the emigration to the north that he is living (unresolved), the unhappiness of life and the heaviness of injustice weigh heavily upon him. He doesn't have the bored look of Martinazzoli, who, he tells me, will be the minister. It is clear, however, that he would dearly like to be at the head of the Italian justice system. What would be better – his dramatic mobility as a Turinese immigrant, or the pacific tedium of Martinazzoli, a lawyer from Brianza? I don't know who will be nominated – Martinazzoli probably, he is the stronger candidate – but I have a certain nostalgia for the restlessness of Marcello G. From his wife and children I get the sense of a life which is not satisfied with its present circumstances. No, this is not the discreet charm of the bourgeoisie. And no, he won't make it to be minister. Contradictory feelings today, while the discussion swings between Kelsen and life (what a distance!), between the image of parliamentary Rome and the splendid mountains of Gressoney. No, he won't make it to be minister. Today he is still a free man. Why? I remember how he came to visit me one time when I was in the special prison. He refused to speak to me through glass. You can't look at the mountains of Gressoney *in vitro*. Meanwhile the escort is still following us. I look at them as they hide shamefacedly, a bit embarrassed after the blow-up of yesterday evening. And among these bright mountains I think of the jaundiced face of Rognoni. (Milan/Gressoney – 7 August)

Folio 73

A hellish day, but with a least one positive result. They have definitely put off any decision about my re-imprisonment until September – the 1st or the 8th. I have gained a month of freedom. It seems unbeliev-able to me. Today is Wednesday. This story – very tense – started on Monday, with a hearing before the committee for parliamen-tary privileges. Very embarrassed they were. I looked them straight in the eye, one by one. You could have got more expression out of the Sphinx. At least the Sphinx was beautiful. This bunch, with the exception of Mellini, are ugly, devastatingly ugly. I present my defence before the 'committee for authorizations' in a moderate tone. I am not in attack mode. I put before them a number of points in my defence, minimal but cogent and incisive. They sit there silently. The ambience and atmosphere of a meeting of carpetbaggers. I look around me. The place where they meet is a long narrow bunker. A bomb shelter. They are waiting for orders. In this half light, their terrible emptiness becomes apparent: they fill this shadow and don't illuminate it. Tuesday: Despite the good press in the morning, in the afternoon the committee decides that I am to go back to prison – immediately. Then pandemonium broke out – I'm not sure exactly why. What is certain, however, is that the bag-carriers had misunderstood the orders of their bosses. There was a MSI-DC-PCI majority for immediate re-imprisonment. But the thing didn't pass in the Communist Party. They are calling for a postponement of any decision until they've had a chance for political discussion. In the course of the night a variety of positions begin to be outlined. A certain Loda, a Communist Party member of Parliament, received a telling off. This is gratifying, but I don't understand the operation, its meaning, and where it is leading. Rossana is making superhuman efforts. Today she left for a few days' holiday and I went to see her off. All very emotional. Massimo is on the rampage – I see him often during these days – and he is convinced that a lot can be done in the party, if only we could gain some time. What is happening in the PCI is certainly important – but I don't think they will have the ability to pull back from their repressive vocation – against myself and my comrades. They have already dirtied their hands too much in this regard. A party led, on occasion, by some rampaging court journalist, driven by motives of revenge, and in dialogue with some of the worst of our hanging judges! What a tragedy, this Noske returned from the dead, this Asiatic face – Sanfedist and brutish – of that once great party! No, they cannot escape from the shame of all this. The efforts of Rossana and of the comrades at *Il Manifesto* have paid off, nevertheless. Massimo is happy – even though he is extremely pessimistic about the future. Already on Tuesday evening we knew that any decision was going to be put off. Today is Wednesday – or is it Thursday? It's so late, and the night is cool. I am not just tired – I am literally destroyed. I feel like I have a ring of iron round my head. I want to drink. In this house where I am staying there is not even a bottle of wine. So the great repressive alliance of the Historic Compromise – the DC and the PCI, with a bunch of fascists supporting them – has been shattered. I have a terrible headache. Marlboros make me sick, and today I have smoked only Marlboro. Tired. Tired. So . . . everything is put off till September. A month gained. This evening I walked through Campo dei Fiori with Paola, on our way to a restaurant run by a friend. In the half light, a boy dismantling the last of the flower stalls asked me for a cigarette. I give him one. He looks at me, recognizes me and says: 'Hey, you're the professor.' I say

'Yes'. I stand for a moment. Then he blurts out: 'Don't let them take you in again.' I walk on. He runs after me, with a rose in his hand. He gives it to Paola. 'Don't let them get you, don't let them get you.' He's right. No, no, I mustn't let them get me. (Rome – 8–10 August)

Folio 74

I am on holiday at last, at Montescudaio in Tuscany. After talking with Scalfaro, the new Minister of the Interior, I have finally succeeded in getting rid of my escort. At last – I couldn't take it any longer. The countryside is beautiful, and the house, rented from Sylvie and Giovanna, is delightful. The whole valley of the Cecina lies below, stretching towards Volterra upstream and the sea downstream. There is a lot of greenery, and always a wind to freshen the heat of the day. I reorder my thoughts, and once again I find a desire to live, returning surreptitiously. My relations with the people around here are good. Of course, I am a public figure, and that's how they see me – people point me out, and look at me, and there are even journalists and photographers making the trip up here. But these are communist villages: many of the local people – some of the communists, and workers from Piombino, and farm workers – are interested in discussing with me – with a communist. So we begin to talk. They tell me about the workers' struggle in the locality, about the crisis in the steel industry and the restructuring of Piombino. I notice that I have not forgotten anything of the communist style of working – and in passing I recall that here in Piombino we were doing political interventions twenty years ago! We keep talking in the bar, and then, in the evening, in people's houses, and they are most welcoming. Excellent local wine. After an inconceivable length of time I begin again to enjoy the pleasures of relaxation. I meet other very dear friends, who come to visit me. We talk about politics, a lot. My situation requires it. And not even the delights of this countryside can lessen the sense of political and institutional tragedy in the situation that we are living. We are in a blind alley – the perversion of the institutions, the breakdown of the constitutional balance of powers, and the cancer spreading through the political machine: these are the results of the political blockage that has been imposed on us, massacring our hopes. Today, they tell me, people in the factories are starting to get angry again. I hope so. But we need self-criticism here. It must be deep, and it needs to attack not only the political class of the parties, but also certain sectors of the working class who, through the blind and exclusionary defence of their corporative interests, have allowed our massacre to take place. First 7 April, then the political sackings at FIAT, then the defeat of 1981 – and then downhill, all the way. Chaos. A chaos dominated by the force of the industrial restructuring that was put into place – and as a political formula dominated once again by creeping compromise. Nor will Craxi and the socialists be capable – not for a long time yet – of discharging the underlying tensions. And it is true that the Historic Compromise is the only possible political formula, the only possibility of governing and of recovering powers of decision-making out of the swamp of the social. It is the only way, given that the blockage of change has arrived at this violence of effects. The problem, the only problem, is how to destabilize the conditions that have allowed this disastrous stagnation to occur. But how can this be done? We know all the negative conditions, but we also know how fiercely they are capable of reproducing themselves and defending the mechanism of their reproduction. Prison, this fearsome weapon of social constraint; the rampant restructuring of industry, which is attacking and destroying the workers' aggregations in factories and in communities; and war – an ever-present threat, which includes Lebanon, the atomic bomb and nuclear terror. All this tends to create a situation of passivity and fear. A fear which does not have the metaphysical strength to develop horizons of higher sociality out of relationships between human beings and to accept antagonism as the basis for guarantees of freedom. No, this is a fear which spreads over everybody's heads, like a cloud laden with misfortune. And everything is flattened by its shadow. In such a situation only ethics – and only a new and very profound action of transformation that can be rooted in ethics – would permit us to re-found politics, outside of this fearsome solitude that we all share. I am reading and re-reading Leopardi, and I find him very much in tune with our times – between imprisonment in his hometown of Recanati and emptiness and passivity of the Italian way of life; between this destructive second nature which dazzles us and the ethical revolt which his poetry expresses, arising out of his solitude. I look around me – I can see these sentiments taking objective form among my children, among my friends, among the workers with whom I discuss. We need to reintroduce the prophetic into our lives. Gradually, as the days pass, my restlessness is growing. Maybe its interference with my reflections on ethics and politics has become part of my character. A malaise which wants to go and find rest somewhere beyond this condition of life and culture, of prison and society, which is imposed on me. It will always be this way, whether I am in prison or a free man, if ethical hope and transformative behaviours do not become the (mass) base of events of radical change for this society and for this state. Giangi, Giorgio, and so many of the others whom I see have abandoned militancy. They work and they have children. This does not lessen their desperation, for sure – but perhaps they, like me, expect a re-founding in all this; maybe they are waiting for a sign. But there will be no sign unless we build it ourselves, unless we transform the ethical unease into poetry, into the production of new signs. There are a lot of shooting stars in these August night skies. We need concrete signs of life, new children, new communities, and justice. Happiness has to be rebuilt as a material element, through restlessness, driving it to its inner ethical limit. Only in this way can we be productive of hope, and of the new. *Peu de gens devineront combien il a fallu être triste pour ressusciter Carthage.* I contemplate with real terror the fact that I am going to have to throw myself back into the perversion of the world of politicians, into that swampy terrain of meaninglessness. Why? The non-truth of that world is such that there is no possiblity of a reply to my question on that layer of significations. Why? These days I have been writing the text of my self-defence before Parliament. I shudder to think of the parliamentarians' faces I'll have before me. I am trying to be as sincere and balanced as possible, in order to lay down some kind of marker of freedom. It will not be accepted, that's sure. And it's right that this is the way it is. There is nothing to be done. Nothing other than our radical and profound ethics, only our re-founded hope, only this producing of positive signs – between us and only between us. The rest is all a machine of hatred and repression. (Montescudaio – 12/21 August)

Folio 75

Today I was at Rebibbia, with the comrades of G12, and then in the women's wing. When I walk into prisons, the measure of continuity between inside and outside is completely a given for me. But inside I experience that desire to break this continuum of repression and of acts of bad faith that you don't feel on the outside. The intelligence of the comrades, in their struggle against this prison system, reaches out to the society as a whole. Outside, in society, however, the signs of struggle and ethical reconstruction are only subterranean. Love for the comrades and emotion submerge my capacity for clear thinking when I meet them, but their intelligence and their attention are so strong that those elements of rupture with the meaninglessness of the institution and of society jump out with startling clarity.

Today I came to see them with no particular problems to discuss
– only the tedium of prison in August. I hope I gave them a bit of
a break. We talk of this and that. There are people being held in
solitary confinement – Aeneas, for instance. I go to see him. He is
angry over a strange tale of things that were lost and then found
again during prison searches. Silly stuff – it is August. I promise to
come back tomorrow and look into it. I hope I can. With Fiora and
her comrades we talk about how to develop the political campaign
for freeing the prisoners, and against the special laws. Finally they
gave their support to it, with all the committedness and vivacity
which these women can put into concrete matters. They are beautiful in their summer clothes. Here, in this unbearable heat of the early
afternoon, life is fresh and cool – here is a sign of a higher humanity.
Actually, if the truth be told, I came here to cheer myself up. And
perhaps to consolidate for good the decision to preserve my freedom.
These comrades are telling me: 'Go, leave, you have done what you
could.' 'Not yet,' I reply – I have to push forward to the very end. 'Be
careful – don't let yourself be taken again.' And I reply: 'No, I won't
let myself be taken again.' But . . . I don't tell them how difficult it is
to regain a grip on life, on your body, your freedom, your soul – in a
world where the institution surrounds you with death and a smell of
cancer. Can't you smell it? I don't tell them that I have a very strong
impulse – a life impulse – to return to prison. They would laugh at
me and would not be amused. But if I stay on the outside, as is my
duty, will I ever succeed in reproducing a high political function and
in responding to the calls for freedom – the freedom of you, men and
women comrades in prison? There are no shortcuts – it is difficult
. . . maybe too difficult. I have to do it. I have to rebuild hope and
produce signs. It is difficult. I have to do it. I have to try. Thank you,
comrades. (Rome – 22 August)

Folio 76

I'm going crazy during these days. In the Montecitorio *palazzo*, wandering round this huge empty building, I have the impression of being
the only person here. If I wanted to destroy it I could. But maybe
this place is so worn-out as a symbol of power that, even if you set
fire to it, it would not shed much light on the scene. The fact is that
this building is a heap of dung. Damp shit doesn't burn. This is its
strength – the fact that it doesn't actually burst into flames – the fact
that people leave it to its own devices – the way in which it reproduces

itself in its own fetid sweat. The only people present in these deserted rooms, in these pointless antechambers, are the journalists. They are the flies on the dung heap, untiring and always there. Either you get yourself paid by the journalists or you pay them. I would prefer the second solution, but unfortunately I am forced into the first. The relationship with them is a relationship of falsity. Their only pleasure is stirring shit. A wretched corporation! Gelli, who has just escaped from prison in Geneva – amazing coincidence! – understood them perfectly, and they were there to allow themselves to be bought. With Valiani and all those of the P1 lodge at the head of the queue. The selection of journalists in the old days used to go via the 'Intelligence Service'; in the '50s, they were chosen through the CIA. The younger generation, poor things, don't even have that good fortune. P2 and vulgarity on every hand. On the edges of the dung heap there are small pools of rampant putrescence – I imagine Scalfari, Cavallari and Montanelli here in their natural habitat. I wander around the rooms of Montecitorio, among half-asleep parliamentary staff and these scum-of-the-earth journalists. I manage to find one or two old friends who are not away on holiday, and I bring them in to survey the rubble. My decision to choose freedom is now irreversible. I tell this to my friends, in the hope that they might offer an alternative proposition. I am very calm, and I think that this society has to be revolutionized and this Parliament destroyed. (Rome – 23 August)

Folio 77

It's a Thirty Years War that we are living. A war of piracy, on the most diverse horizons, against pockets of humanity. A political world reduced to filibustering. If you ask people if we are in a state of war, nobody is prepared to admit it. Precisely as in the 1600s, when people were expecting death at any moment. Terror and restructuring of the state. Hobbes is a great mystifier: he talks of fear as if it were an ongoing reality between humans as individuals. In reality it was hanging over the heads of all humans, taken together. It was not antagonism but fate. The modern state is born from the sense of irresistible and radical change [*catastrofe*], from this blackmail, and not from the struggle for security and liberty. Only the state of the future – and it will not be called a state – will be born from a desire for liberty. Nobody admits to the continuous war of this century of ours. I would like to be able to explain this to the people around me. And I would also like to explain the horrible effects that it produces. *Metus versus* [*ad*] *superstitionem*. But nobody wants to understand. Spadolini is sending people to Lebanon – for the first time we're seeing our children being sent to war again. In '68 this would have been unthinkable. One day, once the Americans have been defeated along with the current bosses of Lebanon, they will all have to run away with their tails between their legs. A nice type, this Spadolini. With the idiocy of a Luigi Facta, he lives this creeping war without understanding its dimensions, its implications and its terrible evolutive potential. He runs to sell himself to the Americans, offering himself as a *Gauleiter* for one of the provinces of the Empire. War. I have fought against it from within the movement, hoping and struggling, so that the state of war between the classes, this war which is eternally present, should not transform itself into open war – poor Erasmus! And now, in the name of dissociation, should I accept the irresponsibility of the likes of Spadolini and the state of open war he is imposing on us? No, really no. If you reject war, you have to reject it in its entirety. Only peace provides the conditions for revolution. With the slyness of shopkeepers, they are hard at work, so that their presence in Lebanon simultaneously is and is not – it must not be seen, but it must be seen by the great chancelleries. They have absorbed Cavour's diplomatic wiles from their high-school textbooks. The Crimean War, Lebanon as Crimea. And do they really think themselves to be so clever? Spadolini. He hopes to have pulled it off with the P2, just as he hopes he's pulled it off in Lebanon – pulling out before disaster strikes. This is exactly what they said about Mussolini when he attacked France – and who would have thought that he'd be forced to send our troops barefoot to Greece and Russia? Bocca has always accused me of ambiguity. But he should look around him – at the dense ambiguity of his friends and bosses, at the way in which intellectual uncertainty shades into cold opportunism – that the people of Cuneo are stubborn is proverbial, but not that they are short-sighted. Peace is the prime precondition for revolution. So we should fight for peace. The Germans – Greens and non-Greens alike – have played a strong hand in my election – conference documents, a very strong stance against the 7 April trial, etc. Important to tighten this relationship, which has always been strong. This is fundamental. In large part these Greens are comrades and old friends – people with whom you can talk of hope. Strengthen the relationship. Lift yourself out of the suffocation of Italian politics and break the chains of the current peace movement and the traces of Stalinism in it. Here, in Italy, not in Germany. Rediscover peace as the precondition for revolution. Puncture Spadolini so that he deflates. I am amazed by one thing only: surely they cannot be sincere in what they are doing. These gentlemen must have at least a moment of intimacy with the boy they go to bed with: how will they manage to tell him that he's being sent off to war? (Montescudaio – 24 August)

Folio 78

Today I was in Capalbio. I met Ettore G. An amazing person. When you see this generosity and this liberating intelligence fully deployed you get a nostalgia for democracy, for what it once was in the hopes of thousands of people. The fascists tortured him in Palazzo Giusti, and then in Vicenza he was tortured (fortunately not physically this time) by all the reactionaries of the first Years of Lead of the Italian Republic, in the McCarthyite 1950s. He is a man of European culture and spiritual openness: it was as a European that he watched the developments of '68 and the regeneration of hopes of freedom and justice in its aftermath. In his children, and in the friends of his children, and in the movement, he loved the reclaiming of that justice and liberty that had been so downtrodden. Here, for the first time, I am proud that I too have been called an 'evil teacher' [*un 'cattivo maestro'*], and I am aware of how far I fall short in the presence of this real 'evil teacher'. If what Ettore G. expresses is anti-fascism, then I am radically anti-fascist – I rediscover myself as such, even in the face of a Republic which hypocritically assigns that title to itself. He is a man, this Ettore. I don't know why, but Brecht's Finland dialogues come to mind . . . That's where I would see Ettore located, eternally in flight from a nightmare that repeats itself – torture and exploitation – and always lucid, like Brecht's worker. The Constitutional Court does not deserve him. It took critical thought to dig this soil. Once the furrows have been opened, they do not close again – this earth which has been opened up remains fresh, and is black and dense and moist, like everything it creates. The seeds are deep sown. We cannot change. Ettore G. brings back to me the Venetian environment of my childhood. He suffered it as a grown man. Together, in our different ways, we have transformed it. He is a demonstration of how it is possible to win, despite the repression – not because he had professional, scientific or political success – no, this is only a piece of blackmail of his, which the political class had to endure – but because he had the strength to be a seminal influence and to stake his life on the boundary between resistance and revolution. This positive relationship is the only one in which I recognize ethical essence. But what does it matter if I recognize it, when he gives you this metaphysical hand with a moral simplicity and an intellectual sweetness that are worthy of the horizons of Capalbio? In the afternoon, in that splendid landscape (I shall be very nostalgic for it when I am far away from Italy – maybe for a long time: everyone is telling me 'Make your escape' and 'Don't let them get you again') . . . in the afternoon Alberto A. arrives, together with other old friends. A powerfully emotional moment. Here's another 'evil teacher' – or maybe just a 'bad friend'. Joking. We discover the meaning of *Geschichte* [history] when you are dazzled by the *Historie* [tale] you have lived. This is a knot of problems – meeting with Alberto again – and probably with Mario T. – a knot which only the entirety of history, and the great variables of the spirit, will eventually be able to unpack. Happy genealogies of dramatic stories. And then? The end has not come yet. With Alberto we do the round of the towers of Capalbio. It's like a reunion of the Beatles. With great humour and great attention. A sweet sensation, of understanding each other even before words are spoken. And it is a great music. Don't let them get you again! Maybe it is precisely in this situation of almost institutional encounters that I sense, not a nostalgia, but a desire for revolution to run through people's consciousness. I am crazy, as is known. And yet I see this naïve sense of freedom in the gaze of tactful people and in the kisses of distant friends. The furrows, once opened, do not close up again. This soil that we have ploughed has lines which, even in their separateness, join together at infinity. Today has been a delightfully sunny day and I am no longer scared. (Capalbio – 15 August)

Folio 79

I am a Marxist. And I remain a Marxist. I ask myself, recalling prison, what it was, if not my trust in revolution, that gave me the strength to carry on working. A re-reading of that strong theoretical hope, of that optimism of the intellect which is Marx. Marx beyond Marx. Spinoza and the logical certitude of possible revolution. And the calm passion of this vision, which went right through the experience of prison. Lessen the anger against injustice by means of the analysis of its structural causes, and through this build a higher level of hate against exploitation and domination. Many people tell me that, like Marx, I too am a corpse – but I don't see humour in their eyes, only fear. The advantage of my hatred is that it is articulated on, and mediated by, hope. Between yesterday and today we have travelled from Montescudaio to Venice, calmly, by car. From one paradise to another. We were talking about all this with the children and with Paola, in different registers – different registers, but the same theme. Big complex family games. (Incidentally, the children are telling me: 'Don't let yourself get caught again.') Marxism: it is the only practice that turns theory into a weapon. So, now, if I leave, what is going to happen to the comrades in prison? In reality, nothing worse than what was going to happen anyway. Whereas my careful long-term work, a work strongly charged with Marxism, is the only serious thing I can give them. Maybe yesterday and today, in the car and in Venice, I allowed myself to give way too much to affection. Despite that, I don't think that I need to modify those conclusions I have arrived at already in prison, and which I am now simply reconfirming, with the pleasure that the concrete gives to me. There is a revolutionary society which lives within this shit of developed capitalism. Marx has brought us to this limit, which for him was hypothetical, but for us is real. This is why I am a Marxist. Certainly not in the traditional manner. I didn't need to wait for Solzhenytsin or Glucksmann to discover about Gulags – I knew about them from '56. But what does this have to do with Marx, we asked ourselves back then. And what does this have to do with Marx and Lenin is what I continue to ask myself today. When it comes to intellectual geneses, Calogero and his ilk are quite enough for me. Here I live the duality of revolutionary society with the same intensity with which I perceived it in the 1950s. I am irritated by the dialectical opportunism of the older Marx. I prefer the theory of antagonism of this rejuvenated Marx. Rejuvenated by what now amounts to long-standing struggles for communism by the whole of the proletariat. We are living an enormous victory in the world. The world has been reshaped by the desire for communism. What has happened is enormous. We have to complete the mission of victory that has been assigned to us. Having come out of prison, I begin to touch and feel this irreducible reality. It is there. Why should we be ashamed of telling it to ourselves, and of telling it to incredulous others? The horizon stretches out as I talk about all this quietly with my children, and the thing seems natural – what we are experiencing is a Spinozan substantialization of hope. I do not know what is going to happen. I know only one thing: exploitation is unacceptable, and it has become natural to reject it – a new natural law has been born. Existence is the source of revolution. We have been forced into retreat, but only in order to attack more strongly. And with greater force. The problem of revolution is the present of our lives. As I write I have the lagoon before my eyes – this Venice lagoon is a consolidated history of capitalist revolution. Now it is rotting. Whereas the cool hydraulics of our spirit creates new generations of fish – and of men. We are waiting for a radical change which has already happened. (Venice – 26–27 August)

Folio 80

Here in Gualtieri, close to Reggio Emilia, I held a meeting on the Po. In the midst of so many people. A world that is strong and open-hearted, a world that I have known for a lifetime. The Po flows as powerfully as ever, here and in the neighbouring region where my mother lived, some thirty-odd kilometres away. A countryside where the horizon is uninterrupted by any kind of border, or by any block-age of the view. No hills here, everything completely flat, and the Po flows like a lord. Mother earth – this place where the history of peasant struggles connects seamlessly with a sense of freedom that only the infinity of the horizon can interpret. Here I smelt the smells and heard the voices and saw the colours of my childhood. In the meeting I spoke about the difference between this history and the institutions of the Italian state, between these horizons of freedom and the squalid regime which dishonours it by dominating it. I spoke calmly, but with great determination. There were many people at the meeting – very dear comrades. I felt at home. And I felt as if, once again, everything was possible – our dreams of liberty and justice – and the possibility of taking these things, with the strength that struggles give us. With this mass potency that the river represents. The village is architecturally delicious, an example of Renaissance perfec-tion. I feel really good in such a place! And how it feeds openhearted imaginings and hard behaviours of struggle! I think of the birth of socialism, of how people found their feet, uncertainly at first, but then with growing confidence, along these same winding banks of the Po, as they spoke of revolution. A revolution which grew throughout the duration of this century, overcoming the counterattack of the bosses, and of fascism, and of capitalist reconstruction. The waters of the Po run fast. And this image of the river's potency must be part of the awareness of the people who work around it: this strength does not abate. It is from the river that you learn the purificatory and invincible function of mass struggles. The work of maintaining the river banks and the irrigation systems which these lands have known for centuries. In people's eyes, and in their smiles, and in the move-ments of the young, and in their dances, and their communal singing,

I find so many recollections of my youth – I remember my mother dancing on the threshing floor. I've been followed here by the usual bunch of little provocateurs (the father of poor Alceste Campanile, who shouts 'Murderer' at me and is drowned in the laughter of the people at the meeting), and a couple of journalistic hacks. I am so completely serene – even though I am dead with exhaustion – that I barely notice their pointless pinpricks. I look at paintings by Ligabue, who spent his own desperate life as a free man around these parts. Here it makes sense to attack the state, the cliques of the political parties, those of the magistracy – because this is a frame of mind handed down through generations. People are naturally communist, and it is as a communist that they welcome me and draw me into their affections. I feel good here. And so many people here. I touched Earth again. Once again I can see those possibilities of mass struggle which political reason demands and which repression cannot have destroyed, either here or elsewhere. (Gualtieri – 28 August).

Folio 81

I have returned to Rome, to this parliamentary cesspit. After the day of yesterday spent in Gualtieri, I understand even less why I should continue to be here, to conduct this impossible struggle. And yet something is moving. By now we have an enormous document-ation on the strikes and struggles of the prisoners – enough to push towards the solution of various problems (preventive detention, prison conditions, the call for new codes, application of the 1975 law on penal conditions, etc.). So they have started, just as they had promised. The forms of struggle are completely new and original. Peaceful struggles. And one has the impression that they have been conducted with great tactical wisdom – they are not allowing them-selves to be trapped in unwinnable confrontations. We have here mass struggles led from the base. News is arriving from prisons all over Italy. I am receiving a load of letters from prisons, from friends and from people unknown to me. I read and read, all day long. And I answer the letters. I have to function as a relay of this struggle, in relation to Parliament. I shall do it, in the very short amount of time still remaining to me. I feel that something can be done. But I am still amazed by the disproportion between the huge quantity of hope for justice which sustains these struggles – and the scary rigidity and the crude, uncaring response at parliamentary level. Those in power do not deserve these struggles, which we, the prisoners, have built with such democracy and correct tactics. But it's good to go ahead like this, because this fighting educates us and makes us stronger. It offers a way out of the alternative of shipwreck or desperation, which are the only options offered us by those in power. I have no difficulty in imagining the course that the struggle has taken, the obstacles, the clashes, the discussions, the decisions. And the nerviness and the tiredness which, in prison, colours each and every one of these movements – not to mention the loss of confidence, which so easily overtakes you. But I also imagine the warmth of those movements, and the popular wisdom they contain – and that act of liberation that is created for each person when they decide, in the course of communal discussions, to make the choice for struggle. The objectives are undoubtedly reformist – they really are the least that could be demanded. But it is important nonetheless – and indeed revolutionary – to indicate this trajectory of the mass struggle, and to involve everybody, personally, in decision-making. It is an enormous sign of the maturity of the people in prison, and probably also a sign of changes in their composition. Nowadays the whole of society is filtered through prison. And yet this force, this generosity, this democracy will be disappointed. Why this incredible distance? Here in Parliament prison is seen as a place of prevention and a terroristic exemplification of punishment, which capitalist countries necessarily have to offer. There really is no possible contact between this conception and the desire for liberty. I try to understand what can be gained out of all of this – in fact it is almost nothing. This country of ours needs a revolution. It needs one on the basis of a transformation of consciousness which has already taken place, at the broadest mass level. It needs an expansion of this root-and-branch change [*catastrofe*] in needs and desires, which has already taken place. Today the Ministry of Justice appears as an archaic monster of wickedness by comparison with the prisoners' groups and the mass meetings being organized in the prisons. How are we to move within this reality, which has now reached such a degree of scission? (Rome – 29 August)

Folio 82

In the morning I met with the chancellor [*il Guardasigilli*], to discuss with him the conference that the comrades want to organize in Rebibbia on the theme of alternatives to imprisonment. The discussion immediately shifted to ways of bringing an end to the state of emergency, and then to the communist project of the abolition of prisons. An intelligent man, with a sense of spiritual freedom and a deep irony – a man who is tired and disenchanted. One can be reactionary even through being simply realistic. He is not a cynic. The conference will happen, . . . yes, no, if, . . . we'll see, . . . the minister is difficult, . . . there's a security problem, and so on. It is devilishly hot today. I return to working on interviews and on the media. I have a long discussion with Gad. The movement and its history. He reproaches me for not having intervened in time to block the disastrous line the struggles were taking. But it wasn't like that, I reply. The problem was the internal disproportion, the unboundedness of the strength of the movement, which made it so that the radical change in the conception of needs and desires and the urgency of appropriation ran up against the poverty of organizational means. We, on our own – too much on our own – did our best to intervene in this conjuncture. The fault of many others who had experienced the movement – a fault which was serious and historically marked in fire – was that they attacked the consequences of this disproportion but did not address themselves to the actual problem, trying to find ways to resolve it directly. This was the mistake that led to practically all the leadership groups in the movement breaking apart. Including the leadership group of Lotta Continua – even before that of Potere Operaio ['Workers' Power'], preceding it chronologically. That the problem was profound is illustrated by what happened afterwards – the Years of Lead and the thousands of comrades who were caught up in the repression. And the present demonstrates it more than anything else: the lack of fibre [*atonia*] of this society and the fragmentation of interests, the impossibility of getting a whole picture of them. Just now I was looking at the endnotes in the Censis report – which offer a Greek-style lamentation over all these things, always supposing that they are not a hypocritical justification for the electoral defeat of the major political parties. As for myself, I certainly have no illusion that everything can be resolved by a wave of some magic wand. But how are we to move forward? There is only one way: by deepening the logic of our history and reproposing the original problem, which we left unresolved. A continuity is possible for us – it is not a continuity of what they are accusing us of, but of what actually happened in the movement, the things you don't see unless you actually want to see them – and which are, quite rightly, hidden from our accusers. We have to study and organize the content of the radical change which our generation has lived and which can in no sense be cancelled out. Is this conception substantialist or non-substantialist, rationalist or irrationalist? I really do not know. I am not interested in defining reductive categories, but in grasping the sense of complexity of things. And the complexity consists in this – that there was a revolution, and that it was inscribed in people's consciousnesses and posed certain central and fundamental problems. And it was prevented and repressed at the point at which it was engaged in this transition – in the transition to organization. But it has remained in people's spirit and it manifests itself in their unhappiness and anguish, because it was not able to find expression in constitution. For sure, it is difficult and hard. I'm seeing Rossana today. We are discussing the idea of starting a research project on northern Italy – on class composition, to be precise. I don't know whether research work like this can actually be done. What class, dear Rossana? The class which is being disaggregated is being disaggregated, and that's that. Then there's the other class, the one which moved through the period of radical change and moves itself only for revolution. This one is intent on detachment and alternative ways of life. I do not know when it will express itself. I have the impression that it is extending infinite numbers of threads and constituting a new web of being. How is this to be grasped? Sarcastically, I almost find myself saying: through travel. At this point I have an increasing detestation for what I see around me – even the intelligence, even the honest self-questioning about where we went wrong. We didn't go wrong, except insofar as we did not ask ourselves the question. We should have lived this incredible tragedy of ours even more to the limit, knowing that this is what it was – and that only by imposing on ourselves a profound asceticism could we have succeeded in interpreting an event which was too enormous to be capable of being contained within our language. The primary inscription of our being is communist revolution.

PS Kafka, *Wedding Preparations in the Country*. 'The first sign of the beginning of knowledge is the desire to die. This life seems unbearable, alien, inaccessible. There is no longer shame in wanting to die. One is asked to leave the old cell which is hated in order to transfer oneself into a new cell which we shall learn to hate. A shred of faith continues, however, to make you think that, during the transfer, the big man will happen to be coming down the corridor, and he will say: "Don't put that one back in prison, he's coming with me . . ."'
(Rome – 30 August)

Folio 83

Interviews again, and work on the media. My endless refrain: 'Parliament is the only armed gang of which I have ever been a member' – highlighting Parliament's distance from the real problems of the country and the fact that it is a perverse image of the state. My words are not much appreciated. But, while the press attacks me in its customary ranting style – I am referring to the press of the likes of Cavallari and Scalfari, of the P2 and FIAT – there is not a single member of Parliament who dares to reproach me. Why is that? Because, obviously, I could answer easily, showing how absent and distant Parliament is from people's real everyday lives. But also because there's a certain shamefacedness among the younger parliamentarians – at least among those whose faces have not yet become frozen into the customary, chilling grimace of cynicism. However, dealing with the problems is what protects me, what keeps me in the saddle even after these two months of freedom, what enables me to maintain a high profile both in defence and in the attack on the perversion of the institutions. Now [we have] the problem of the great struggle going on in the in prisons. The movement continues to grow, the forms of struggle continue to be extremely peaceful. There has not been a single incident yet. Good – they won't manage to set in motion the usual provocations, which give them an excuse for repression. But here, in Parliament, not a word. I talk to the radicals – they tell me that it's very hard for them. The only people who are moving – with their splendid generosity – are the comrades of Democrazia Proletaria. A handful of true Catholics and people from the independent Left are also beginning to discuss the problem. For them – as befits the administrative (and only incidentally political) persons which they are, to perfection – it will take a long time to weigh the arguments and to propose, discuss and quibble over the complexities of the problem. And meanwhile the movement moves ahead. For the rest, nothing. And yet, I keep telling myself, here we are witnessing a generalization of the experiences of San Vittore and Rebibbia in 1982, a generalization which is almost a typical representation of a qualitative leap of consciousness in the social composition of the prisoners: how is it that people who claim to be the country's representatives are failing to notice this extraordinary process? On the other hand, I know that the military and civil prison authorities have certainly registered all this: this development of the struggles reveals in a grandiose manner the modification, which is now definitively in place in prisons, in the relationship between the prisoners and those who hold them in prison. Furthermore, the problem of prison is now a fundamental intersection point of modern consciousness, almost a paradoxical slice of society and of its problems. How can they not notice all this? How can a Parliament be so external, so empty of understanding? So lacking in response? The situation scares me. Is there too much ambiguity around? It is certainly the case that, if Parliament is tone-deaf, the social is deaf. However, this does not seem to me to be a sufficient justification. What is the social, in the face of this Parliament? Is it still a force which, in all its differences, is capable of making its voice heard? No, most certainly not. Here we no longer have channels of general communication. There is only the invasion which a few corporations make, every once in a while, into the spaces of the political, bringing some of their servants to guarantee their expression in politics. Fragmentation and segmentation. At this point I feel almost nostalgic for the old notion of general will, of the autonomy and force of the political. However, the illusion lasts only for a moment; I am mindful that this nostalgia borders on fascism. No. The only way is for the prisoners to express themselves, to express and impose their problem with force. There is no longer any mediation of the political in relation to society. Parliament is a clandestine gang. The comrades in prison, on the other hand, have begun to walk along the only line that is correct: the abolition, elimination, end of prison. ('Don't let yourself be taken again' is the word from all the comrades who write to me from within the prison movement – escape is the only form in which we can today conceive of the abolition of prison, in the face of a ruling class that is so inept.) (Rome – 31 August)

Folio 84

Yesterday and today saw a continuation of the meeting of the Authorizations Committee, and it finished badly. Yesterday I made a very powerful speech, unlike my presentation at the first hearing. Calogero is mad and should be locked away; the power of the magistracy must be restored to a correct constitutional positioning. These were my basic points. Not that they understood much of what I was saying. They decided to send me back to court, with a request for my re-imprisonment. However, the clash was very strong over postponing discussion until the end of the 7 April trial and until a decision [was reached] that might take account of the sentencing. These months of parliamentary work have not been in vain. I don't think in the slightest that the proposal for deferral will pass; it is nevertheless true that, unlike in the committee, in the Chamber there is an abstract possibility that it might be passed. This is a compromise that I can accept. The communists and socialists have fallen into line with this proposal. This strikes me as important. A great job has been done. I have many comrades to thank for this. I harbour no great expectations: I just hope that the debate in the Chamber will bring about further contradictions. It is clear that the Left is unifying around this proposal for compromise and postponement – for the first time we are seeing a breaking of the DC–PCI axis, which up until this point had been the 'party of no compromise'. Albeit with extreme caution, the PCI is abandoning that position on questions of civil rights. This is the hypothesis entertained by those at *Il Manifesto*, and it is Rossana's great hope. How solid is this hypothesis? Will it succeed in transforming itself into a tendency? Today Mellini, for the Radical Party, abstained from giving his vote. I begin to get a whiff that Pannella is not prepared to accept, under any circumstances, the formation of any such front on the Left. The thing terrifies him; he hates the unity of the Left, and in particular he fears for a unity of the Left that might rob him of his monopoly on the defence (painless, when he does it on his own) of civil and political rights. Pannella is an American – sometimes a progressive (I mean on civil rights), but above all an American (I mean he is dead-set against the communist point of view and against the unity of the Left). Mellini, who is only from Civitavecchia and is generous and intelligent, clearly suffers under this political stance of his boss. On the other hand, you certainly can't say that things are particularly clear on the Left. Lula B., a member of Parliament for the independent Left, was taking issue today with Rossana for the passion with which she is committing herself to defending the 7 April people and myself. She is saying that we should be more cautious in order to achieve our ends – and she is sincere in this. I conclude from all this that I am stuck in a big imbroglio – I really do not think that any of this is immediately resolvable – in this I agree with Lula – but I do not believe that it is resolvable in the future either, through good tactics – in this I disagree with Lula. The situation is politically perverse, and good intentions and correct tactics are not sufficient. This perversion is structural, and there is always an ultimate institutional instance founded on repression. Even good will and daily work can bring about perverse effects. It is strange to have to spend time explaining this to the only people who, despite everything, sincerely passed through the experience of 1968 – Lula and her comrades of the independent Left. They have a naïve notion of the state.

As for Rossana, it is clear now that her generosity and her optimism of the will have caused her completely to lose sight of the terms of the situation. She sublimates everything: the violence of the institutional relationship which is implicit in the 7 April trial and the dense contradictoriness of the political relationships involved. We probably have totally different evaluations of the inertia of the institutions (which for me can be blocked only through a radical change) and of the PCI – for her the Historic Compromise is now definitively behind us, but for me it still lingers.

On the other hand, how could she fight this battle if she did not still nurture these illusions? In order to move in the world of parliamentary politics you need to get the realistic measure of it, take its measurements and dress in its stuff. And, anyway, there's no saying that every once in a while illusion doesn't win. Was it not perhaps on the basis of an illusion that I got out of prison – even though it was only to fall into this new parliamentary prison? The one who scares me more than Rossana is Pannella – this evening, after Mellini's abstention and after strong insistence from Rossana (from what I understand, she has started counting the potential votes) – I asked Marco if he, too, intends to abstain on the vote in the house. With his usual clear-sightedness, Gianni F. today reminded me that even ten votes would be no small thing. Marco answered neither yes or no – he reminded me of the code of conduct of the Radicals (not to support laws that strengthen the partitocracy nor to involve themselves in theatricals), but he also added that nothing would be done to prevent the passing of a solution that would leave me free. This discourse in negatives gave me the shivers. Let's keep hoping. I don't have many options other than hope. Thinking back over things, I am anyway satisfied with the work that has been done. In these two months – less than two months, and with the holidays in the middle – we have succeeded in creating a possibility and defining a spiral. This is not tactics but strategy. This possibility is a knife plunged into the institutional inertia, which cuts away its ties to the ideology of the state of emergency. Modestly said, 'Bravo, Toni, well done!' They may fuck me, but I'll leave them with a hot potato in their hands. (Rome – 1–2 September)

Folio 85

What a day today! I spent the afternoon in Pisa, a few hours on a phone-in on a local radio station. Then, in the evening, to Livorno, for the *Avanti!* Festival. A load of people. I am sitting in a hotel in Livorno, extremely tired, trying to sum up my complex and difficult perceptions of the situation. But first, within this tiredness, there is the continuously drumming repetition – I don't know why it was so continuous today – of the phrase *mai più in galera* [never again in prison]. I had this from the autonomist comrades of Pontedera, and from the ex-Lotta Continua people of Pisa, and from the socialists in Livorno. Ten, fifteen people. Why? Why this very strong value attached of the symbol of escape? Because this escape is a claim to autonomy in relation to the institution, it is a freedom asserted in the face of a state that is perverted.

But would my escape not be in contradiction with the declaration of dissociation, with the politics that follows from it, and with all the small steps we have taken towards a political solution? I ask this insistently of everyone close to me. This escape, if it is going to happen, is coming very close – we are well beyond the point of talking about it as an abstract principle. Now, if it is necessary, I have to do it, and all the consequences need to be weighed up. And yet in this *mai più in galera* there is a force, a solid feeling of autonomy and freedom, which grips me and moves me. Perhaps this is precisely the key to today's events. Autonomy and freedom – put solidly, in the manner in which these Tuscan comrades know how to express themselves. Including the ex-Lotta Continua people (sometimes they express a past of which they accept the value, but from which they protect themselves; and sometimes they almost desire to repropose the dream of revolution but are incapable of carrying it through). A whole cocaine scene here. This is not to say that drugs necessarily eliminate the truth. However, the general scene seems to me anarchist more than political or communist. It is quite the opposite for the comrades of Pontedera – they contacted me when I was on holiday in Montescudaio. Then there are the autonomists from Lucca – all new working class: here libertarianism has lost the stamp of the artisanal, what we have here is abstract labour. It is good to be able to touch the abstract with your fingers and to kiss these comrades.

It's completely different in Livorno. Thousands of people. The taste of the sea is tangible, and the music is as solid as the air that carries it – salty. I do the meeting with Andò, from the executive of the Socialist Party. I proceed to attack – the emotion of the moment is very strong, in the chilly and vengeful silence of a big hall that is packed – these are the people who want me back in prison. In particular I attack the magistracy. Andò manages to get himself a hearing among the audience, which had not paid him much attention at the

start. He is very good. He explains, through the emotionality aroused
by my presence, how the special laws are evil, not only because they
cause unjust suffering but also because they give the magistracy
powers outside the constitution, and those powers end up being
destructive of political representation. I have to applaud what he is
saying. I talk about prison and the prison movement, and I say that
the only way these problems can be resolved is through a profound
renewal of the constitution. I speak of the material constitution, of
what actually is, and not of the great principles which a degenerate
political class likes to claim as its own. I am in tune with the meeting,
there is an incredible emotionality to it all. Some people are crying
– and people tell of the injustices that they themselves have suffered.
There is soul in the whole thing. They come up to me, they embrace
me. Ex-prisoners cry like babies. They break through the stewards
who are there to protect me – big chunky stewards, local dockers –
and what a sweet thing it is to hold these unknown comrades close.
For god's sake, leave me a bit of time for the political project of
reorganization and liberation of the comrades! Leave me some time!
Then, more calmly, I talk with the socialists. Here, in the port area,
I discover in them a libertarian will which under the arches and tap-
estries of Parliament all too often disappears. Basically, throughout
the 7 April affair, the socialists have never behaved badly – even if
they did keep themselves at a distance, fearing that it was all going to
fall on their heads. Anyway, I am completely wiped out with tiredness and now I'm going to bed. In Gualtieri, in Naples, in Padova,
and now here in Livorno I have experienced those emotions which
certify that another society, proletarian, is alive and reproduces itself
in the face of the inertia and perversion of power! I should sleep
soundly tonight. I see the light of dawn coming up – I like the analogy
between the landscape and our political and revolutionary hopes.
(Pisa/Livorno – 3 September)

Folio 86

My escape is necessary. I talk about it with all the comrades. Not
one of them tells me no. Today, between Venice and Padova – the
weather is crystal clear – I see not only comrades from the movement
but also old friends. Feliciano B. is a great and old (now) bourgeois
intellectual. He has the cynical lucidity of the reactionary. He doesn't
believe that the world can be much different from what it is – but, on
the other hand, inasmuch as he is an intellectual, he is often seized

by theoretical imaginings of transformation. However – precisely as a pure intellectual – he keeps his theoretical imaginings to himself, and in no sense applies them to the world. It is truly wonderful, this schizophrenia of his, which becomes frankly cynical when it has to deal with the real world and enlightened when he examines his own thoughts. He is rarely wrong in his views of what is likely to happen institutionally, and as a result he has a clear view of how things are unfolding. Theoretically, on the other hand, he would have a dialectics of liberty which does not exist, or which has been repressed – and he is confident of being able to handle it because, anyway, that's the way the world goes.

I really enjoy his sense of irony, his reactionary iconoclasticism, which is the lucid proof of a free intelligence. In historical terms, he reminds me of Paolo Sarpi and the crisis of the Venetian Republic. I wonder whether his defence of liberty is a hope, or whether it is nostalgia. It is the latter, for sure – and this is better. Nostalgia, only this gives value to thought. Set against this we have the fierce will for conservatism of others of his generation. Somehow it takes you aback – but the same thing can be said of so many others of my friends in the Veneto – the way in which they allowed the terroristic demonization of Padova and of the Veneto (not to mention of myself) to pass without lifting a finger to stop it, even though they knew that the basis of the charges was false, even though they were sickened by the madness of the media. In my view this was basically laziness. (Their view of the University of Padova was a bit like Voltaire's comment on the University of Coimbra: 'After the earthquake which destroyed three quarters of Lisbon the country's wise men could find no better way of preventing total ruination than to give the people a fine auto-da-fé. It was decided by the University of Coimbra that the spectacle of a few people being burned alive, in a big ceremony, was an infallible secret for preventing further earthquakes.') A combination of caution and aloofness – from people who don't want to get involved in dirty business. Those of the magistracy in particular. With their smoking-caps on their heads and their cats on their knees, they sat and waited for the institutional frenzy to pass. Always playing things in a low key, never explicitly defending what was happening. Living a disenchanted view of power, surviving in the crisis. Maybe they were right – but why accept to live such unhappy lives? Sometimes craziness consoles. Massimo C. is, basically, one of that kind. One time I used to be disturbed by his intelligence; now I am amused by his desperate desire to survive in the crisis. His disenchantment has taken on tones of asceticism. For the pure reactionary disenchantment can

be also a way of not getting involved, and of allowing yourself to continue (with irony and detachment) in making money or a career. For
him these things are derisory. For him, what counts is knowledge –
but a knowledge that shuns horizons of hope and raises the possibility
of a comeback only in an act of knowing, in a dimension of ethical or
aesthetic transcendence. Here cynicism is not neutral multiformity in
the use of the concrete, but a contempt for the whole of the concrete,
in absolute terms, as a horizon, with a blind faith in the power of a
destructive and liberating intelligence. Except for the generosity of
intervening and of applying oneself to the particular case – a generosity which is undermined by sarcasm – but all the greater precisely
on this account. Politics becomes application to concrete cases. The
subtext here is a despairing judgement that there is nothing to be
done – maybe a few small battles can be won – 'We're doing our
best for you, Toni' – but with no illusions, and let's leave it at that.
Really, only in asceticism can we decant unhappiness. I am probably
strongly affected by this world, in a negative sense. When it comes
to the transcendency of hope, that hard nucleus of values, I overturn
it, I try to see it in its concrete aspect, in its totality. This quest is
equally desperate, but inexhaustibly filled with hope. Is this my great
fault? My escape is necessary. It offers the possibility of rendering my
protest concrete, not only in relation to these infamous court proceedings, but also in relation to those people who think that hope is
no longer on the agenda. There will be many difficulties, enormous
in fact, but only in freedom will it be possible to resume that work
of thinking and acting which, precisely here in the Veneto, enabled
us to develop and innovate in relation to a tradition of cynicism and
disenchantment. Here we have dug deep. Today has been a calm and
beautiful day – the sky merges with the green of the earth. (Venezia/
Padova – 4 September)

Folio 87

Everyone was playing at war in '76 and '77. But among these
Milanese intellectuals you would not find even one who would be
prepared to admit to it, not even if you promised them that their
books were going to be published *chez* Gallimard. They were all
involved – and how they elbowed each other out of the way, in Nanni
[Balestrini]'s 'Area [Cooperativa Scrittori]', and then in his *Alfabeta*.
I understand the fear, and I also understand the disgust with what
happened during the Years of Lead. But why has none of these intel-

lectuals, not one of them, contributed to the collective self-criticism? Why did they hide away? It's hardly the case that they were not right there in the thick of things, en masse. One more than the other, and all together, they toiled away to prove that transversality was more important than discussions about organization – and they informed us that such discussions could only end up in ideology and violence and Stalinism. Then it turned out that precisely this sprouting of groupuscules and sectionalism, and the dispersion of that small amount of political intelligence which was being formed at the centre, degenerated into blind violence; whereupon transversality turned into a killer. That led to a situation in which the repression started striking out blindly. And they all fell silent. Or rather they all met up again, very cosily, at the dinner table, to talk about other things. So why not set up a journal? *La Gola* – an 'open journal', naturally, because anybody can talk about *gola* [throat/gluttony] – materialists or idealists, traditionalists or postmodernists. But things had not hit bottom yet. When the final tragedy hit Milan, with the killing of Tobagi – and our trial has shown the extent of the degradation of the red and cultivated bourgeoisie and the perversion of the state, so that both sides made use of killers in order to solve problems of rank and to make sure that the socialist parvenus never made it through to the inner sanctum of power – both then and now, nothing happened, except a headlong race to justify *pentitismo*, or, for the more astute, to bundle up everything together – autonomists and terrorists, judges and police, *Corriere della Sera* and Mondadori. There was a crisis, and this was the magic word that pacified their consciousnesses. I am in Milan, talking about this with Primo M., with Sylvie, and with other friends. Everyone is at their wits' end. What needs to be studied here is the axis of repression–perversion: and the transformation of fear into resentment, and that cancellation of memory and intelligence which is tantamount to a death wish. There is nothing tragic in this. There is only failure in intellectual and ethical duties. Every generation passes through some moment of crisis. But here we have seen too many crises, and now you can say that a certain slothfulness dominates the scene. This red generation of Milanese intellectuals has seen too many corpses. It watched impotently the passing of a whole parade of corpses, even before those which blind terrorism left in its wake. The corpse of the Resistance, the corpse of Stalinism, the corpse of the economic boom and the corpse of '68 . . . so nothing surprises them any longer.

And all the time you find them inventing alibis and disguises. I ask people if there is any hope that out of this sequence of traumas they might still be able to re-emerge with some kind of life energy. And they tell me: look, you were in prison for four years, you don't understand . . . What has happened now cannot be compared with the big crises of the past. The intellectuals saw those crises on a screen, projected onto the big dimensions of universal history. The crises of recent years have been different. The dramas ran through whole families. Criticism and self-criticism became our daily bread. Intelligence should have reacted. But, instead, it did nothing. This is not failing in functions and historical responsibilities – this is pure and simple betrayal. It is weariness and cowardice. We no longer want to understand anything, we are hurt and affronted. Then, when my friends go, I spend the rest of the day thinking over our discussions. On the one hand I see many things growing, and it really does not seem to me that this Italian proletariat has abandoned its desire to change, to transform itself and the world in which it lives; but on the other it seems to me obvious that we have to rebuild a scenario of thought and a dimension of communication through which this desire can reinvent itself in effective ways. However, what is certain is that we cannot rely on that circuit of traditional Milanese intellectuals. Their desire to live has mouldered away, and they have betrayed the mission which alone justifies the existence of the function of intellectual. (Milan – 5 September)

Folio 88

Is it a betrayal, to escape? That's how I experience it. But rationally it seems to me absurd to think like that. There is an infinite number of things you can do when you are free, for the comrades in prison, and above all for the rebuilding of the movement. It is obvious that the radicals are not a means for doing this; and, while Democrazia Proletaria is an important historical nucleus, its traditionalist limitations mean that it is not up to the task of rebuilding. It is obvious that we have to build a European dimension, as a basis on which . . . and so on.

Nor does it seem to me misguided or wrong to escape when I look at it from an *emotional* point of view. When Lauso and Paolo Virno went back to prison after they had already been released, I told them with profound conviction that I would not have done that. I don't think that the desire for freedom, which you feel with such force from behind the prison walls, can be cancelled out. I live it in its entirety, and I find that I'm always living that desire when I'm out walking and my imagination runs riot, representing every possible route of escape. So is it wrong in *political* terms to make my escape? Here too, I don't think so. Escaping is a political declaration of dissociation which, for me, has good practical effects – removing oneself from the state of emergency – and which also leaves the comrades in prison the possibility to act. My politician friends are of the opinion that the battle of the trial can be won. I think so too. The *pentiti* can be destroyed.

But the 7 April case is not a just a courtroom battle, and it would be idiotic to reduce it to that. It is a political battle, and we have some prospect of winning it. People are starting to tell me: a few more years in prison, and then the European elections, and then I don't know what . . . But the cost of this gamble would be the acceptance of their rules of the game – and this is exactly what I do not accept, because those rules are irrational and therefore cannot be counted upon; furthermore, they do not promise a rebuilding of the movement and a project of revolution. It is I who will choose my limits, within an analysis of the rational possibilities. So why is it that, having said all this, escaping still strikes me as something of a betrayal?

Why is it that, even though there is only a week to go before the resolution of the matter, I cannot yet decide to give the go-ahead for my escape to be prepared? Between the abstract of truth and the concrete of community there is an infinite distance. And it is difficult, this inhuman acceptance of abstract truth as the only rule for action. It is not only difficult, but also desperate. We have to gamble on the truth – but is it possible? I am not a gambler – in fact I detest gambling. On the brink of making the choice to escape, I find that I am paralysed.

I talk about it, over and over. There are many indisputable reasons in favour of my escape. Reservations are useless, objections are stupid and tied to petty electoral interests or concerns about public opinion. And yet I still cannot decide. This evening my escort suddenly popped up again, unexpectedly. I was coming out of Pier Giorgio's house, and they followed me to Mauro's house. I immediately called the Ministry of the Interior, but they claimed they knew nothing about it. Anyway, the escort disappeared during the night. I am expecting subtle systems of surveillance. All this raises the problem of how exactly I'm going to make the break, as and when I decide to get away, in case I want to get away. I am resistant to thinking about it, but I have to. Between the abstract of truth and the concrete of community the gap is enormous. It does not seem to me that my escape will have disastrous consequences, either on the comrades or on the trial, even though some imbeciles claim that it will. I reply that it is rather my presence that is having a disastrous effect, and this I truly believe to be the case. But the problem is different. It is the problem of loyalty to a habitual way of thinking; of community and loyalty to this family, which is our life together in prison. It is the problem of breaking this with an anticipated and unilateral choice of timings and themes of political struggle which are not those of the community – or at least not immediately so. The choice of a different timescale, in the community and for the community, but outside of its immediacy. The tearing of a fabric. I don't know how to resolve the problem. I am going almost crazy with this. I hear the voices of thousands of comrades who have told me to get out of here and not to fall into the pernicious trap of institutions and of perverted politicians. I am aware of the silence of the Rebibbia comrades on this question. I am aware of the desperate desire for my freedom on the part of all those people who love me. I think and think again and I cannot see a single rational, emotional or political reason that even faintly suggests that putting myself back into prison would be a good idea. And yet I am unable either to decide or to clarify for myself the reasons for this desperate perplexity. Between the abstract and the concrete I have always allowed the abstract to win. But is it correct to do so at this time? After the experience of prison, and after the struggle? Is it correct? What kind of frightful gamble am I committing to if I make my escape? And yet I must win this fight. It will be difficult. (Rome – 6 September)

Folio 89

Last night Marco P. called me in urgently. He talked to me about his own crisis, and that of his party – in a way which seemed to me to be sincere. Then he suggested a possible scenario for my escape: to leave just for the period of the vote. Stay in France for three months. Then, at some point around Christmas, to present myself at the Strasbourg Parliament and at the Court of Human Rights. The idea is that I would get myself extradited to Italy. For his part, he says that he will support me during my escape and would get me elected in the European parliamentary elections of June '84. Honestly speaking, the scheme strikes me as crazy. I do not share this way of working – so tied to the media, to calculated illegality. I tell him that today the problem is to guarantee the passing of the communists' proposal for a further postponement – and at the same time to do nothing that might obstruct its final stages or impede its approval. As for his suggestion, I shall give it some thought. But, already this morning, Marco was trying to be clever with the foreign press in the press conference. While I was blandly reassuring everyone that the matter of an escape was not on my agenda, he was openly encouraging me to escape. I am beginning to think that he sees me as some kind of puppet that he can stake in a risky game of hazard. The man is obviously a gambler, but this is a strange sensation for me, to find myself being used as money in this kind of gamble. Money and symbol at the same time. All hell has broken loose over my presence in Parliament and what it represents symbolically. On the one hand those in power and the journalists are trying at all costs to destroy me as symbol. (Today we have the latest vile stunt [*vigliaccata*]: Biagi ran my TV interview alongside an interview with Captain Genova, the torturer of Padova, thereby invalidating it through recontextualization. And today there was another cheap operation of taking my words out of context, by Bonsanti (who, not accidentally, is a close pal of a communist boss in the Palace). This journalistic operation makes a pair with the total falsification of the facts published in *Der Spiegel* earlier this summer. And yet another article today, an interview with a wretched little hired *pentito*, Coniglio of Milan. Once again I am accused of being an 'evil teacher', on the grounds that, about ten years ago, I drank a toast to a mass appropriation which had taken place in a supermarket. Cretin! Tell us why you killed. Did I teach you to do that, you runt?) On the other hand, Marco P. wants to maximize, for his own party, the symbolic value I represent in party-political terms. In particular, it is becoming increasingly obvious that he has no intention of allowing my figure to become a symbol for even a temporary unification of the Left. He will continue with provocations designed to prevent the formation of a majority – just as he did this morning (in a first simple preparatory *essais*, by telling me 'Escape' and quoting Salvemini and his opinions about preventive imprisonment and the judicial corporation). But, I ask myself, if I do make my escape, would I be extracting myself from the area of significations that the symbol represents? No, for sure. Escape is part and parcel of the symbolic content of me as a figure. So, if I do escape, how is Marco P. going to react? If I withdraw from Pannella's party-oriented agenda the objective content of my escape – a content of getting out of prison, of liberty: a content voted for as such by my electorate – how will he react? Presumably by teaming up with the journalists and with those in power to destroy me as a symbol and to muddy my image. Or would he be more intelligent and wait for things to become clearer? I don't really know – but I do know that I have to be very careful. Money-symbol: that is certainly not the way that Rossana sees things. I had a sharp meeting with her today. Jaro must have told her of my uncertainties. She came on heavy, reminding me of Socrates and various other fine things. She sees the problem as being two-fold: on the one hand, the push for a unification of the Left around the issue of civil liberties; on the other hand, winning the 7 April case . . . I agree about these two threads. But there is a third one, which is missing. Namely my freedom and my possibilities for continuing the struggle. There is nothing egoistic about this – only my natural right. Socrates doesn't come into it, because he was saying that the just laws of Athens should be obeyed even when they are badly applied, and if necessary even through one's own death. But here we do not have just laws. We have laws that are ferociously unjust, and nobody is obliged to accept their consequences. Nor does the democracy which we enjoy offer any hope of rapid modifications of the picture, or any prospect that the law will ever operate fairly. Nevertheless, my uncertainty remains. And I explain to Rossana that, if I decide against escaping, it will certainly not be because I have been persuaded by her arguments. If I decide not to escape it will be because I have understood the silence of the comrades in Rebibbia as a tacit lack of agreement. A disagreement tied to a culture and a sense of right which have nothing to do with the money (other people's money) with which the wretched Marco P. is so spendthrift, and have nothing to do with the immediacy and the importance of a political battle over rights, here and now, which Rossana is proposing to me. Rossana, the basics of life are powerful in another way, when they break servitude and build community. Only that could keep me here. Deciding to stay as a revolutionary act. Who knows! (Rome – 7–8 September)

Folio 90

A really fine demonstration in Brescia yesterday. A thousand people – so many people have not been seen together for a long time. A tense, focused discussion – the people, together, are beginning to see freedom. I am very tired – today I arrived in Milan from Rome, by air, and then we were stuck in a traffic jam for hours. Then, here in Brescia, together with the comrades of Democrazia Proletaria, in a working-class environment where I feel very much at home, the people in Val Camonica started telling me: 'Don't let them put you back in prison again.' And the sister of Stefanino, a comrade from Rebibbia, said the same, and this moved me hugely. And so did many, many others – it went on and on. I am a symbol of liberation, not something tied to the vile dialectics of infamous laws and of this equally infamous state. Set them free! Free all the comrades who are in prison! The people, as a whole, give you this impression of strength.

I think of the techniques that power uses to divide people and remove the strength of their unity – like a reverse path, a musical fugue turned on its head, moving from ensemble to separation, to the point of destroying that sense of ethics which only the collective can construct. The people, as a whole, give you a *potenza*. Here talk of freedom is common currency among people of all ages and generations. I lay down a strong attack against the magistracy – in fact I am increasingly convinced that these constitutional ruptures, this coercive, separated and non-accountable power, are among the most bestial instruments of the reaction. The magistracy represents the triumph of consolidated political relations over all forms of social mobility that might develop potential [*potenze*] and be political transformation. My speech was warmly received. Today, in Milan, I see Alberto again. A comrade since forever. He is being destroyed by his sickness. It is beyond me why nature has to take this terrible revenge on the intelligence and lucidity of its project. The other evening I met Bifo – another comrade forever and since forever. We talked about war. And about Lebanon – and the sparks fly – they stink of death, of pain, of rottenness. Only Spadolini feels comfortable in all this. Bifo says a lot of trivial things, but they are true: war has become the inescapable horizon of our being; and in California they have taught us that there is no escape from this situation, but that at least you can save yourself through an ecological discipline of the mind . . . and so on. But he takes the discussion onto another tack, trying to be intellectually detached when in fact he is only defensive – with that implicit recognition of his, of weakness and of the insuperable disproportion between the potency of war and sickness on the one hand, the weakness of mind and life on the other. And yet, if we could only stand together, we could reverse the relationship between life and death, between war and liberation! And Alberto and Bifo know this.

This evening in Brescia I was completely convinced of all this. What is capitalism, if not the power to divide the masses and then to destroy, in a negative dialectics permanently poised between sickness and death, consciousness and freedom? What is communist potential, if not the possibility of producing an opposite path to that? Increasingly and with increasing intensity, I grasp the abyssal

difference between the institutional world of bourgeois and capitalist democracy and this desire of ours for a free and collective life.
The tensions which I feel in society and in people with this head of
mine, which has been once again rendered virgin by the experience
of prison, continually confirm me in this. Revolution is possible. The
transformation will happen, in Aristotelian style, around a formal
cause which embraces entirely, like a reality already lived, the material cause and its efficiency. I have to start over again. I protest against
the timid and wearied ghosts of my consciousness!

That's what I'm saying to everyone – we have to start over again.
This evening in Brescia, like a man in deep water, I found something
to cling to. I am beginning to entertain a hope of extracting myself
from the shipwreck; I see a collective consciousness that is capable,
again and anew, of mobilizing itself. Maybe only to live. During the
evening I see Alberto again. How I understand his sickness! And how
I shall live it if I decide to escape. But both of us need to free ourselves from it. With the collective, with the masses. The desperation
of having suffered oppression, of bearing in our flesh the scars of the
enemy's violence . . . we can only get over that through an operation
of revolutionizing life! It is possible. Until and unless they kill us.
(Milano/Brescia – 9–10 September)

Folio 91

They came right up to the front of the platform. I looked them in the
eye and saw the same violence I had seen in the eyes of those who
wanted to kill me in the special prisons. They hurled coins and bottles
onto the platform. Today, in Piazza Navona. This is a meeting I shall
not forget. But why all this hatred and all this violence? In my speech
I tried to explain what is both necessary and possible to do in order
to get at least *some* of the comrades out of prison – but they came
up and said that this was not an option, because *all* the comrades
have to be freed. They may well be right, but at least let's discuss
it. What I can't stand is this homology, in terms of hatred and violence, with the police and the state killers, with the judges and their
prefabricated sentences – at least let people speak, and maybe we'll
all gain something from it. This evening, at the start of the meeting,
I felt that same emotion and that same solid, sure sense of justice
and of an alternative society which I had encountered elsewhere. I
addressed myself to that. So why, instead, this hatred and this ritual
of destruction? I know well this kind of street action: I invented it.

But in those days it was life and *potenza*. I do not experience what is happening today as a repetition – and not as nemesis either. When, for the first time, we attacked and took over the trade union platform in San Giovanni, in 1969 if I am not mistaken, we were a majority of struggles. We brought working-class Turin, Marghera and Milan into that people's square, and against that bureaucratic platform. But today the hatred is fed by a memory that is static, vengeful, full of bad feeling and not of life. Nor of struggles either. Whereas I was talking of struggles. Of struggles in prison, of struggles for freedom. And all they could answer was 'grunf grunf'. However, as usual, my thinking in this regard is too rational. What needed to be answered here was a stupid action, which was only provocation. Pannella prevented my comrades from intervening (there were lots of them, and they were experienced in the best stewarding situations . . . vintage, DOC bodyguards). He was wrong. We could have given a lesson to those arrogant idiots, filled as they were with resentment against the fact that I was a free man. This was nothing more than a masochistic revenge for their own defeat. A good kick in the pants would have done them good. But Pannella is totally non-violence. Except when it comes to making political use of situations that are not clear to me. Here we are not administering a vaccine, *à la* Martin Luther King, to the current mass violence in order to turn it into a political and organizational force – here we are being subjected to an idiotic violence, which comes from a few people drugged on ideology and ritual. There is no project for organization here, not even a promotion of consciousness being put into effect. Pannella is engaged in an operation that is purely symbolic. It is of no interest to me. Piazza Navona: there you have it, the fruits of terrorist irreducibilism and of the 'no compromise' stance of the partitocracy – really there could not be a more fitting image of a modern hell! They were slavering. At a certain point somebody told me: 'Be careful – they're passing round plastic bags with guns.' Careful of what? Of guns? Sure, they can shoot, but I am both too close and too far – too close in understanding their madness and in reacting to it with a contempt of equal intensity – and too far for them to be able to burn up, in stolid immediacy, the time of revolution which I want and live with intelligence. My contempt for these imbeciles is as great as the desire for revolution that I feel in my body. Enormous. These idiotic, fanatical manifestations of extremism!

Look at their eyes. Their hatred says it all. They are a mere flash, not the continuity of the revolutionary process. They will never get aboard the Finland train. Be careful, they've got guns. They can go fuck themselves! Meanwhile, like a good Jew, while Pannella is jumping up and down spouting his usual pacifist nonsense, I bend down and pick up the coins – a few thousand *lire*, which should provide the price of a decent pizza this evening. (Rome – 11 September)

Folio 92

In Rome today, waiting for the final round. Very heavy pressure from the press, total provocations, a complete scandal. They are gnawing at my image like a pack of rats. I find it hard to fathom how much of what I have represented in the past few months will remain in the collective imaginary. Maybe nothing. Maybe it will all disappear very fast. I am very tired. I have been working too hard. Maybe after four years in prison my re-entry into the world could have been organized more cautiously. But what else could I have done? It was important to play this moment of opportunity, to use it to the hilt, to place the problems of a political resolution on the table of the institutional negotiations. I think I have kept my promise, without sparing myself. As they used to say in the old days: my conscience is at ease with itself. More than this I could not have done. Now it's up to other people to do the talking. If they let me move forward I shall move forward. And if not . . .

Another discussion with Rossana today. I have the impression that the possibilities of the confrontation have been exhausted. How can one hope to create anything positive out of hopes for justice and struggles on the one hand, sickness and institutions on the other? Some people regard the need for a relation with the institutions in the same way a doctor might envisage his relationship with a fatal illness. An unequal battle which nevertheless has to be fought. Pessimism of the intellect. I can only respect people who see things this way. However, this is not the way to get a grip on the world. There is a point in this process of disease where, vice-versa, the sickness is the one that gets hold of you and clouds your brain. Personally I prefer alcohol, and drunkenness, and delirium – the scream of the Furies to the lament of the Fates. Death is not any less distant – the ghosts of my night-time dreams, which return to haunt me during the day, speak only of that. Here, in my forehead, between the eyes, I have a black and painful hole. My spirit becomes strained in trying to understand why so much pain. And I think I am also experiencing this strain in my relationships with people – too much uncertainty, maybe ambiguity, intensity of concentration and a frightening rigidity in understanding. In reality, as the institutional deadline creeps gradually closer and I have this foreboding of unavoidable disaster – I understand at this point that the material conditions of this political operation of mine, and of this institutional existence of mine, are poised on absolute precariousness. You cannot build on precariousness. On the other hand, freedom – my freedom and that of the comrades – has to be built. During these two months I have lived moments of struggle and the expression of a desire for politics that are irreducible to this institutional mediation. To the same extent that the latter is irreducible to the former. And so? The sickness is beyond curing, and at this stage there is also a risk that it will turn infectious. (Rome – 12 September)

Folio 93

Here, in the Radical Party group in Montecitorio, ever since I arrived they have obliged me to use a room with no windows. Completely panelled in wood. I work in artificial light all day long. It is here that I see people and do interviews, in a continuous and undifferentiated night-time meeting. I hate this room. At night I go a couple of hundred metres down the road, to a studio flat in a building in Campo Marzio. There is a folding bed – which I open with enormous difficulty; and that is where I sleep my nights. I hate this room, so pompous in its furnishings and dirty in its décor.

Has the debate in the House started yet? No, not yet. It seems, however, that the heads of the political parties intend to prolong it for a whole week. Oh well! It seems that I have a very large number of enemies. I live between these two loathsome rooms like being trapped in a den. My energy is destroyed in an impossible defence. Like a hunted animal, caught by its hunters now, in a trap from which it feels it can't free itself. I remain, however, a fighting animal. Comrades arrive from the south. They tell me about the resumption of organizing work and the building of new social centres – this is happening a little bit everywhere. For the freedom of the comrades in prison, for peace, for proletarian recomposition – this is what they talk about.

I take a long hard look at this place in which I find myself. Italian democracy is, unfortunately, nothing more than a gang of criminals. Here the incompatibility, in a period of crisis, between capitalist development and democratic government becomes caricatural: crooks, thieves, businessmen with their hands in the public till, *mafiosi* – the scene is like something out of the *Threepenny Opera*. What can I say to the comrades who come to see me, except 'Take a look around you – what is to be done?' We are in need of something different. We need to rebuild movement and power. We have to strip of all its credibility this corpse-like institutionality and pull people out of their passivity. They need to speak out and tell their truth and their needs! The work is long, but at least this time we know where we are trying to reach – if power is this perversion, we have to build a different power. And now the news has just arrived that the party begins tomorrow. (Rome – 13 September)

Folio 94

Today I read this document in Parliament:

Madam Speaker and honourable members, in what follows I am turning to you to call for the 'authorization to proceed' regarding the trials against me which are currently under way and which all arise out of that single complex of trials known as the '7 April case'; and, on the other hand, to ask you to reject the call for authorization to proceed to my arrest for the trials involved in that case. Inevitably I will have to summarize for you, extremely briefly, the history of this trial and of the four years and five months that have elapsed since the whole thing began.

The first phase began when I was arrested in Padova on 7 April 1979, on the charge of being the head of the Red Brigades and of other armed groups hierarchically and functionally linked to the Red Brigades, and of having taken part materially in (a) the kidnapping, (b) the so-called negotiations and (c) the killing of the Hon. Aldo Moro. Within a short time the charge was extended so as to include a charge of armed insurrection against the powers of the state, and the trial was taken on by the Rome magistracy.

Honourable colleagues, I know what the kidnapping of Aldo Moro represented for this House and for the institutions of the state, and I fully understand the high drama of that period and your emotions at the time. At the same time, however, I have to ask you to understand what those accusations meant for myself, who was innocent of them.

Then came a second phase. On 21 December 1979 and during the early months of 1980, the accusation that I was the leader of the Red Brigades and that I had taken part in the killing of Moro collapsed. It was replaced by a series of other charges, related to the part played by myself in the organization known as Potere Operaio in the period 1968–73 and to my involvement in the birth of that diffuse phenomenon of social opposition which was known as '*autonomia operaia*' ['workers' autonomy'] in, and exclusively in, the period 1973–5.

In other words, the context of the charges against me was completely changed, but it retained its pharaonic extension into charges of armed insurrection against the powers of the state.

During the course of 1980, precisely in the period of the collapse of the accusation that I was part of the Red Brigades, I was the subject of about twenty further arrest warrants and notifications of investigation for a total of seventeen despicable murders, including that of my friend Judge Alessandrini.

On 30 March 1980 a third phase began. The authorization was issued for me to be sent for trial. Nothing remained of any of the preceding charges, either the ones related to the Moro case or those that had emerged in the second phase of the proceedings against me. However, various elements of the initial theorem remained in place, on the basis of an alleged unity between all the subversive forces in existence at that time and of an organizational continuity which the prosecution claimed to have existed between the movement of '68 and the autonomist social movements of the '70s.

On this basis the accusation of armed insurrection against the powers of the state still stood. As regards specific facts – or so-called facts – in the document which sent me for trial, we saw the collapse of the charge related to the odious killing of one of my dearest friends, Carlo Saronio. But other specific facts remained, for which I was accused solely by virtue of being the presumed head of a non-existent and completely undefined organization: the famous 'O', a responsibility which I have always denied, and which I am certain that I can refute in the course of the trials for which I myself am requesting the authorization that they be restarted.

In the light of the relative fragility and continuously shifting nature of the charges in terms of specific facts, and, on the other hand, in the face of the solid and permanent nature of the accusation of armed insurrection, it seemed to me, and to a broad swathe of public opinion, that the continued application of the charge of armed insurrection had more to do with political responsibilities than with material responsibilities and that the '7 April case' was a political trial – driven, promoted, conducted and guided by political motives. This feeling was confirmed by statements made by not inconsiderable sections of the magistracy itself, who had analysed the 7 April case and had (belatedly) admitted that it was based only on a political intuition. I should say that this is also the substance of the report drawn up by the Hon. De Luca, which identifies the procedural irregularities that underpinned the theorem and multiplied even as it was being constructed – except that the report then went on to say that they were irrelevant and reproposed the political and prejudicial notion of the unity of the whole subversive project, an accusation which not even the final charges of today have been able to sustain.

Honourable colleagues, I am not asking you to declare that I am innocent. I am only asking that, in your role as members of this House, you do not accept the positions of those who have pre-judged the issue.

So the 7 April case is a political trial. Unlike many defenders of civil rights, I fully understand how the state and its normal juridical powers should have the option of embarking on political trials at times of major threats to constitutional order. But at the same time I do not accept a situation in which this function is concealed behind a formalistic hypocrisy. I refuse the fact of having to defend myself against charges of another kind and in another place. When things become political, I affirm my right to discuss them politically.

Furthermore, I would remind you that, when political trials become a function of the state itself, there is a very strong danger of a degradation of the institutions; when everything is subsumed under a logic of 'you are either with us or against us', some of the fundamental rules of democratic legitimation inevitably collapse.

Now, when behind all this talk of major threats to the institutions party-political interests are also concealed which attempt to subordinate a very high and delicate function of the state to contingent political ends – and at this moment of particular peril they start setting in motion dubious compromises and coalitions – then, honourable colleagues, it seems to me that the problem becomes extremely serious.

All this, therefore, has to be opened up to debate and discussion. Not only because I am here as a representative of the people, and hence I exercise the function of representing a significant sector of public opinion in this country, but also, honourable colleagues, because the nature of the thing you are judging cannot possibly be eliminated from the judgement you are called upon to express.

So: I have been charged with political and moral responsibility for the social struggles which took place in Italy during the 1970s. I do not deny these responsibilities, and this is what we have to discuss here. I simply want to offer my contribution.

Of what political and moral responsibilities do I feel myself to be guilty? Certainly not of having maintained, defended or directed terrorist activities, associations or groups. I have absolutely nothing to do with terrorism. In fact I have always fought against terrorism, in a manner that has been linear, coherent and continuous, both in prison and outside. I accept, however, the responsibility of having taken part – through my writings and thoughts – in the movement of social transformation which developed in Italy throughout the '70s, on the side of the exploited classes. These were movements for the transformation of life and of the relations of production. From 1968 onwards, albeit for a brief period, they pitted a social majority against an institutional minority.

These movements gave expression to a concrete utopia of changing consciousness and of changing political relationships; subsequently they also developed into the mass hard-line positions and violence which characterized the movements of antagonism in the years of crisis.

The passions that were nurtured at that time by great masses of workers, women and young people were not abstract passions – they were concrete needs. Needs for freedom, for community, for wages, for housing, for culture, and for a different quality of life and social relations. We believed that the crisis could be resolved without any institutional compromise. That this did not happen is demonstrated by recent history and, not superficially, by the very physiognomy of this Parliament. We believed that alternative spaces of freedom and new forms of popular participation could be built.

These problems have not been removed through repression, and indeed their resolution remains incumbent on this Parliament. Our hopes could not be realized. Certainly, in the clash with the blind forces of reaction – often, too often, these were lurking within the actual structures of the state, and demonstrably within various corporative and party bureaucracies – the movement and its desire for transformation can be presented as elements subversive of the institutions. I do not deny it – but in this crisis of ours, and within this troubled relationship between society and its institutions, let he who is without sin cast the first stone, as they say.

On the other hand, it is absurd to create vicious circles within which the clash between people's desire for change and the institutions' urgent need to control such movements creates moments of exclusion and criminalization – of repression pure and simple. The events of 7 April 1979, following on the shameful initiative by the procurator in Padova, which was then picked up and amplified by the procurator in Rome, have created a dramatic situation. The claim that the autonomy movement was the same thing as the forces of terrorism – which lived alongside it, certainly not without mutual contaminations, but parasiti-cally, on the basis of organizational traditions, ideological driving forces and strategies which were in no sense unifiable – has created a dramatic situation for many social subjects, both individual and collective. Every possibility of internal political mediation within the movement was removed; all possibility of political representation was denied. The alternatives were all too easily at hand. Some people went into drugs, as an individual solution (the terrible death toll from drug usage is rarely if ever cited). Or they went into retreat – the withdrawal of an entire generation into voluntary exile from the political life of the country. Or the organization of desperation led to the creation of scattered group-ings, engaged in the murderous and destructive activity of terrorism.

I am unable to say whether there were specific collusions between individual judges and the party-political and bureaucratic apparatuses which set up the 7 April operation. However, I do know that, in objective terms, that repressive operation erected an institutional wall in the face of the various forces that were calling for transformation and participation. I know that, in objective terms, this repressive operation had the effect of opening murderous political spaces for terrorism. And I know that, in the name of a repressive state of emergency, this operation succeeded in sustaining coalitions of forces – both old and new, both within and outside the institutions – which were seeking to defended their own common interests by blocking any movement towards social change.

I do not claim, as the founding fathers of socialism always used to do, that proletarian society in revolt is the only force capable of effecting social transformation. But I do insist, stubbornly, on rejecting the validity of the reactionary reflex which, on 7 April 1979 (as also today), saw in law and order the sole guarantee of society.

Honourable colleagues, I am neither a *pentito* nor a turncoat, and this is why, at the same time as I reject what the facile defenders of the 7 April operation are claiming, I can also develop the theme of political responsibility to the point where I recognize my own errors. The illusions, the utopias and the (often devastating) effects of these impulses were as much a part of my own thinking as they were of the entire generation of '68.

We were living in the midst of social upheavals. I made some mistakes, but on the other hand things were changing, and I am not ashamed to affirm my own change within the reality of that movement. I am accused of having been an evil teacher for students at my university. Perhaps I was; but here again this happened in the midst of things: within the terrible marginalization of thousands and thousands of young people, in the face of the impotence of the institutions to respond to the most elementary requests that were being put to them. I have never said that violence was the sole solution, and where there were violent responses, those responses cannot be considered as having been incited by myself. Nor have I ever killed anybody – as was irresponsibly claimed by a member of this House just the other day. Nor have I ever organized criminal actions against people and their lives. I moved in the real world of that time, between utopias and the reactions of the force of law and order, between a tumultuous upheaval of demands and institutional responses that offered nothing but blockage and repression. So the problem of political responsibility is actually far more complex than people are prepared to admit, particularly when my own political activity was immediately marked out as criminal activity.

Let us never forget, honourable colleagues, that 7 April is located at a pivotal point in the extraordinary production of emergency laws. Now, what are the contents of these laws? We know what they are. Preventive detention, which can be extended for life; denial of bail; the law permitting the use of *pentiti*; a maximum extension of the repressive efficacy of the accusation of association; and, above all, exceptional procedures. All this is accompanied by a configuration of extraordinary powers for the judges and investigating authorities, and thus by a virtual termination of the normal processes of balancing the evidence in the investigative phase and of a correct articulation of the regime of evidence. The rules of the game have been turned on their head. For example, take the law on *pentiti*. Try to imagine the development of a trial which uses that law. Even supposing that, at particular periods, in various aspects of the juridical system, efficacy is allowed to prevail over the force of law, this prevalence cannot be carried to the point of overturning the actual evidence. I have always considered the state of law [*stato di diritto*] to be a utopia; I have always pointed out the fragility of its mechanisms. However, it remains the case that, before and beyond any other juridical ordinance, we must have rules which prevent the abuse of judicial processes and put limits on power.

Honourable colleagues, political responsibility cannot be formed in these conditions. You should know that, when contemporary philosophers define political responsibility in contemporary society and try to give it a critical definition, they speak of 'an institutional conjoining of evidence and legal validity, of consciousness and intersubjectivity'. This means that the political decision, in order to be responsible, in order to be rationally founded, has to nourish itself on debate and on a consensus which is neither prefigured nor extorted. The emergency regulations and the exceptional legislation have rendered impossible the formation and expression of a real political responsibility on the part of many of the subjects involved in the struggles of the 1970s. In particular, we, those of the '7 April case', have been caught in the hystericism of the media and 'opinion makers'; we have been pre-judged. And the functional outcome of the mechanisms of preventive detention has been continuously to reconstruct presumptions of guilt, regardless of the fantastical nature of the charges brought against us. The more the facts failed to fit the case, the more we have been accused of political responsibility.

Four and a half years later, not one of us has yet seen our accusers face to face, despite the fact that they were prisoners like us. There are prisoners who, after four and a half years, have had only one hearing, which lasted at most for a couple of hours, even in cases where they were willing to collaborate in the trial process but wanted to reject the accusations that have been brought against them. I set before you all the case of Luciano Ferrari Bravo, whose case has been taken up by the European Court of Human Rights and by Amnesty International. Nor do we understand why it has taken two whole years to move from the stage of permission to proceed in the trial to the actual opening of proceedings, despite our insistent requests for the trial to be started.

However, my purpose here is not to complain about violations of the law and of public opinion. The problem lies elsewhere. In this case there has been a breaking of the principle of the plurality of subjects participating in the justice process. There has been a dissolution of the condition in which it is possible to exercise not only the power of rendering justice, but also the power of accepting that justice.

The democratic state takes on board the division of powers that is traditional in the constitutional state. But the order of things is no longer simply constitutional – it is also democratic. And in this latter respect there is no conception of justice which is not established solidly, or at least conflictually.

Both individually and collectively we have asked to be represented as part of this mutual process, or at least of this conflictuality. The answer we have received is that the rigidity of the material constitution, and of the equilibria and historic compromises within it, would not permit that.

So what political answerability are we talking about, then? Of whom? And how and when?

On our side it was politically responsible – I reaffirm this – to struggle for social change and to suffer – in the environment of a social struggle that marginalized terrorism – unavoidable forms of mass violence, never murderous ones, which were often productive of a new and more democratic ordering of things.

It was, however, politically inadequate to think of overcoming a deeply rooted social crisis through the exclusion, marginalization and repression of new and irreducible social subjects.

Thus I accept my political responsibility, honourable colleagues; but I also denounce those who pose as the saviours of democracy but at the same time deny the very preconditions of that democracy.

Perhaps I made mistakes. In fact for sure I made mistakes. But this does not justify the deafness which, in the 7 April case, has produced the conditions for an 'ecological' disaster of the legal system and the democratic establishment.

Mistakes are always implicit in grand circumstances; but they are also present in my small circumstance. I do not intend to deny it. At the same time, however, I reject the claim that the *autonomia* was a cradle of terrorism. I cannot deny that contiguities were created. But this was not because the movement was organized in some vertical sense, as the prosecution is claiming. On the contrary, the contiguities actually developed at the time when the movement was coming apart of its own accord. In the Veneto, we only started to see the killings a year and a half or two years after the start of the '7 April trial'. Before that we had outbreaks of violence, which I condemn; and I categorically refute before this House what has been falsely attributed to me – even recently – by various journalists. Never, either at that time or now, did I approve of those acts of violence, nor was I responsible for them. I insist, however, on the fact that it was only after '7 April' that the violence slipped across into the barbarism of murder, being brought there from the outside by the likes of Savasta.

Continuing on the theme of political responsibilities, honourable colleagues, I would like to add some further elements of reflection.

After '7 April' there was a strong temptation – both for myself and for my comrades – to accept the solidarity which was offered to us in prison by the terrorists, in tune with what the '7 April' situation had determined in the movement, both inside and outside of Italy's prisons. But we resisted that offer. Against everyone – really against everyone – in terrible solitude.

The Ministry of Grace and Justice put the '7 April' comrades into the special prisons, together with the terrorists. Good sense, which normally means finding ways of living with people, would have meant seeking a *modus vivendi* with them. But our history, our responsibility would not permit that. Despite the daily confrontations and the not always inefficacious death threats, we succeeded instead in building and consolidating that pole of political dissociation and in reconstructing our identity as militants for life and against death, against the violence of terrorism, and at the same time against prison and torture. In short, a front of hope for social change.

When we dissociated ourselves politically from terrorism, we did not do so for us, but for all those whom the combined mechanisms of repression and a blocked desire for struggle had driven into the arms of terrorism. Here we are talking about thousands and thousands of young people, women and proletarians. Political dissociation became our banner, against the *pentitismo* laws and for a political resolution of those Years of Lead.

Honourable members, do you really think that this was easy – or hypocritical, as some people have claimed – and that it was 'simply a matter of words'? If so, you should have tried saying those 'words' in the prison at Palmi in 1979, or in Trani prison during the revolt of 1980, or in Cuneo, where two young men, guilty of having succumbed to torture, were killed; or in Rebibbia, where we were being sent repeated death threats in 1982!

And do you think that it is easy to utter 'words' such as 're-finding of communist identity' and 'political dissociation', when the honour of these declarations is turned on its head by the media and by the regime's persecutors, and the word 'dissociated' is used in cases such as that of 'the animal' ['*o animale*'], Pasquale Barra?

So perhaps you should try it for yourselves, carrying forward this kind of politics, when the deafness of judges and party hacks destroys the very preconditions for a resumption of democratic requalification on behalf of subjects who have conducted – with mistakes, but also with generosity – struggles for social change.

However, despite all these misrepresentations, our battles have achieved important results, extending beyond the growing number of political prisoners, to become a mass agenda for all prisoners in the system. Today we are witnessing a major struggle in the prisons, where there has been a reduction in the strategies of the big clans and in the irresponsible behaviours of the irreducibles, who always push for taking the fight to extremes. We are seeing important openings towards a democratic order of things and towards the kind of debate which is indispensible today for a solution to the prisons problem.

When for the first time, in 1981, we proposed democratic delegations of prisoners, in Rebibbia and elsewhere, and we battled in order to introduce – against the logic of violence – the method of discussion in assemblies, we found ourselves caught between two fires: the deafness of the institutions and the threats of the irreducibles. Honourable members, I do not want to say that the one is the same as the other; but it is certain that, since I first entered this system of repression, I have always found myself crushed between the one and the other. Preserving our own lives and identities has not been easy.

So, honourable colleagues, today, inside the prisons, there is a large majority of political prisoners who ask to be reinstated into a democratic order of things. And they are doing this on the basis of a critique of the mistakes that have been made. I am very well aware that there is no easy solution to this problem. But I also know that reasonableness and responsibility require that some sign of hope be given by the governing classes.

The disregard for human rights in prison and the exceptional juridical measures which were imposed during the period of emergency have to be subjected to criticism and gradually eliminated. A sign needs to be given that a start is being made along this path. A reversal of things is needed – indeed it is overdue – also in order to avoid (and this is not a threat, or blackmail, but a simple forecast) desperation turning in on itself and producing new incitements towards terrorism and new impulses towards death, not only in the prisons but also outside.

But let us not concentrate on despair as much as on the hopes of the generation which has been caught up in this vicious circuit of terrorism and repression: crushed, with no other means of expression, by the institutional blockage of political development; and at the same time carried by Italy's particular historical situation to a richness of desires and impulses for change that found no satisfaction. Let us look at the hopes of a generation which, albeit with serious errors, had conceived a dream of justice. The plague has touched these young people, but it has not killed them.

Honourable members, this is what we represent – my comrades and myself, and everything else that is summarized under the heading of '7 April'. We represent a relationship between the past and the present, a hope for social change in which anyone who so wishes is welcome to join us. And a political tragedy for which all of us are responsible, and which needs to be resolved.

So, honourable gentlemen, I urge you not to opt for imprisonment. That would be a negative sign; it would impart a sense of blocking a necessary tendency, and it would lead to a new and terrible disillusionment regarding the ability of democracy to resolve its contradictions. (Rome – 14 September)

Folio 95

The discussions continued in Chamber. My speech was well received by our friends, but it was not much appreciated by our enemies. Immediately after I finished the Chamber was deserted, but I stayed in to listen to the debate, albeit with some boredom. There were many speakers – both friends and enemies. Among the former, the formidable Giacomo M. – I appreciate his warmth, his intelligence, and his parliamentary practice. Then various people spoke in my support – Fiandrotti, Felisetti and the good Franco P.; then Stefano R., and, with great emotion, Gianni F. and many others. Speaking against me, and fiercely, was a band of fat Christian Democrats and hysterical fascists – plus various parliamentary clowns among the republicans and the social democrats. Such is Battaglia, in the midst of this pack, demonstrating the most excited sense of the state. Ignorant of things, but with arrogance. Big confusion among the communists. Loda made a speech – he had already distinguished himself in the Committee, with a heavily sermonizing, inquisitorial tone. Occhetto, on the other hand, spoke in favour of postponement. The ferocity on the one side is barely lessened by the sense of opportunism on the other. I do not understand how a proposal so timidly presented can have any chance of being passed – as a mediation, it is presented in terms that are solely formal – it says nothing about the substance of the trial, or the exceptional laws, or the problem of how to emerge from the Years of Lead. In the PCI there is a clear rank-and-file call for a political solution to be found (the debates at the Festa dell'Unità festivals this summer showed this) and a leadership which evaluates this possibility. However, there is also a series of utterly ferocious intermediate levels who have no intention even of discussing their deadly loathing of the *autonomia*. On this issue the party bosses are deadpan; because the truth is that, like the sorcerer's apprentice, they have set in motion a dreadful dance, which they do not know how to stop. Here, both yesterday and today, the main people to speak have been these intermediate cadres. They tell me of very hard-fought discussions apparently taking place in the PCI parliamentary group. I don't understand this very well – I have the impression that the proposal for postponement is biting on a void, that it is politically sterile. On the other hand, it is the only political alternative to returning to prison, and those who are good at number-crunching assure me that it is going to pass. Despite the customary absences (what a sinister impression the Chamber gives when it is almost empty!), the debate is tense, with a sense of urgency. I don't think it's only my nervousness that produces this impression. However, I feel in myself, a sense of detachment, a schizophrenic repulsion, more and more as the hours go by. OK – better to head back to Milan, to talk to my friends. I'm on a plane now. Tommaso M. accompanied me to the airport. With his great affection and considerable legal skills, he gives me good advice. Remember, Tommaso, when I was in prison and I told you that we were not going to get out of this ugly story – or, better, that the only way out was by political means? You looked at me through those bars and that glass, as if my optimism was insane. It may have been insane; but, as it turned out, it was realistic. And now? 'Toni, be realistic,' you tell me, 'there's nothing more to be done.' You're right, Tommaso, but is it not possible that this realism will also turn out to be insane? Anyway, I have to decide. But what a wearisome thing it is, to have to live these different dimensions of one's consciousness – on the one hand, the timescales of institutions, and, on the other, this hope for liberation. And to have to act decisively and to choose between them. Not that my spirit is not totally inclined towards freedom . . . and not that my head has not been rendered almost impotent by the relationship with the insanity of life in this institutionality – but this time of freedom seems to me to have been too short, and almost voraciously destroyed. You say: 'What you promised to do has been done: (1) the political and parliamentary dramatization of the 7 April case and of the problem of finding a political solution; (2) the opening of up of the legislative debate in the institution and the opening the historico-political debate in the country; (3) support for a reopening of the prison struggles front, and its capacity for undermining the institutions. What more do you want, Toni? You could not have done more than that. Now the problem is entirely theirs.' You're right, you're right! And yet . . . The plane is flying over the sea, with excellent visibility. Down below, to one side, you can see Sardinia and Corsica. This sea is beautiful. (Rome/Milan – 15–16 September)

Folio 96

Good, so the decision has been taken – I am to leave even before we know the results of the voting. Pointless risking further delay. My exit route has been arranged by sea, assuming that the weather doesn't turn bad. So in the course of the day we need to check out a land route as well. Splendid friends, they take on this task immediately. Also, as regards organizing an easy and safe return in the (impossible?) event that things turn out all right in Parliament, everything has been arranged. It is evening. I've had a hellish day. Paola is in a state of total nervousness. The children are very sweet and strong and decisive. I see Maryse and Christian, and many other brothers and sisters. I see Giuliano S., in fact I've just seen him off. It's the middle of the night. We talk of Spinoza and communism – a maximum of tension, but also a very strong sense of the values of life and liberty. Communism – the necessity of resuming the struggle. And then the timings of the struggle, unavoidably tied to, and necessary to be detached from, those of the institution. The dilemma, the mystery of this antagonistic temporality. It is a wound that begins to open in my consciousness – and the pain is strong. But so is my critical ability. This house – maybe I shall not see it again – I never particularly loved it, except from prison, when Paola and the children came to live here. Now even the dog is gone – it was always present in the photos they used to send me. And the trees of Piazza Vetra, which came in through the windows and spread over the terrace, seem to have dried up. They're calling me. I have to leave. It is hard. Will I have to start a new life? Caught in this necessity I find myself – for the first time since my release from prison – hoping that the vote in Parliament will turn out in my favour. And that this horrible separation from too many things that I love will not be definitive. The trees of Piazza Vetra are not dry now, but laden with night-time dew. They're calling me, I'm leaving. I'll have to change cars a couple of times, to make sure that I'm not being followed. What a business. Then the goodbye, which may or may not turn out to be definitive. Goodbye everyone. They're calling me . . . (Milan – 17 September)

Folio 97

I am in Rome, in a small apartment in the suburbs. I travelled down last night in a state of extreme calm – sleeping in the car for a couple of hours, in the light of a Tuscan dawn. A strange calmness of my heart and in my veins. Maybe I am getting old. Minimal excitement. I am not representing the future to myself. It is flattened on the present instant. I'm imagining nothing. This morning they had me doing a very fast run-around on a motorbike – to be absolutely sure that we'd shaken off anybody who could have been trailing us. Is this a foretaste of what life is going to be like for me in the future? In front of me I have one of the books in this apartment, a copy of Lucretius. *Avia Pieridum peragro loca, nullius ante / trita solo. Iuvat integros acce-dere fontis / atque haurire, iuvat novos decerpere flores.* I snooze for a bit, waiting for the friends to come. The word arrives: the comrades are waiting for me in a boat at Punta Ala. So it's all working out. The weather is excellent and the sea is good. (Rome – 18 September)

Folio 98

Monday morning. Somewhere near Punta Ala. A pleasant little house. Friends of friends are putting me up. Everything is very simple and natural. I read the papers while I wait. In *La Repubblica*, Arbasino rants against me. Insults, pure and simple. This rosy Spadolinian is so vain that I cannot prevent a feeling of revulsion. I remember him dancing with Letizia's tutu. Firpo writes in *La Stampa*, attacking my *La forma stato* and *Il dominio e il sabotaggio*. Describes it as opposi-tional thinking which finds no possibilities of mediation – because the thinking in them is so maniacal, etc. All of them weighing in with their two pennyworth. However, unlike Arbasino, he is against the idea of my re-arrest. In this very brief stopover I run through the problems one last time. It seems to me that my leaving is necessary, accepting all the risks involved in the decision. This is not only a generic choice of liberty – it is also the choice of a particular kind of freedom, which escape can construct. Maintaining the symbolic value of liberation. Certainly the dialectic I am living is without mediation. But at this point it is the crisis of capitalism and the degeneration of its state that are devoid of mediation. Maybe the only problem is how to lessen the values of death that this negative exit implies – not out of a dialectical moment but out of an entire historical episode. It is not by denying the nature of the crisis and its horizons that we shall succeed in bringing about any kind of future at all. I have lived the experience of the Palace. I have seen at first hand its irreducible perversity and the impossibility of opening, within its space, any dis-course which is other than tactical. Certainly tactics does not mean simply political cunning, and many discussions of political solutions have been powerfully posed within a tactics – *à la* Machiavelli, or rather *à la* Baltazar Garcian. But tactics in itself does not suffice. Here we have a world that has become separated. A revolution has already taken place. This particular power is wallowing in perversion. Is it the case that, with my exit from Italy, I am perhaps giving value to an objective scenario and, when all is said and done, to those same unjust accusations that are being levelled against me? No. Rather I am revealing and confirming a truth. Inasmuch as they don't want to leave me in Italy, to fight my battle for the justice to which I have a right, they are saying not only that every strategy of liberation must be repressed, but that every tactic of liberty is burned out. Soon they will have terrorism on their backs again, and these *signori* of the Palace will each come to feel the terrible precariousness of their own lives. Why should they be so stupid as not to negotiate peacefully over their own euthanasia? This was what I was offering them; and it is something preferable to the slow revelation of functions which by now are only destructive and degrading. They have not seen fit to rise to my suggestion. So, this morning, in the midst of these merry discourses – the pitiful obscenity of Arbasino and the funereal incomprehension of Firpo – I wait. It is a long wait. The weather is beautiful, and from here the sea seems very calm. My internal weather is also excellent. (Punta Ala – 19 September)

4

Freedom

19 September to 30 November 1983: Folios 99–135

Folio 99

So everything began yesterday, at about half past one in the afternoon. Two friends came, very happy, to collect me from the comrade's house where I was staying.

I went down to the port with them, and then boarded the boat. Worried that someone might recognize me. On the boat we waited for half an hour, then the skippers arrived and we set off. A splendid sea. A calm crossing. The sun shining, and then a full moon. The sharp profile of Elba, then the deserted profile of Pianosa. The happiness of love and the formidable complexity of the unexpected. With a bit of luck (fingers crossed!) I am on my way to freedom. Goodbye semi-liberty, hello freedom. Last night I slept happily in Corsica. This morning, with a crazy driver in a very fast taxi, we raced down to Île Rousse – and then the hydrofoil to Nice. I'm on board now, and the sea is still flat. I get the feeling that freedom is beginning. I don't know – or I pretend not to know – what it means. It must be a fine thing. In my body I have an immense happiness. Here are spaces of liberty, of joy, of alternatives. In addition to this short and pungent time of the experience of freedom, there is space and broadness of horizons, spaces capable of being defined and circumscribed the same way you would describe the alternative time. (But I don't know – in front of Pianosa, at the point where Italian territorial waters come to an end, there time stopped and it seemed that the boat was immobile, that we were not going to be able to get past that last obstacle.) Next to me, as I write, some children are playing with little toy lorries – they're having fun embarking them onto tiny ferryboats. They believe in their make-believe. The youngest one is towing a little train of overloaded ferryboats, taking care that they don't tip over. The children are transforming reality into illusion. I, on the other hand, am already living an illusion which is reality.

I pinch myself. No, I am not dreaming. I am happy for the freshness of my attentiveness to the real. My voyage towards freedom continues. Our train of hope rattles along. What an effort – but at the same time we can increase the speed of our hope and raise our sights enormously. Aiming at freedom and happiness. Meanwhile, in Parliament, the debate continues. I listen on the radio. Really incredible how distant I am from all that. This ship and that sea of yesterday have opened a deep caesura in my life and have brought hope seeping into my tiredness.

Yesterday evening I was watching with the soul of a Renzo Tramaglino as the coast of Tuscany and the profile of the islands went by. A new life is beginning, heightened by the joy of escape. Time presents itself to me as liberty. For sure, there is a huge task awaiting me and a terrible amount of work to be done. But my consciousness is now illuminated by the sun of this Mediterranean September. Why did I not have equally positive and powerful emotions when I came out of prison? On that night too there was a full moon. Why? Why is it that this experience of yesterday and today fills me with such happy eagerness for projects? Why do I finally feel myself to be a whole person? Perhaps because when I came out of prison it was an event overfilled with the past, whereas this is an experience of the future. That must be it. It is a choice which is beginning to be concrete and operative. There are ontological differences between the two situations – I am living a humour of liberty and the warmth of hope. Escape means rebuilding a free body. A renaissance. I experience the moving mass of the ship and the quiet throb of its engines as spatial–temporal signs of a future which is approaching. I have an incredible enthusiasm inside me. I exchange smiles with the comrades who are accompanying me, intense smiles, of great freshness and love. I feel again the spray of the ship in my face – and once again a sunset, this time behind the mountains of Corsica, and the appearance of the first lights in the night. Right then, the skipper brought me hot chocolate: it's been at least thirty years since I last drank hot chocolate. I experience my tiredness with the soul of a teenager and am looking beyond the edges of life. Once again I hear, with joy, people's encouragements that I escape, extract myself from the perversion of Italic justice. I am living an illusion which is real – it does not have many differences with reality. I am fascinated with freedom. (Punta Ala/Nice – 19–20 September)

Folio 100

Yesterday I was in Aix, staying at Morgan's. On the radio I heard the result of the vote on the deferral of my imprisonment. The unbelievable has happened. On the proposition put forward by the socialists and communists there were 293 votes in favour, 300 against. The radicals did not vote. If they had voted, I would now be able to go back to Italy. A crazy situation. I listened to three radio news programmes in a row – I could not believe it.

This morning, despite the abstention of the socialists and communists, there were seventy-five votes against my arrest. Between abstentions and votes against my arrest, the total number is favourable to me. A broad majority, in short. Yesterday, after the vote, it seems that somebody spat in the face of Marco P. They did well.

What scum, that Marco. What a vile mystifier of the popular will! How dare he assume the right to decide against my freedom? How dare he, with his short-sighted party-political interests, come out against the desires of so many people to see me free? Cowardice – a stab in the back. So three cheers for desertion, and down with Parliament! Long live my escape. I'm in another world now. Tonight is the night of the autumn equinox – there ought to be portents. They are happening in my conscience. Not even the drab realities of Italic politicking can spoil my sense of serenity. Today we left Aix, after my long conversation with Morgan and the joy of seeing the life he has built for himself there. We set off for Paris. A big car, a long journey, and all the most beautiful skies of France open to my frenetic attention. I am browsing through Heidegger – *Gelassenheit* – serenity? – I hate his permanent, fabulous ability to manipulate the truth – but he has great strength when, from within being, he counterposes the various figures of existence. I too live his *Offenheit für das Geheimnis* – this sense, not of mystery but of discovery. This evening, a long discussion with some very dear friends in Paris. They have started immediately preparing a document to legalize my situation in France and to get me granted asylum. There will be difficulties, for sure, but they have good hopes of overcoming them. I am staying in an apartment in Place Monge – in the Latin Quarter, a place I have known for twenty years. I feel good here. I feel at home. Then I phone Italy. Long calls, to argue, already this evening, with certain unfaithful friends. Anyway, they tell me that there is a determined drive under way to destroy my political image. This job has been left to the *pentiti* – it seems that Barbone and Coniglio have already started. *Pentiti* sounding off about my escape. How much longer do

I have to put up with the moralistic invective of the likes of Fioroni, the murderer? I am expecting the worst, but I no longer care. I am calmer than I have been for very many years. I think of the comrades with the greatest of affection. Thoughtfully I summon up their faces, one by one. Equinox: mystery and discovery divide the night between them. And remembrance and hope. I shall need to start work again, immediately, and continue in my newfound freedom the battle that has been started. And yet, even in the quiet of this night, I find myself unable to lay to rest my anger at what has happened in Parliament. Every now and then I get up from the table where I sit writing and curse loudly. The friends chatting sleepily in the next room smile at me sympathetically. They are foreigners who cannot understand what a tragic overturning of the real happens when you have to deal with the vanity and cowardice of Italian politicians. They don't understand the grinding lack of civilization – for them this is all, in some sense, comical. As for me and the excited state in which they see me, perhaps they think that this will pass? The first question they put to me to me was: 'And what are you going to do now?' I replied cautiously that I'd have to think about that. They replied: 'It seems to us that there's not much to think about – you can't return to that world of mad people.' They are probably right. But I have to wait and see. My life is not only my own, and my present freedom is the fruit of a collective work. We shall see. (Aix/Paris – 20–21 September)

Folio 101

A day of prison today. We are waiting for news from the government. So far the only news to arrive has been advice to proceed with caution. Don't make waves! Don't move, don't make a fuss, don't publicize your presence here. All of a sudden, the right of asylum seems to bring with it an obligation of passivity: control on their side and silence on my side. Is the *République* maybe a remnant of the past? Certainly – but why is it that this remnant lacks the powers to defend liberty, immediately and with vigour? Anyway, I am waiting with caution. I read the newspapers of the last few days, with the description of what has been happening in Parliament. It must really have been a major fuss. What strikes me most is the quantity of ambiguity in the conduct of all the politicians – from the mealy-mouthed ambiguity of Marco P. and his media-directed opportunism to the cynical ambiguity of the communists. It is beyond doubt, as the newspapers have said after examining the voting figures, that the communists did not apply the party whip. In fact this is exactly what must have happened: from non-left sectors there must have come a lot more votes in favour of my freedom than was expected – in any case, they outnumber the ones from members of the PCI who voted against me. It is probable that Pannella did not understand this; and, because of his short-sighted stupidity, he ended up being the decisive element in my re-incarceration. But, whether this was cynicism or stupidity, we can no longer rely on him – if it was stupidity, it's even worse than if it was cynicism. As for the newspapers, they really don't know what to say. They must be saying to themselves: 'OK, we need to be against Negri, but this time the operation to put him back behind bars seems a bit too dirty.' So they are taking their time. Their attacks are not particularly hard-hitting. But I ask myself in exasperation, is it possible to continue having a relationship with that world? Is it maybe the case that, during the period when I was out of prison and in Parliament, I made such mistakes as to make possible this reproduction of persecution, be it even among all this ambiguity and filth? I don't think so. Actually, at this moment I am unable to fix a terrain of self-criticism which is sufficiently articulated – maybe I have made mistakes, but those mistakes were contained and integrated along a firm line – that of not selling myself to anybody, of preserving my integrity and of keeping intact my capacity for struggle and choice. Transparency instead of ambiguity. A powerful transparency. Even if only from this point of view, I feel that I have held my ground. Succeeding, perhaps, in dealing with some of the problems that the antagonism of the media has thrown up. In other words, despite everything, I have succeeded in upholding the figure of the immediacy of liberty, of the significance of escape, against the flattening and erosion operated by the media. So I don't deserve the perverse ambiguity of these operations in Parliament. Maybe I brought this about as a perverse, destructive and inimical effect of my transparency. But that is a paradox. What should the comrades and our friends do now? They should press again and again the image of freedom; it would be good for them to speak of my decision to leave Italy as a continuation of my release from prison, which was achieved through the popular vote. I have respected the will of my electors. Only if the comrades and our friends keep up this level of attack shall we be able to do something and to continue and enlarge the battle. We have to give technical form to the intensity of my choice of freedom. Probably the fundamental point, as of now, is to come out directly with an attack on the court, pointing out how it is utterly complicit with a perverse political class, within a perverse

framework of repression. The social force of my liberty, however pre-
served, has to be transferred to the political level and made to work.
The real antagonism which I represent cannot be forgotten – it has
to be insisted upon – it is strong. Only through ambiguity and illegality can they succeed in denying it. This is exactly what happened
in Parliament – they never actually won a majority vote against me,
only a vote which was valid according to illiberal and partitocratic
rules. Thought a lot about prison today. I am a bit alarmed at the
situation which seems to have come about: a vertical split in the
defence lobby as a result of Pannella's cheapskate operation. Surely
Rossana will not want to see him again. The Democrazia Proletaria,
the PdUP and the independent Left have spat in his face. And what
about the comrades – what will they do? Will they have the strength
to sustain yet another betrayal? Today there absolutely has to be a
project of attack, of forward response, solid and unwavering. But
with what forces? If I made one mistake during the period of my parliamentary bail, it was that of not having prepared my escape from
a political point of view. An error of generosity, as usual: I was so
tied up in building the conditions for a debate on a political solution
and on prison reform. But – maybe – my escape is a different kind of
problem from that? (Paris – 22 September)

Folio 102

Two days of discussions with the Guru. Very tiring. In his relations
with me he seems like an *agent provocateur*. I am trying to explain
to myself the development of events. He turned up yesterday, as if
nothing had happened. Or rather he told me immediately that it was
only thanks to his deep knowledge of the parliamentary mechanisms
that things had gone as well as they did. He is an idiot pure and
simple. The sympathy he enjoys here is minimal: people who know
him tell me to beware of him, because he is an actor in the style of the
Grand Guignol. He makes me furious. Then he uses moral blackmail
by telling me that I have to think of the comrades in prison. Vile man.
But of course he is right – I *do* have to think of the comrades in prison.
He offers me a rendezvous this morning, to do an interview for the
Radical Party TV. I go to the appointment. He arrives. He brings the
police in his wake. He denies it, but the house is surrounded, and I
have definitive confirmation of this when they photograph us at the
window. I become completely hysterical. I understand; and he, with
cynicism all wrapped up in smiles (today he was smiling, yesterday

he was not), tells me that I have to accept his plan. In other words he thinks that I should give myself up to the police in a very few days. Or indeed, he urges, I could do it straight away. Whatever happens (I say crazy things during the interview) I have to get out of this apartment, and that is definitively the last time I go to Rue Rambuteau. As for him, I see that he has not lived forty years of partitocracy in vain. Like a reactionary, I find myself hoping that one of these days he will die in one of his hunger strikes. He lards his triumphant cult of the institution with a tawdry moralism, simple-minded and eighteenth-century style. Like Indian gurus, he is able to talk only to those who want to listen to him, uttering banalities that only he thinks are anything other than banal. He lives on inquisitiveness. He is closely related to all those who, hypocritically, do wrong while denying that they are doing so. He is an individualist Jacobin from his feet to his head – I say feet first because there's no point talking about his head, it comes in a poor second. The only advantage to be had from discussing with him is that he is so emphatic and obviously insincere that you see immediately where he is heading. Fortunately, in his psyche circumvolutions do not exist. He organizes his illusory game, however, in the tones of a revolutionary Jacobin. Poor man, he is the perfect product of Italic non-culture, lay and bureaucratic – a mixture of books not read and resentment towards those who have read them. He is only bad in individual relations – he has never known collective and disciplined levels of working. However, despite my compassion, he really should not have played the joke of bringing police around the house. Enough, he can go to hell! With incredible fear, helped by Emma, I finally manage to get out of that house in Rue Rambuteau. I can't take any more of this! Furet says: the Jacobin knows how to be dumb. When we talk about this, Jean Pierre F. adds: Sade is the only hero for Jacobins. Enough! This evening I see a fine bunch of old friends, and I do an interview for Ramsay, for *Les Nouvelles*. Socialist journal, first issue. We have to liberate the power that exists in society and give it organization. We have to break with that fetid separation which, in the crisis, the organs of the state bring between themselves and society as a whole. Corporate interests and power. I talk at length about all these things with the comrades. They agree, and we shall work together to develop these themes. They tell me that there are people in the government who are open to grasping their centrality and full implications. I doubt it, but let us try anyway. I am very tired this evening. I try to phone Rossana – I can't get hold of her. Is her institutional story btry to eginning once again to separate itself from ours, from the class struggle? Escape is an act of class struggle, nothing more and nothing less. But there are too many people these days who see class struggle and insubordination as the projection of an undefined subject. Not at all – here we have person and flesh. It seems that in Italy certain old comrades are angry about the fact that I have made my escape. I wonder whether this is a general attitude. I don't think so. But if it is, so much the worse for them. It would not be the first time that so many comrades have fallen on the accident-ridden road of re-founding the movement. Escape is a powerful symbol of it. And, as always, only the analysis of the tendency is capable of winning. (Paris – 23–24 September)

Folio 103

The discussion with the comrades here has been frank and hard-hitting. They are all French. I have neither the desire nor the interest to see the Italian refugees. The comrades are insistent in what they tell me: first, it is absolutely necessary that you put an end to your remaining doubts about whether or not to return to Italy – it would be madness, and we have no intention of following you. This position is put most forcefully by people who have followed the trial. Second, if you do stay in France, you have to get it into your head that you are in a foreign country. You have two possibilities, but your choice has to be clear: either you move as an intellectual or you move politically. Third, if you decide to move politically, you need to realize that, as things stand, your possibilities of doing anything around Italy are minimal, and it is only by working through political forces at the European level that you will have any chance of effective intervention in the medium term. In short, dear Toni, you are going to have to recycle yourself and to set aside thoughts of immediate interventions. I protest loudly. Today the trial is resuming in Rome. I imagine the terrible tension among the comrades, the arrogance of the court, the provocations related to me coming from the press and the media in general. From Italy they tell me that the lawyers are being timid in the face of such an unfavourable climate. I protest at the positions advanced by the French comrades. What am I supposed to do? Must I be the lone crusader? If I go ahead, will it be with no support whatsoever, either from here or from there? The contacts I was hoping for not only do not exist between France and Italy, but will be very hard to set up, given the position of the French government. I also have to take into account one very basic fact, namely that our Italian defence 'lobby' has fallen apart. This has happened because of the vile behaviour of Marco P., the (over-imaginative) freedom of judgement of Rossana, and the justifiable anger of the Left at the betrayal which has been perpetrated. In Italy, my only remaining points of reference are the lawyers and a group of friends. Even my comrades in prison will shortly be swept away by the immediate concerns of the trial. No political battle that I may envisage can take for granted their involvement. And yet I protest – how can I abandon the comrades, even for a short period? Today, as I say, the trial started again, with Paolo Pozzi on the stand. The radio is very short on details. In my mind's eye I can hear, see and share the chill of the situation in that damned courtroom. Go for it, Paolo! How are we to get out of this imbroglio? Only if the lawyers and the comrades immediately raise their sights and maintain an aggressive profile in the daily confrontations in court. This is the only way we shall get a good result. But it seems impossible, now that our defence 'lobby' on the outside is so weak – and in fact has more or less dissolved. At the same time I should not underestimate the strength of the enemy. In the two months since my parliamentary release from prison, our call for a political solution managed to get a vote of 293 for and 300 against, and that fact is going to generate a ferocious and determined reaction. How will the court react? What will be their strategies for effecting a political restoration and for cancelling out that fact? The political forces – except of course those of the far Left, and maybe the socialists – have not yet succeeded in creating a stable policy for a potential political solution. The PCI, in particular, is flailing about incoherently between a nostalgia for a hard line and for the Historic Compromise and a desire for the unity of the Left, understood as a project for hegemony in which perhaps they will be prepared to pay some kind of price to find a way out of the state of emergency. This means that their policy moves are being dictated by strategic choices – and the outcomes could therefore be unreliable, or even monstrous. So what is to be done? I feel an incarceration of my spirit hanging over me. My opting for freedom, as a symbolic act which is full of life and hope, is at odds with the future. We have to build it, this future. But the comrades are caught up in the immediate demands of the trial. Freedom and future. It is a terribly wearying task, but a passion that is nonetheless untameable. We can't afford to set our sights low by going for medium-level solutions and an artisanal approach. No, the French comrades and our friends here are right. Once again the project has to be large-scale and capable of sustaining the tendency. I know this both from my own experience and from the history of the movement: each time, we have re-started at a higher level, without turning back. But this does not mean that we should not look back. And, as I see the comrades and review their faces one by one, imagining them walking and mixing in the cells during their recreation time, imagining their very strong desire to live and their righteous and dearly held desire for freedom – well, I begin to feel the tragedy of this next step. But it is the only way. (Paris – 25–26 September)

Folio 104

From what I read in the newspapers and from what friends have confirmed, the 7 April trial is falling out of the news. The whole focus of interest has shifted to me and to whether or not I am going to return to Italy. The comrades have attempted a strong push on the question of freeing the prisoners – calling for imprisonment to be replaced with house arrest. The court is taking its time – it will reply when the cross-examination of the defendants has been completed. At this moment they are cross-examining Francone – from what I hear it has been a very heavy examination, but from the little that I find in the newspapers it seems that he is defending himself well. What is certain is that the situation of the comrades is difficult. The court's reply as regards house arrest will almost certainly be no. So we need to proceed to a direct challenging of the court. We need to denounce the prejudicial attitude of the judges and the way in which they have conducted the trial thus far – taking apart its heavy accusatory mechanism. What we have here is not a courtroom which is trying to arrive at the truth of the charges, but a new accusatory horizon. They will try to give me a life sentence, of that I am sure. And what about Pannella? I saw him again yesterday evening (this time I protected myself in case of eventual provocations – a couple of comrades took him all around the houses first, to make sure that he had not been followed). He refuses to see the disastrous implications of the parliamentary stunt which he set up. With that operation not only did he push me right to the brink of re-imprisonment, but he destroyed that miraculous unity of forces for a political solution which we had built with such effort. A miracle which was having results even at the institutional level. Now, when he calls for me to hand myself over, he is trying to get himself out of a difficult spot. He wants to restore his 'good daddy' reputation. He is cynically playing power politics; but it won't wash in my case. I think he is starting to realize this. His problem is not our defence 'lobby', which he set out to destroy, but how to restore his image in the eyes of those thousands of people who voted for me – and who could have been hundreds of thousands. If I do not hand myself over he will become my worst enemy, because he will have to help in the destruction of my image – in fact he will have to do it directly himself, in order to regain the confidence which my voters very definitely removed from him. But is he really such a fool? He cannot superimpose himself on the symbol that I represented! Anyway, at this point Pannella has become extremely dangerous. I have to stop meeting with him. He suggested that I do an interview with Biagi – a good chunk of money, about a hundred million *lire*. For that reason I accepted, on the understanding that I shall give the money to the comrades in prison. I am very tired. And I have been very ill. Today I collapsed in the course of the day. (Paris – 27–28 September)

Folio 105

I see Enzo Biagi again today, with Gregoretti and the Guru, for an interview. We have to wait for a few hours for the camera team to arrive. During that time the three of them indulge in every kind of mischievous gossip about the current political situation. Apparently in the past few days Carboni has stated that Andreotti was the head of the P2. That provides enough material for a good hour of jokes and insinuations. I sit there listening to them, shocked not so much by what they are saying as by the fact that they see me as one of the family. The family. For Pannella and Biagi there is always this senti-mental invocation of the family. Personal stories. All very affectionate – like those good capitalists who exploit people but say that they're only doing it for their children. Gregoretti intervenes only to talk about a particularly nasty incident involving his son. He is very reserved. But Biagi goes over the top. He seems to feel the need to talk about his mother. She pops up everywhere in his conversation. Mothers are a great stereotype in communication. I wonder what percentage she gets of his contract. Indeed, I wonder, did Biagi even every have a mother . . .? We start the interview and complete it in short order. Biagi and Pannella make a big deal of me as a person – they are totally uninterested in issues of *pentitismo* or the emergency legislation. For both of them the interview serves as a way of accusing me. Given the conditions, I think I did well. Today was perhaps the last time I shall meet with the Guru. He seems to realize that he's come out of this adventure with a bloody nose. Today's interview has been important for me. It opens a new phase, marking my definitive abandonment of the parliamentary adventure. I am restarting from the bottom, rebuilding a serious political discourse. I am beginning to get a sense of its dimensions and subjects. I shall write about this shortly. The most important thing today has been that the irrational and rancorous element, present in my departure from Italy, is beginning to pass. And at the same time the elements of rationality in my choice seem to me increasingly obvious and clear. How could anyone ever willingly involve themselves in those worlds that I have traversed? The world of the law courts, politicians and the media, with all their perversion. Certainly it was not tiredness that exhausted my desire for any of this; and it was not frustration, either. Indeed I think that I have behaved well. It is a fact: beyond the malevolence, slanders and provocations of the media, I managed to pull in a majority in my favour. If it had not been for the cowardice of the Guru and his political stunt . . . But when all is said and done, it is the vulgarity, the cheapness, the provincialism, the small-mindedness of those worlds that makes me so angry. What saves me is the fact that I can rise above it all. I shall never be able to respect Biagi's posturings and his cheap emotionality. I find myself thinking that I would like to live in a world which accords with his sentiments. In Japan, in fact. Then, with the Bolognese bonhomie that is customary in those parts, I could send him a noose to strangle himself with, or a sword for him to commit hara-kiri. I cannot stand parasites. I have traversed a world in which not only pity is dead, but imagination too. What would a man like Pannella be without the endless repetition of these rites, which are accountable to nobody? What would Biagi be if he could not shed tears for his mother and transform tawdry emotionality into fat cheques? (Orsay – 29 September)

Folio 106

The discussions with friends and comrades here are getting heavy. They are trying to force me into drastic choices. They lead me to understand that my chances of staying in France depend on my deciding not to do politics any more. 'You'll be an intellectual,' they say, 'you're capable of it.' Meantime operations have begun to get me nominated to the council of the Collège International de Philosophie. That will provide a cover, and also a possibility of work. But no more politics. I reply jokingly that the 'either–or' [*aut–aut*] is a level of metaphysics, whereas for my part – as always – I prefer the 'and–and' [*et–et*]. I don't think that it will be possible to impose very general criteria on my experience of life. Let us leave open the question of possible reconstructions of political discourse. They are pressing me, and giving me a sense of the dangers in store. This evening I received a dramatic proposal from the French government – to go to Algeria, where I would be protected. I said no. It seems that the Italians are applying massive pressure, supported by that old para-Berlinguerian Martinet, the French ambassador in Rome. Negri is on his own – that is the message from Biagi, as repeated by Pannella, and then by Gilles Martinet too – and by Marcelle Padovani as spokesperson for the former. So this is the moment of attack. But I am not on my own. I think I have succeeded in making this clear to the comrades here, who are too jaded to want to believe it. I am indeed defended here. I am not alone. I am defended by a tradition of asylum and by a practice which is part of the material constitution of this state and of the libertarian beliefs of certain important socialists in the government. But, above all, I am not alone because I am moving in the context of a political and social situation in Italy of which I am completely a part. It is true that I have to succeed in changing my life, but this must mean transforming my removal of myself from Italy into a long-term victory. Certainly the situation is hard. But it will not be that way for ever. The suspended state in which I live today is the suspension of political struggle in the current political, social and economic structures of this Europe of ours. But behind this suspension there is the growth of the communist community. The solitude of this genesis and of this perception does not negate the reality of it. I am within that solitude. All their machines, their justice, their politics, have hit the buffers. The ugly irrationality of their violence is met with silence. But for how long? This blockage of reason and expression will inevitably bring about a radical change, an innovative break. Never has there been such a blatant need for a new politics and a new system of justice. I have very little to say about anything else, almost nothing in fact. I think only that the reason of the masses, the intelligence of the community, will express newness. Radical newness. That which is currently mute will express itself by rising up. It has to happen. There is an ethics which I feel to be growing beyond the conditions of oppression in which this world organizes itself. The crisis of the crisis-state has no possibility of finding a resolution, except through an enormous revolution of the means of mass participation in power. We have an experience of this desire: the crisis of all the nomenclatures of the state and of its very form – the state cannot be confronted and transcended other than through the recomposition of the will for revolution. This revolution which is silent, but which nonetheless constitutes the ethical grounding of the singularities. The only obstacle to participating in the development of the new ontology lies in the fact that I am old. During the past few days I have felt old age creeping up like a marshy tide – my body tried, once, twice, many times, to get out. But each time it just fell in deeper. It was difficult to move. I licked the surface of the marsh, thinking that it was human skin. I allowed myself to be carried on my back by the water, hoping that a wave would not overturn me. My wonderment, my amazement at the new vital expressions of being, my passion at its renewal – I find these things lacking in me. But old age can be serenity – and it is not to be confused with death. No, Rossana, no – I too fear a tumour growing inside me, but this ageing, this exhaustion of the animal spirits, I cannot say that this is death and, with that, say that it is the justification of the sickness organically existing in our current institutions. No, I do not think that the idea of death is rational. When we used to say (as the comrades continue to say in court) that we are for life and not for death, we believed, naïvely, that the phrase was acceptable. Correctly, from their point of view, the judges replied by saying that we are extremists. So: is it the case that the only realist is the person who sees death as being indissolubly connected with life? And therefore the stink of death that stagnates in our courthouses is a sign of reality? No, I don't want to believe in, I can't believe in, this dreary funereal ceremonial of the institutions. Here I understand the revolutionary value of Epicurean and Spinozan thought – not to think of death because when there is death there is not life, and when there is life there is not death. Even in old age I reject death. So for that reason people should not expect from me an institutional loyalty that I cannot give. There cannot be loyalty in the face of death. I claim my habeas corpus, my liberty, my life. With this I realize how much I am, and remain, a revolutionary. Down with death – this is the slogan of revolution. During the past few days, among comrades, while we await the government's decision, we talk and talk – about this and other things. Meanwhile someone has been shuttling to and fro to the ministry. They return bringing various proposals which offer expatriation. I always refuse. Finally the word arrives that I have been granted asylum. I take the opportunity to confirm, with caution, that shortly we shall start doing politics again. To return to Italy. Emerging victorious – and sweeping away the filth of the politicians – down there. (Paris – 30 September–1 October)

Folio 107

The Makno polling organization says that 62 out of 100 Italians want me to be arrested. That sounds good to me – it means that 38 out of 100 don't. Always supposing that these polls actually have some kind of validity, there is no doubt that I am holding up well in the midst of the brazen and insolent propaganda that the regime is stoking against me. As for the Italian authorities, they want me dead. I had a precise account of what has happened in the past few days from a French functionary who has been literally terrified by the violence of the Italian demands. As he sees it, at least the forms should be maintained. They have been asking either for extradition or for my expulsion from France. The *Corrierone* confirms the news. Obviously they are hoping to get me expelled to some South American country, where they can get me kidnapped! I have no intention of departing from here. This morning, at dawn, I went on a splendid motorbike ride through the streets of Paris. I had spent the night talking to friends, and at dawn we returned home. It is Sunday and there are there no cars in town – especially not at dawn, when the weather is so blustery. How beautiful this city is, with its order and its intelligence. A rich arabesque carpet. My second home. Will it end up becoming my only home? The memories are piling up, of so many years spent in Paris, ever since I was a teenager, and of many friendships, and of dear teachers. I talk at length with Alexandre M. – an excellent philosopher and a great friend. He laughs like a lunatic when I tell him that certain people are advising me to take a Socratic attitude – in other words, to return to Italy and drink the hemlock. Unless of course I am elected to the European Parliament; but that, too, would mean swallowing the hemlock. No, he tells me, it really isn't even worth the effort of reasoning with such ignoramuses. He reminds me that Socratic formalism did not consist in the *sic et simpliciter* acceptance of the law, but in honouring just laws against their wrong application. Formalism in the *polis* is certainly not on a par with what we can expect of the Italian state, which is notorious for the very bad laws on which it is founded. In Alexandre, good sense triumphs over high-school misreadings of the classics. We talk at length about Spinoza – it is Spinozan to save one's own life and not to give in to compromises. 'Anyway,' he asks, 'are you interested in the European Parliament?' I tell him no. And what about the comrades . . . Today they were supposed to start the cross-examination of Oreste Strano – my old friend, how I love you. I cannot succeed in getting the comrades out of my head and out of my heart, not for a single moment.

I turn over in bed, sensing that they are close by, like in the cell. Someone is breathing heavily – I smile . . . Yes, night time in prison is full of noise and of the troubled dreams of the people sleeping next to you. (Paris – 2 October)

Folio 108

Today, at last, I got to see Paola again. Her enormous tension – she is continually followed and bothered by the police. But also an enormous positive tension: she is a communist, without embarrassment and without doubts, and she combines this great strength of hers with a sense of protection and a generosity which make a great woman of her. A formidable fighter? Her sweetness is matched by a willingness to discuss and by the broad horizon of her discourse. A great tenderness. Anyway, we try to get a grip on the situation. It seems to us that the trial of strength we are traversing is not going too badly for us. But it remains a trial of our strength, and we shall either win or lose. The margin we are treading is very neat and hard. Furthermore, there are urgent things about the trial that need to be dealt with, and I also need time in order to rebuild a capacity of intervention. What to do? Correctly, given the situation, Paola is also advising me to proceed cautiously. No more interviews. OK. As for the friends, God preserve me from them . . . *Ils ont déconné*. Paola brought me the back numbers of *Il Manifesto*. I read the bitterness in Rossana's articles and her rhetorical postponement of any 'moral judgement', but actually that moral judgement is entirely implicit in the mawkishness of the piece. I read an abstract 'let's forget him' article by the restrained (but evidently irascible) Ferrajoli; then there is an outrageous attack by Cases – the 'snob' *signorina* does not play out of character. I connected with these people with too much emotion – today they reveal themselves as having not much intellectual staying power. I am saddened by this. On the other hand, I am amused by the apoplectic ragings of the great buffoon Montanelli. And of all the likes of him. Let them take it out on Pannella – what do I have to do with loyalty to the institutions? Together with Paola we laugh about it. As we leave, she seems serene. 'Wait and see' seems to be the best option. Certainly it seems that they are mobilizing their forces in order to destroy my image, and with this destruction to open new possibilities of repression. Maybe they want purely and simply to kill me: OVRA still lurks in Italy's administrative structures. But first, if you don't mind, destruction of my image! And they have to do this destruction, first and foremost, for the ex-friends. How boringly manualistic and repetitive the operating systems of the state services are! And how naïve the ex-friends! I have no fear of being destroyed, but I do fear being killed. (Paris – 4–5 October)

Folio 109

Today I see the Guru again, after he's been pushing and pushing for a meeting, creating incredible misunderstandings and strains.

We discuss calling it off, on both sides. I really don't think that we shall meet again. But he promises me loyal support in the coming months and years. And so I do the same. Will he keep his word? I dare to hope so. As for myself, in the tiredness of these days, I still set to work. I am completing a long *mémoire* for the French authorities – on the whole business of the 7 April case and on the undertakings I shall make once I receive a residence permit. *Moi Philippe Rivière . . .* I hope this is going to work. I still have not seen any of the Italian refugee comrades in France, not even the closest friends among them. I know that they are looking for me, and in so doing they are making problems for me. I would like one of them to read my *mémoire*, so that I don't write something that could damage someone. I know that they have their own, ongoing negotiations with the French government, and I don't want to jeopardize them. I discuss this with the French comrades and they offer to act as go-betweens. What's more, they say, here among the emigrés there are perhaps more political families than there were groups in Italy. I can feel a strong tension building up inside me – to begin again. To begin again with political work, in line with, and matched to, the tasks which are required by the present – and not by the past. It is important that I manage to carry through this leap in consciousness – a leap forward. It is decisive. I am winding up the spring. When it is released I must be perfectly prepared to receive its impulse. Otherwise I run the danger of falling flat on my face. I have to pay a lot of attention to the French situation. This is now where I live, and I live protected among scientific and bureaucratic congregations (I mean, of the high public sector). Here politics is second nature. Today they see me as being part of their milieu, unlike previously, when they used to look at me curiously and half ironically, like at some kind of savage. A miracle due to the fact of my imprisonment, a transformation brought about by the way in which I conducted myself in prison and by the fact of having won a battle. Thus, if I want to revive my work, it has to develop in relation to the given political conditions. We shall see. These are difficult problems. Making your exit is an art.

PS In yesterday's *Corriere* even one of the heads of the P1 lodge, Cesare Merzagora, was attacking me as a 'coward', a 'destabilizer of the system' (sic!). But how is it possible that such a ruling class manages to continue to reproduce itself? What difference is there with fascism? What difference is there, let us say, between Merzagora and a fascist freemason, for instance a Grandi or a Bottai? Why this never-ending pitiful tragedy? (Paris – 6 October)

Folio 110

Dying a bit in order to begin again. The bureaucratic difficulties are numerous – administrative difficulties related to the granting of a residence permit, difficulties which then affect the preparation of my nomination for the Collège International. (On its executive council there are representatives of four separate ministries. My closest friends preferred to defer the naming of the foreign components, so as to avoid creating scandals – and at the same time they have produced a warm letter for Ton-Ton.) And political difficulties such as the lack of contacts with Italy, the media baying at my heels like a lynch mob, the enmity of the French ambassador in Rome, and so on. I am finishing the *mémoire* – if it is used properly it could be decisive in the environment of the French high administration. But it is true to say that I am in a situation of very heavy isolation, and when all is said and done I cannot even count on being able to settle here. Given that, I have to programme this isolation and this uncertainty. How long will they last? It's hard to know. However, there will be elections in France in 1986, and the Right is growing, and, despite the fact that the right to asylum is written into the material constitution of this republic, if a right-wing government gets in, it would certainly be more inclined to accept requests from the Italian government. Thus the problem is how to organize a basic political work which can move from Europe to Italy during the coming two years. It is not the first time when I find myself moving in uncertainty, within a defeat and on the look-out for a re-foundation. But on the other occasions (halfway through the '60s; and at the start and in the middle of the '70s) at least the material conditions of my existence were assured, and the fabric on which we were working had been created over a long period. Now, if I take a closer look, it is evident that the problems are dramatic. But probably it is precisely this radicality of the problem, with all the desperation and the risks which colour it, that guarantees the intensity of its unfolding. And the importance of the result, if we manage to achieve it. This isolation is distance, but it can also be (and will be) an immediate coming close to the situation and a radical change. The tendency is moving within these limits. We are living an enormous paradox – the fall of the Empire is not the same as the centuries-long process described by Gibbon; rather it is a rapid and deadly implosion. It has the rhythm of a heart attack, not of TB. It is within this tension that intelligence has to be organized. This separateness, which I discovered during the class struggle in the crisis, and which was bizarrely imposed on me (and heightened) in prison and now in exile, is beginning to present itself as a hegemonic rule of society. Deep, dark, ontologically determined and without future. We need to die within it and be born anew. They accuse me of being a coward – let them continue to do so. I have always avoided notions of being strong and being weak; in fact I have preferred to embrace weakness, and if I have been strong it is certainly not by vocation but by constraint. Anyway, strength of spirit is a purely intellectual fact: it means locating oneself practically and theoretically on an average point in a possible history, heightening the independence and the separateness of the possibility, of prediction, and thereby building their strength. We have to cover in the mind what the proletariat and all the exploited live in their everyday lives and obscurely construct in their concrete history.

I have to turn myself into a marginalized person. I am that anyway, so why not make it a key element in rebuilding? The political situation in Italy is perverse, and the European situation is threatened by a Right which is on the rampage and is increasingly fascist in ideological terms. However, alongside all that, sometimes in total separation and sometimes crossing the same institutional level according to rules which are no longer corrupt, there exist currents of thought and a will for struggle within which one can rebuild. Dying a bit, in order to be able to begin afresh. A terrain of immediate intervention, of direct protest, of effective denunciation is almost impossible, and anyway it is unrealistic to think in terms of going down that path. Now is not the time for a *vox in deserto clamans*. But it is also true that this is what a lot of people want; it is true that we can collectively construct the modalities and the *potenza* of it. Time is playing in our favour, because it is a new time, an alternative time to the slavery of work and oppression, a new time, which has been internalized at a mass level, and with unexpected dimensions. God help me . . . within this choice of a new time, of a new immersion in the deep substrate of the desires of the exploited. The risk is enormous, and only an extreme lucidity of analysis can permit us to construct the light-filled determination of conscious rebellion – a new capacity for constitution. From physical uneasiness to a rational undertaking, from rational uneasiness to the constitutive strength of the masses. Avoiding the temptation of suicide. So many times I must, yet again, traverse frontiers. Recover reason's desire for living, and its joy. Once again I have to bring a fleshly reason to bear on the surfaces of the world. (Paris – 7–10 October)

Folio 111

I am working on Leopardi again. I have written several letters to Italy. I have resumed contacts with the German comrades. I am beginning to draw on the affective relations that surround me. You get over the tiredness of separation and isolation also, and above all, by re-learning a real tiredness of the body, and by re-establishing a balance between affects and reason. The sweetness of life is not an extra, but a stimulus and a colouring of rational consciousness. Work and freedom can go hand in hand. I have to arrive at a criticism of myself, of the quantity of mechanical that there is in my existence and my thinking. Prison and the prison community have been an excellent propaedeutic in all this. But only in one respect; the necessities of preparing our defence, the fact of being in the basements of the Palace, the urgencies of material reproduction have instead boosted the inhuman characteristics of the spirit. These have to be eliminated. Every homology with power has to be removed from the spirit, and every residue scraped away. This is a fundamental presupposition in the methodology and epistemology of rational rebellion. I have to define at the earliest possible opportunity a form of analysis of myself. Freud would be a good place to start. (Paris – 11 October)

Folio 112

Le Monde of 11 October carries a strange article, rather weird in fact. There is a Libyan whom the Italians accuse of being a murderer – do the Italians want him extradited or do they not? *Le Monde* claims that they don't want him extradited because it would cause too many problems with Libya, and this leads them to expect that the extradition documents will not arrive. (NB Additional note of 13 October. The Italians did not send the necessary documents, and the Libyan has been released from detention by the French.) But then, *Le Monde* adds, why is it that this Italian justice system, which is so concerned with political relations – to the extent of dropping the extradition of a multi-murderer defended by Gaddafi – why is it that this same system has it in for Negri, who is certainly not an international killer? Obviously for internal reasons that cannot be stated publicly. Therefore, *Le Monde* concludes, necessary caution on the part of the state and the republican tradition of liberty would suggest that Negri should not be handed over. The article made rather an impression on me. While I am happy to know that an authoritative newspaper thinks that I should not be extradited, I am a bit surprised – unpleasantly so, very unpleasantly – to find myself being a commodity in these kinds of international bargainings. My friends, and various functionaries and lawyers whom I see, are all happy. They tell me that they had warned me about this internationalization of my case, since – given that I am a member of Parliament – I am a bit of Italian sovereignty transported abroad. I don't recall the reference, nor do I appreciate it. I am extremely puzzled. Should I perhaps accustom myself to living with this kind of risk? A continuous, unknown and destructive gamble? No, my friends tell me. Given that the political nature of the case has been recognized (as indeed seems to have happened), it is obvious that you have been granted an informal right of asylum. All right, that may be so – but I am still puzzled. This is the least I can say. Meanwhile news arrives from Italy of a sixth charge having been raised against me – this time for the killing of Alceste Campanile (following the fifth one, for the revolt at Trani, and the other four already discussed and accepted). When will they finish coming? Will there also be a seventh set of charges, as seems to be promised in Barbone's statements and in Spataro's obscene persecutory mania, for the Custrà killing? The number seven seems to have an irresistible appeal for the judges in my trials. They have been seized by a will to destroy, a maniacal repetition of a deep political hatred, which is accompanied by resentment towards the fact that I have often demonstrated the falsity of their evidence. This maniacal persecution has become a structural element of the 7 April case. I remember the teachings of my old professor Opocher: justice as the ascertainment of truth, as judgement, as a process of trial. My dear teacher, much as I respect your utopia – and it saddens me to say so – this is really not the way things are. Instead we have justice as a machine, as a dehumanizing structure, as a process without a subject! Unless it is, as in my case, pure and simple vendetta. Without even that modicum of solidity and blood that there is in real vendettas. I am experiencing here the vendetta of a corporation. The only element of dignity that there is in my case, apart from my suffering and my rebellion, consists in this extreme and exemplary dehumanization of justice – this is perhaps the most specific characteristic of the Italian crisis, and its revelation and denunciation are therefore an expression of theoretical dignity. However, I derive no pleasure from putting on this medal of representation. Just as I am not amused to find myself treated as a commodity in international transactions. I wonder whether I might end up being exchanged on the European market for a few barrels of south Italian wine or a delivery of Danish butter. Bah! Anyway, during these days, less than a month after my arrival, I have a clear sense that progress has been made in my situation here. My presence here has been accepted as a political presence. This means that I have substantial, albeit limited, guarantees of freedom. So now to work. Rebuilding, rebuilding conditions of liberty and communism, with a maximum of strength and intelligence. It is time to begin. (Paris – 12–13 October)

Folio 113

I see from the newspapers that Pertini too, the voice of the people, has said that Toni Negri has acted unworthily! I am sorry that our fine president did not take this splendid opportunity to remain silent – but then this was the man who signed the laws on preventive detention and *pentitismo*, even though he pretends to have forgotten this. And, for my part, I cannot forget his congratulatory telegram to Calogero on 7 April 1979. Nor do I thank him for having publicly admitted that the telegram was a mistake – after two years during which I had been desperately defending myself and affirming the truth of the matter. Anyway, the fact that Pertini expresses himself in these terms is a sign that the balance of forces has changed.

Institutional unanimity – because this is what we are talking about – is particularly dangerous when it is exhibited by policemen and judges. The law and its execution should never exhibit signs of unanimism. Today I saw *Blade Runner*, the first film I've seen since I came out of prison. The protagonist is a state killer, and, as he hunts down the 'mutants', he gathers and applies the unanimity of humanity's interest in the preservation of the species. I feel myself to be a 'mutant' here – and in any event I fear this fierce and deadly struggle into which I am forced. I converse with my ghosts – why, despite everything, do I continue with the struggle? And what is this profound memory of rebellion and of refusal, which I feel that I interpret faithfully? Sometimes I fear madness in my pursuit of this ancient dream of transformation. Recently I have been re-reading Hölderlin. How enlightened humanism can be! An enormous difference from the thought of dialectics and of the 'general class', of the bureaucracy and the institution, which little brother Hegel achieves. Hegel understood and served unanimism. Hölderlin lives the ancient phantasm of freedom and revolution. Why do these ghosts always seem to be ancient? Why this enervation of the world? Only reason sustains me – but it is an optimistic reason. A delightful afternoon today – not even Pertini can spoil it for me. It is raining on and off, a typical Parisian autumn day. From the window of the apartment where I am now living I have a fine picture-postcard view of the Pantheon. At night its dome is a glowing presence in the orderly and jumbled accumulation of Parisian rooftops. I talk to the ghosts of freedom and revolution that have illuminated the nights of Paris. It all continues, and will always continue, until the liberation of all becomes a reality. Why is it that the 'mutant' carries within himself this most ancient dream, which humanity holds dear? Why is it that this business of ontological repetitions is always so amazingly new? Today I also meet with the band of economists. All excellent people – and in this period, in their attempts to trace the causes of the crisis, they too are involved in discussions with their historical ghosts. In the fever of liberty we find common cause. (Paris – 14 October)

Folio 114

How hard it is to return to life after these four years of imprisonment and two months of institutional bail. And particularly at this difficult moment, when I am pursued by the dogs of repression! But I know I'll manage it and my work will gradually become productive and collective. Certainly, for now, the landscape is not like that – endless flight, weariness, conflict in my consciousness. I am studying Leopardi and re-reading Roth – in both of them flight becomes a source of knowledge. This has nothing to do with romanticism in its exoticist or 'beat' traditions – for me, in this act of fleeing there is imagination and contact with the future. I live and feel the future as something that I am beginning to possess. My hope is the only thing I own (plus, as of today, I have a good winter jacket). Revolution means conferring validity to hope. From tomorrow I'll start to see the French comrades regularly, to discuss politics. Our central topic is the shifting of all the terms of the debate and political propositions of the past few years, a shift that has taken place on the ground and now has to be grasped by the political project. Here in France the victory of the Left in 1981 threw everyone slightly into disarray, closing the dialectic of the positions around the need to hold on to power at all costs. From what I understand, the interest has shifted away from playing dynamically with contradictions in order to excite reformism; it has moved to the problems of restructuring, as they relate to the preservation of the welfare system and to the maintenance of consensus. The modifications in the composition of the proletariat are huge, and this is where we need to do analytical work. A crisis of the methods and parameters of research.

The problem is how to give a dynamic representation of these contradictions within a political framework. We do not see clearly the possibility of a vertical rupture – rather, we have the possibility of many forward-moving, transversal ruptures. The Left's critique of power is that it does not grasp in an open fashion this system of small break-points and has no desire to carry it forward. The Right is counterattacking – it is very strong. It plays very astutely the transformation of the general picture of things, inserting itself into every little fracture and heightening its corporative character. The Left in power seems entirely incapable of finding itself in this new framework, armed with a reformism of some vigour. The shadings of the situation are rather obscure. Reading the newspapers and comparing those of the Right with those of the Left, one has the impression of a civil war under way, because (particularly from the Right) the attack is ideologically hard and insistent. But in reality this is only smoke. Actually the whole political situation is folded back onto itself. And sometimes it seems that, through all the polemic, the Right is convinced that it will soon be back in power and it applies pressure on the government to get it to resolve the most important problems. Particularly the dirty business of the big restructuring and the creation of mass unemployment in the traditional factory and industrial sector. What a difference between today and 1978, the last big struggles in the steel industry of Lorraine! At that time there was a real hope of being able to create a coordination between different class sectors. Today the analysis is blocked – many comrades seem to believe that it is no longer possible to do analysis. But it is obvious that, without a deepening of analysis, there will be no political shift. Because such a shift can only take place through the identification of new subjects of political development. New social subjects. Who are they? The discussion is not moving very far in terms of identifying them; here too, as in Italy but in different forms, the vectors of the formation of wealth and those of exploitation pass increasingly through the levels of the tertiary sector, science, and informatic innovation of the social. Within the labour movement insufficient attention has been paid to all this. There is a complete lack of agitation on this question. Our discussions will go forward on this terrain. We shall see. The fundamental problem, however, is that of method.

PS News arrives that a young member of Prima Linea got himself killed during a 'hold-up' here in Paris. It is very sad to hear of the death and desperation and loneliness of this boy. And it is terribly bad news, this reappearance, wild and isolated, of terrorism! Here, apart from anything else, it could create a very, very dangerous situation – both for the absolutely peaceful colony of Italian political emigrés, and also for my own position. Furthermore, I do not see how these residues of terrorism *all'italiana*, now deprived of a base, are going to be able to reorganize themselves, except on an international, inter-state basis. And this makes things even more complicated. (Paris – 16 October)

Folio 115

During the past few days I have seen various other old friends, social scientists and economists. I saw Benjamin – I continue to be fascinated by his narrative about the OS, the mass worker on the assembly line. He tells very fine stories of struggles. But the situation is certainly not such that you can construct a linear interpretation of reality on the basis of those struggles. I also saw Félix again, and he proposed that I start working for the Collège on the theme of the 'production of subjectivity'. To see how the juridical–statal mechanisms have appropriated this production – to the extent of monopolizing it – and how the alternative spaces, ignored and repressed, find no way of expressing themselves except through war. I see Virilio, who further emphasizes this expropriation of the possibilities of struggle and of its multipliers of the speed of antagonisms and of war. How to emerge, scientifically, from this impasse of an objectivity that is too powerful? As for the pure economists, they defend themselves from this kind of propositional impotence by returning to the origins of their science, to try to find keys for a re-reading of the present – with a very advanced disciplinarization of their research.

The only openings are in the field of philosophy. Yes. And here there are both a limit and a hard thickness, traditional in some respects, but incremented by the crisis – the seeking after an epistemology which, since it is no longer able to transform, now tends to consolidate itself on the transcendental terrain. Even Thom comes to be translated in transcendental terms! I find many Kantian elements in the course of discussions, and increasingly I have a sense that this current is making headway. Critical Marxism seems to me to have been completely eaten up by this generation of researchers and social scientists. I see Jean-Paul. He tells me frankly that he is absolutely convinced of this fact – at the level of research. For that reason he has decided to become a grand *commis* of the state – he is working like crazy, in the universe of the possible, he tells me – having set to one side a passion for science which he felt was becoming sterile, in order to try to gain knowledge through practice. It is strange, but he communicates a lot of vitality to me. I think over and over about all the themes that have been transmitted to me. I think of my scientific production in prison – *Il comunismo e la guerra*, *Spinoza*, *Macchinatempo* – and at the boundaries of my work, which has traversed all the themes of the crisis, arriving nonetheless at a blockage with a conception of subjectivity which is increasingly corporeal and substantialistic. I feel the need to return to *Il comunismo e la guerra* – one of the finest things I have written, a thoroughly open work. The Finland train, in this phase of enforced political rest, needs to have its machinery and its theoretical instruments set in order. It is evident that war and peace are becoming the background of a revival in theory. The crisis has by now expanded so as to permit us to grasp, at its sophisticated height, the elementariness of fundamental human terms. A very long discussion with Cornelius on these problems. (Paris – 18 October)

Folio 116

I meet Jean-Pierre Faye. I get to know Châtelet and Derrida. Very different people, both in personal terms and in terms of their cultural and political history. But they have a great generosity and a deep and intimate understanding of the need to defend my escape, to consolidate freedom as an essential precondition for work, to do philosophy and to conquer a new freedom for all. We talk at length.

With Faye – a historian and a poet, an extraordinary sensibility for the concrete and an incredibly gentleness in touching things. With Châtelet – an old and untamed philosophical lion, who never ever confuses potency of thought with the misery of reality, and always succeeds in being a man of the future and of hope. Derrida – very sharp analytical instruments in traversing and reconstructing an *Umwelt* of chaos. With all of them I raise the problem of the relationship between the objective production of subjectivity and the *potenza* productive of the subject – that knot which we no longer know how to resolve. My self-criticism goes deep. A subjectivity that is bodily and contingent, at the limit between the eventual and the possible, is what I have been able to grasp and heighten as a function of resistance and of escape. (Just one month ago. Among the islands of the Tuscan archipelago – the haziness of Montecristo, the looming island of Elba which, like a benevolent patron, shelters us from the winds and sometimes slips in a few little gusts for fun – and then the flat nightmare landscape of Pianosa, with its penitentiary and its motorboats at anchor, a nightmare which the evening, and sleep, love and tiredness have removed. The terrible contingency of that space of liberty. But how am I to resolve this condition of contingency, for myself, and for everyone . . .?) I communicate my uneasiness to the friends. The quest for a hard knot of ontological hope is what I feel to be open and living in this whole environment. For the first time in the general crisis of the human sciences, philosophy does not seem to be turning to superficials, as fashionable consumption. Uneasiness with the collapse of the traditional models of knowledge and epistemology seems to be affecting everyone, in various different ways. The obstacle does not succeed in becoming transparent. And it represses us. The dislocation of theoretical knowledge and of ethical action which is happening in the crisis does not happen without us noticing it, but without us being able to contain it in any way. No point in hiding from ourselves the difficulty of the situation and all the pain it carries with it. This can be immediately felt even in this cultural world, which succeeds nevertheless in keeping the terms of the debate clear. (How I hate the dirty ambiguous and priestly mush in which the Italian debate is suffocating, even though it deals with the same problems.) The philosophical problem is thus one of setting in motion an excavation of the crisis through which we are living – an excavation carried out in accordance with its own terms, *iuxta sua principia*. And of redefining transparency and subjectivity in traversing the obstacle and its blind objectivity. I am reading Deleuze's book on cinema – the image–movement. I cannot be enthusiastic about his clear-cut and precise Bergsonianism. But what a lucidity in his way of constructing, through the problem of the image, the theme of imagination and movement in the conquest of time and space! All the themes of escape, of the *libertas philosophandi*, are thus linking up together – and transferring themselves operationally towards the problems of practice. Never so much as now, in the traversing of the philosophical, scientific and political circles of this country which is hosting me, and which I know and love, have I felt with such urgency the proposition of re-founding. From this point of view, my escape – this fact of being like Ulysses, naked and exhausted on a deserted beach – constructs a good opportunity. (Paris – 19–20 October)

Folio 117

I see Gabriel A. He brings me news of the machinations of the Italian embassy against my presence – as keynote speaker – at the Marx conference in Madrid. First they tried applying pressure in university circles. Then, given the short shrift they got from the various university rectors, they started pressurizing the government. The result of this is that Negri's presence in Madrid is deemed to constitute 'an element of destabilization of Spain's democratic government'. Incredible. I have a long conversation with Gabriel about the situation in Spain, about the repeated coups, both threatened and attempted, about the seriousness of the situation in the Basque country – and about the terrible social conditions which are beginning to appear in Andalusia, as well as in the factory-city. Poverty, unemployment, disorganization, hunger . . . I think to myself that these terms have been of no importance for us in recent years, but now they are starting to explode. Not only in the south, but here in Europe. Gabriel insists strongly on the originality of many of the local cultural and political phenomena – in particular as regards the Basque country; and he tables a theory of the autonomy of the social movements, which is extremely concrete in the relation it makes between politics, culture and history. It provides a terrain for future work. But behind these problems of method I have another question: once again, what is the reason for this extreme distancing between power and *potenza*, between state command and the knowledge and liberty of the common people, of the workers? The total disproportion of the relation is patently obvious. The thing has exploded everywhere, all over Europe, and the victory of the social democracies has not been able to close this massive hysteresis. Why is it that reformism has not only been incapable of intervening actively around the class relation, but has also been unable to understand what it actually is.

Why do we have this – definitive – degradation of political language – this caprice that a non-signifying political language introduces into command and into administrative and political organization? With Albiac I discuss how we have to see self-valorization as a moment that is absolutely innovative – as a supporting element not only in the scientific study of rebellion, but above all in the analysis of the conditions and articulations of the new constitution. The problem is not only how to recover the power of subversive knowledge (which was that of the mass worker) within society as a whole, but also how to rearticulate it at the social level. This is the task that awaits us. We have a science which is up to the job, even if it is temporarily somewhat latent: the science of rupture and refusal.

We need to find ways to express the full constitutional positivity of the refusal. But the major problem is how to rebuild the subjects of transformation. When I think of the people whom I have seen to be active in recent years – and the new ones that Gabriel has indicated to me – there is no doubt: the south is within the north. The person in prison stands in relation to the social proletarian in the same way as people hit by unemployment and hunger stand in relation to the new workers and technicians, possessors of invention power. It is within this complex subjectivity that the new constitution of liberty and communism can be built. Gabriel tells me about the weight of the blackmail which the reaction continues to exercise on Spain's democracy, through the presence of the army. I ask myself, what difference is there (apart from the more elegant form) with what the magistracy is doing in the Italian situation? The full disarticulation of these perverse dialectical determinations of the material constitution is a job that cannot wait.

It seems to me that we absolutely have to move in this direction what remains of European political and social autonomy: towards taking apart the perversion of the institution. This strikes me as a necessary precondition. In short, for the obstacle to be reduced to transparency, it has to be disaggregated and subverted. The epistemological value of subversion has to be entirely reinstated. Now, as I write, I get sudden flashes: Judge Francesco Amato and his stolid provocative manner as he interrogated me on this, on the theoretical value of subversion. What difference is there between his behaviour and that of the officer of the Guardia Civil who went into the Cortes? I was carefully considerate in contesting that ideological agent of repression, just as the Spanish parliamentarians were cowardly in not standing up to his challenge. No. Even the word on its own has a power of subversion. So let us go forward, to reconstruct new horizons within subversion. Constitutional innovation, a new regime of liberties for the new proletariat. This shit world can be subverted from the bottom upwards. The network of class relations is huge, and its contents are ineradicable. The irreversibility of the revolution that has passed – and is already embedded in people's spirits – has to be affirmed, expressed and shown. I am not tired, not any longer. I just wish I were among many. Soon. (Paris – 21 October)

Folio 118

This morning I took a car ride round Paris with a friend who wanted to show me the crazy underground topography of the new organization of this city. One tunnel after another – will this not result in a dark state of consciousness, lived by a subterranean humanity? It is all different, and infinitely more inhuman than the Metro. It seems that a popular sport among the youth of Paris is to go down into the catacombs, sewers and underground passages of the metropolis. I have a sudden flashback of the journey from Bastia to Île Rousse last September: an insane race, with cows lying in the middle of the road and tiny roads that were more or less impassable. The driver told me that he was a Formula One driver, and I could well believe it. What incredible blues and greens, and what a joy, as I held on tight. But here it is entirely different. Now I am living in the subterranean spaces of this city and in the darkness of a semi-clandestinity that offends my hope. But this is the world I am going to have to traverse. In its depth. And on the other hand I have the world of Italy. I read the back numbers of the last few weeks of *Il Manifesto*. As can be expected, every kind of thing is happening *chez nous*. Martinazzoli, the 'good' minister, has presented a project on preventive de-imprisonment which is absolutely disgusting. Meanwhile the comrades of the UCC have started a hunger strike. As for me, Biagi says that I give him a pain – good for him – the feeling is mutual. The *pentiti* of Milan are attacking me. Their lawyers and their families likewise. This makes me happy – no danger of confusion here. This Babylon amuses me, but at the same time it disgusts me. Trumpets braying out of tune. Long live liberty – I shout it with the simplicity of a René Clair. Then I think again of this absurd play between sunlight and the subterranean – and of the fact that the Italian scene generates only contempt and a sense of shame. Martinazzoli presents a law that is contemptible,

Valiani supports it, and the final outcome is simply that the comrades do not get out. These people are butchers, and that is all. On the other hand, what should one expect, in the face of the kind of politics embraced by the likes of Craxi? A politics which maintains the corporative groups, both at the social level and at the political level, within their enclosed space. Refusing either to put them together, because it is impossible, or to create new forms of dialectic by pitting them, as they merit, one against the other. A politics in tatters. What happened to the much vaunted capacity for government? A swamp, more than a government. But we have to shatter this squalid image of power. It is possible. It is possible to emerge into the sunlight. The re-founding of a politics of the Left, in Italy, will have to take the risk of driving hard – the adventure of that Mercedes racing between the two coasts of Corsica, among mountains that are no longer inhabited. A shifting of the political problematics, this is the central point. The political generations of the Resistance and post-Resistance have to be completely eliminated from the scene – they are not our teachers, they are the ones who have erected the ambiguous art of institutional compromise and corruption, both administrative and political, into a method. The 7 April case is a phenomenon of corruption no less important than the cases of Sindona and Calvi. Corruption, in the Italian context, has become so much second-nature to power that it has corrupted it. I do not think that honesty is an absolute virtue in politics – but dishonesty, if it wants to have margins to stand up, at least has to come to recognize the new vices of the new subjects. Dishonesty cannot be archaic. This is the reason why everything is so wide of the mark *chez nous*. A revolution, a revolution that is simply conservative (on the basis of an effectuality that has already occurred – as Tocqueville said of the great French Revolution) is the minimum that we have to impose. We really cannot tolerate these Romans any longer! We need light, sun and clarity. Once again, a presupposition which permits us to follow the level of shifting which takes place in the situation, and gives us the strength to attack the obstacle with subversive intelligence. (Paris – 22 October)

Folio 119

I changed houses this evening, and I expect that I shall be staying in this new place for a long time. It's costing me an arm and a leg. The money from my interviews is about to run out, and my member of Parliament's salary is being eaten up by lawyers' expenses. We'll have to wait and see what happens. The view from up here is superb. I see the outline [of the city] like from the top of a skyscraper. Down below, the world goes past like so many ants. They flow. Slowly. And yet, what a potency there is in that flow! I have a telescope, which came free with the apartment. Food for thought arising from that – near and far, present and future – unique sensations and strange perceptions. How great and splendid the world is, down there. How much richness and how much intelligence flowing past. The only way I have of imagining the future is as political struggle and as time organized for the *multitude*. I am re-reading Spinoza, from among the few books that I own and haul around in my baggage. In the coming days, from this apartment, I shall be better able to reorganize my life. As a machine of work and war. War for hope and liberation. I am very grateful to you, you my friends who have helped me! And how many comrades there are, close to me, and hoping with me, both in their happiness and in their desperation! Certainly, sometimes you look at me as a person would look at a wild animal – a man of surprising vitality. Surprising when compared with the overly pallid nature of intellectuals in France. However, here there is an incredible nostalgia for politics, communism and revolution – and also for everything which buries it or submerges it or postpones it. Why? Why is it that all these forces are not capable of being present on the terrain of constitutive practice? Sometimes this great race of intellectuals risks ending up as a kind of waxworks – wax dummies, horrors, superficial recollections. No, this cannot be. Sometimes they are prisoners of the various traditional taboos of French culture (hatred of Germans and of the idea of German unity, a pallid nationalism, a certain tired-ness when it comes to challenging political stereotypes, etc.), but this cannot permit the extinction of a transformative intelligence, which is the only thing that nourishes reason. In all these comrades I feel that there is a blockage – between an analytical intelligence which uncovers the unbearability of this world and a will that pursues only general solutions to the problems. A kind of frustrated athleticism of the spirit. I think of the problems and of the people, one by one. I don't think that the blockage of the spirit can be allowed to translate into an exhaustion of hope. Here we have the finest brains in the whole of Europe. What is needed is that this intelligence, so sleepily sunk in desperation, finds a way of expressing itself again. We have to set in motion a series of European links and connections, so as to develop our hopes in common. I do not know how it is best to proceed – but this has to be done, and until it is done we shall not be able to produce very much. I talked with Félix at length about this project. He is completely convinced of it – but equally incapable of involving himself in it. This is implicit in his *Mille Plateaux*: I have myself tied up, like Odysseus, in order not to hear and be taken over by the formidable effect of that siren song. And yet he will have to make a move and take the responsibility for a new political initiative – for himself, and for all those who believe, correctly, that the sirens are right. His *Mille Plateaux* is a formidable European book. The finest thing that has been produced in the past ten years. On the basis of this ensemble of ideas and projects which traverse the real we can undoubtedly construct a network of connections and transformation. As for the antagonism – that is growing, and it is our task to identify its constitutive parameters on the basis of the developing subjectivity. Europe – shattered internally in its institutions, and, externally, cracked by Yalta into East and West – is the greatest country in the world. Its intelligentsia has to rebuild itself. This determination seems to me absolutely fundamental. Today we are battling to construct the theoretical conditions necessary for understanding, development and struggle within the general dislocation that has taken place. Breaking with East–West, and destroying even the memory of Yalta. Who would be better at doing it than these intellectuals, who are of the same race as those who destroyed Westfalia and the peace of the *ancien régime*? Enough of the profound masochism of our experience of Europe. Europe no longer has a metaphysics – we need to rebuild it. We no longer have the secular religion of communist militancy. On the European terrain we can rebuild it. I have been talking in these terms continually over the past few days, and launching these hypotheses. My associates are in agreement. The European perspectives of our work need to be organized – and soon! (Paris – 23 October)

Folio 120

On Sunday, hundreds of thousands of people marched for peace, in Germany (particularly in Germany), and also in Britain, Italy and Belgium. Willy Brandt has taken up a position against the missiles. Poor Europe, capable of this last big dream. Peace! Meanwhile the dirty war in Lebanon is moving ahead. Suicide trucks against the French and the Americans – hundreds and hundreds of dead. Reagan has occupied the island of Grenada – a strategy of transversal response, they tell me. That's Bishop's island – poor comrade, I remember you from the Potere Operaio conference in Florence!

Europe, confined between East and West, is sucked into the conflict in the Middle East. An irresistible dynamics of destruction. Here, in our own situation, the problem of peace is completely enclosed within that of urgency, the urgency of a crisis that is no longer controllable, and within that of having to defend ourselves from too many enemies – often terrorist enemies, invisible and suicidal. Responses of reprisal. Moving in a vicious circle, which is absolutely rigid. The problem of peace is felt as a problem of defence of life. We cannot go on like this. In this urgency, the debate about peace is castrated, crushed on the boundaries of estrangement. The urgency removes from peace its particular shadings. It is a Hobbesian operation: one is disposed to sacrifice everything to peace. This is a reactionary and suicidal ideology. In this way peace becomes a formal negative, which provides the basis for a right of exploitation. If I were an African, I would care nothing for this peace. Here in Europe only a few forces are moving decently on a radical discourse of peace. A European peace capable of both breaking the blocs and extending towards the south – on a north–south axis – an action of resolutive political and economic construction. Is this only a dream? I talk about this with many friends and comrades. For all of them, particularly here in France, there is a preoccupation with rebuilding a political content of the peace movement – political and democratic. Peace as a terroristic 'no future' thematic is rejected – this thematic, like that of war, should be denied. The blackmail has to be overturned. If there is no alternative to peace, at the same time there is an alternative within peace. Alain says that, for the maintenance of peace, the only effective means consists of transversal war – this little world has to be considered for what it is: an ensemble of strategic borders. So, he concludes, we have to move realistically on the segments and to abandon the dream of peace and liberation from the power blocs. I reply that this will not do. Our realism disarms us. I prefer utopia, the great utopia which gives hope, rather than this way of proceeding through short-sighted perspectives and the acceptance of blackmail. Europe has the possibility of imposing a major project – European unity versus Yalta, and the opening of debate with the countries of the south, to recover a prospect of real peace. Only such a terrain can offer a chance to emerge from the blackmail of war, which the crisis poses as its fundamental bulwark and which functions in defence of the existing power and against all transformation. We need to link together, even if only within a single frame of analysis, the three great themes of peace (namely the breaking of the East–West axis; European unity; and a new north–south relationship). Only in this way will it be possible to break the hangman's knot, which was made at Yalta and which now strangles us. The discussion needs to open out. What is the so-called French power of dissuasion? Maybe it really is an illusion – but it offers possibilities of international debate to the powers hereabouts. Chauvinist leftovers complicate the question. In reality this 'dissuasion power' is simply a diplomatic tool. The debate has to be sharpened up, it has to go into things more deeply, and it needs to push the terrain of analysis forward. War hangs over us like a spectre and paralyses the spirit. The pages of Hegel's *Jena Philosophy of Nature* and *Phenomenology*, where he deals with terror: re-read them. Tragedy is born on the margins of uncontrollability – but the tragedy could be avoided by a radical change in subjectivity, huge, the kind of thing which is possible within these dimensions of the conflict. Therefore we have to come out of a purely strategic debate and insert the perspective of the great change which is under way: a change which has already happened in people's consciousnesses, and now has to make its appearance in an organized form. Now more than ever, the watchword of the autonomous reappropriation of politics – of the decision over life and death – are completely of the present. The spirit can extend itself in constructiveness only if we entirely pick apart the political contents of peace. Being against war cannot produce the result of desperation and terror. The ecological movement and the anti-nuclear movement have been almost swept away by the hysteria of peace. We need to reconquer the theme of peace as the thematic of a project. I undertake to work on these problems with seriousness, humility and determination, as ever. I feel, for all the confusion of the situation, a certain solidarity with my determination. (Paris – 24/25/26 October)

Folio 121

Other meetings. The problem is how to define a social base for the discourse on peace, and how to identify the subjects who can (and wish to) align themselves with this project. How is it possible to proceed otherwise in this night of grey cats? The discussion begins from a series of basic observations: the south is already within the north, with millions of unemployed. And then: within the north, we are seeing the establishment of new social and racial aggregations; the multinational European worker. In England, the Jamaicans and West Indians; in France, the Maghrebi; in Germany, the Turk – are they only shooting stars in the current class composition? Perhaps so – but they indicate a direction in analysis, and an entirely anthropological mode in their definition. Culture, sensibility, historical and moral elements (and also religious) of class composition. A new elasticity of class composition is born precisely from the irreversibility of the elements and of the elementary subjects that form it. And then there are the aspects which are, in the most absolute way, characteristic of our world: the abstraction of labour power, its dynamic nature, the explosion of invention-power as the substance of value. Science, permanent education and training, communication as the substance of value. This great *Vergleichung* which is in the process of developing. Lyotard confronts the problem in his latest book (see the excerpts reprinted in *Change International*). This is a strong theme. But how are we to relate all these analytic elements to a problematic of subjectivity? Here is the basic sticking point. No longer, certainly, on the oppositions between society and state – no, the antagonism no longer represents itself simply at this level; on the contrary, it traverses also many of the pathways of the state as producer. Nor is the separation of society from state any longer possible. But, having said this, what is the dialectic between the possibility of, and the reality of, the recomposition which is being determined at this level? Peace, the breaking of the perversion of the international treaties and of the state-based policies that are founded on them, the opening of a dialogue and of cooperation between the great invention-power of the north and the proletarian energies of the south, the constructions of conditions for European independence to this end, and so on – all the debate and all the possible richness of projects is blocked by the impossibility of grasping, here and now, the mechanisms of subjective recomposition. The repression which has devastated Europe during the crisis also bears this heavy responsibility: that of having broken the continuity of the processes of emergence and of subjective reconstruction. And, today, anybody who has an interest in social transformation must address the effort of rebuilding things on this terrain, which has been stripped of its greenery and burned by chemical bombs. But is it inevitable that our research should be blocked by these obstacles? Not at all. Because peace on the one hand, and on the other hand the construction of the political conditions of liberation, cannot wait. I know that the times of political re-founding are long – but we have to begin to traverse them. Probably we are at a good point – the possibility is based on the universality of the movements of rebellion we have lived, on the materiality of the conditions we have posed. Certainly, at the level of real subsumption, the definition of antagonism as subjectivity is a problem which is almost unresolvable – but this is the problem . . . *Hic Rhodus, hic salta!* It is at that level of the shifting – on that general equilibrium of the repression of life, over-determined by the extremity of the desire for nuclear destruction – that we have to concentrate all our efforts of intelligence. Loading that abstract dimension with a maximum of physicality. I am working a lot. I am tired. But finally it seems to me that the fact of my freedom is beginning to produce new ideas and a political concentration on the necessary revolutionary transition. However, my urgency is being dissipated over timescales that are too long. I worry about this. I shout at myself – remembering the comrades who are still in prison – There is no choice, we have to do this! *Hic Rhodus, hic salta*. (Paris – 27 October)

Folio 122

A long discussion with Morgan. He is on a high. He poses the problem of creating a link with Italy. He describes the first steps of recomposition that can be glimpsed in the social – in the big *banlieues* of the metropolis. He gives an evaluation of the peace movement which is not entirely negative. He insists on the necessity of creating a network of information which is continuous and effective. My only objections have to do with the absolute priority of connecting with an international network. I talk to him about possible contacts with the German Greens and with the Socialist International. We have to match the project to our means – it is clear that the intervention cannot happen as regards Italy, except at the level at which we have already pursued the debate, in our documents 'A generation in prison' and 'Do you remember revolution?' The relative scale of things is difficult to grasp. The problem is one of political cadres and direction, and only in these terms can it be posed. He tells me that he agrees. He outlines for me the work that has been done in France for the consolidation of the project – at the highest level. But he adds that it is urgent. Certainly, I believe so too – but our forces must be up to it. We shall be intervening in a perverse environment. The obstacles that our action will face are terrible. We have to fight against an action of the state which uses the means of repression in order to delegitimate us as a political cadre. This is done through the *pentiti* and the henchmen of that state.

Not only do we have to go beyond civil liberties arguments, to propose a new substance of political and historical evaluation; we also need to find the strength to destroy the perversion of a machine that is structurally predisposed to war and repression. This force, which must be built within the given realities of European politics – in the awareness that it is in the interests of all free people – needs to identify new social subjects in Italy with whom we can develop a debate about transformation and peace. At this point Morgan stresses the importance of deciding what our means of intervention will be. Given the blackout imposed by the media and their complete submission to power and its perverse characteristics, what means of communication are there left to us, other than the samizdat? The idea seems excellent to me. Therefore we shall soon begin to move on this terrain. We return to more immediate matters. We discuss prison, the trial, and exile. Discussing all these things with him, I find again the impassioned firmness of this eternal comrade and the sweetness of his intelligence. And also a certain deep weariness with the wretched situation in Italy. What atavistic punishment is it, that condemns us to have to endure a political class like the one we have? And what is it, this incurable sickness of the institutions? Why is there so much corruption – in people's ideas, let alone in financial and economic affairs? Why is there so much corrupt practice in the public sphere? None of us, dear Morgan, has any desire to set ourselves up as paragons of ethical virtue – but why is it that the vileness of politics in Italy is able to continue forever, reproducing itself in this way? Nevertheless, our hopes cannot be allowed to die. Because, whatever happens, Italy and Europe – and liberty, and the idea of justice – are not dead in people's hearts. They continue to move – and will always continue to move, this disutopia of communism and this practice of autonomy, which are the irreversible characteristics of our make-up, and are increasingly marked in the new generations. (Paris – 30 October)

Folio 123

I tell stories about prison to my very sweet *compagna*. I see the fright in her eyes. Prisons have to be destroyed. I think again of my comrades, of the harshness of our destiny. The trial is racing ahead, according to the news that I am receiving – it is beginning to present itself (as it always has been) as an antechamber of the execution squad – but now publicly so. The judges have lost all restraint – paranoia and prejudice exploding on every hand – contempt for the trial process on their part, messianic and ferocious expectations of the *pentiti*. Listening to these stories, my imagination is hard at work and I can see immediately what is happening. The comrades have resumed their work. They have defined my 'flight' as a 'very human mistake' – but I don't care. I think that their behaviour is 'very human' too, in that damned cage where they sit, and facing the ferocity of the court. The Guru, on the other hand, has pissed outside the pot during these days. I was expecting enmity as a possible outcome of his enormous vanity. I did not anticipate bestial behaviour. But what can you expect from a priest who sees the *pentiti* as human beings – and the breaking of community loyalty, the enslavement of truth to the needs of the market, as perfectly legitimate facts and operations? The *Corriere della Sera* has offered the Guru the front page – to insult me. It's not worth the effort of replying to him – really not. From Italy, everyone tells me that I should ignore him, because replying would simply give him life and enable him to continue reproducing himself in this vile way. I agree, I won't reply to him – except to remind him that he was the one responsible for getting me voted back into prison, so he had best shut up. I am angry, really angry. He is a low specimen of humanity – first because he knows that he's playing with me like a cat plays with a mouse, and that I don't have the opportunity to respond adequately; and second because he is encouraging the court in its persecutory behaviours, not only in relation to me, but also in relation to the comrades in prison, weakening their defences and blackmailing them; and third because he is now shouting from the housetops that he believes what the *pentiti* are saying and that I am guilty. Pannella is showing himself for what he is: the anti-party of the partitocracy, a man of the P1, on equal footing with Merzagora and the others. People tell me about his friendship with McNamara and the IMF – not bad for a character who claims to be an upholder of the rights of the starving. But how is it that I ever imagined that the decrepitude of the Italian institutions could somehow allow a flower to flourish? Anyway, the problem is not the Guru. May he drown in the swamp. The problem is the trial – its linearity as a showcase trial, and the non-resistibility of its violence. The problem is the *pentiti* and the pre-figuration of our eventual sentencing in their dirty accusations. I look at my own situation and I think about the accusations that the *pentiti* have been throwing at me. What barbarities! I am innocent. I shout it aloud. But they do not hear me, and if I were there, in the trial, they would not want to listen to me, they would block their ears and they would laugh hysterically – true demons of injustice. I imagine the *pentiti* pontificating – pigs like Barbone and schizophrenics like Fioroni; worms like Ricciardi and ideologues like Ferrandi; cretins like Romito and manipulators like Casirati; monsters like Marocco and pathetic figures like Donat-Cattin . . . Oh my God, what a filthy house of beasts. And I imagine the tiredness, the contempt and the desperation of the comrades in that courtroom cage, having to listen to all this monstrous falsification of our history, to this insult to the truth of our struggles and of the communist project. I would like to be an exterminating angel when these fantasies grow in my mind. Then a strong jolt of consciousness brings me back to myself, and again I understand that liberation can only be a collective fact, built and rebuilt within the boundaries of a practice of transformation. But how am I going to manage to say this to the comrades? How can a correct political line replace the horrible tedium of day after day in prison and the daily injustices of repression? (Paris – 31 October)

Folio 124

From inside prison it is hard to get a clear view of the world – it is like looking at things from a distance, or from high overhead: you can only make out the big aggregates. On the other hand, when you are free, your attention tends to get dispersed among the infinite articulations of reality. Sometimes this is useful; at other times it is dispersive. However, it is very good to be able to tie threads together and construct a project, passing through the many possibilities – this is what it means for people to be free. And this is what I finally feel myself to be in these days. So here I am again, alive. I look around myself, and things have a new, warm reality for me. Future, things to come – we are starting over again. Only today Ferruccio gave me an ashtray which I had for years on the desk of my office at the Institute. When he left Padova, Ferruccio brought it with him, as a memento. A strange ashtray: a printer's plate, made of copper, a photograph of a workers' demonstration in 1969, folded up so that it made a rectangular ashtray. Francesca R. had given it to me – she'd taken it from the print room of L'Unità. Now I look at it, and I recognize more or less nothing of the image – maybe a placard of a demonstrator in one corner is just about identifiable – maybe a clenched fist too, maybe . . . The cigarettes stubbed out in this ashtray have erased everything – copper, like memory, is absorbent, which means that all certainty of an image disperses. Time has passed. The old has been transmuted into nothing – at best, the ashtray bears witness only to the thousands of cigarettes I smoked, and to my weariness. For years I kept it there on my desk – Ferruccio, I thank you for having brought it away with you. But this piece of metal is no longer any use for anything. The image cannot be retrieved. But I, for my part, have a whole life ahead of me waiting to be rebuilt. With what intensity I feel that desire! A life to restore, by renewing it. I feel precisely, all over again, the complexity of freedom and of the project. I stitch together again consciousness and will. Paolo C. arrives from the USA. He brings me messages from friends. He tells me that we should reorganize ourselves politically in order to return to Italy. On what basis, I ask myself. Certainly, we have to organize a communist discourse of liberation and establish contacts with all the forces in Europe which are moving on this terrain. But, for God's sake, we should not nurture impossible nostalgias. Any return can only be the fruit of a revival of communist struggle at the level of the needs of the present class composition. This has always been our real continuity, our style in dominating historical break-points. And now it is clear how the big themes of the new phase are taking shape – themes of liberation, peace, Europe, and north–south relations. Escape is this declaration of liberty – in positive terms. No, enough of nostalgias, once again, only functioning brains will succeed in producing community. I throw the ashtray in the bin. (Paris – 1 November)

Folio 125

Sometimes I have the impression of a kind of deep disorientation. Certainly I have the will to start again – and the project of scientific and political work is gradually becoming better defined. But shall I have the strength and the control for it? Life is a system, and I ask myself whether, with one or many of the orientations changing, it is possible that all the values of my life will fail, like in some kind of meltdown. I mean those values that have governed it for all these years. My existence is somehow in suspension today. I force it towards an outcome, but I also fear a great falling apart, a great collapse of its values. I struggle against the grating of my senses, the absence of desire, the emptying out of life forces, the weakening of imagination, the disorder of initiatives – to which four years of prison have confined me. And I fear the shadow of all this on that act of re-founding that I am demanding of my consciousness. I need love, in order to mediate this transformation of life and to rediscover gentleness and sweetness. I am not tired – I am disturbed, emotional. I think that I can succeed in the undertaking of re-founding and transformation, but I absolutely need to organize it within a process which is broad and human. I am not tired, I am only enervated by the perpetual prolongation of tensions – often I feel that they are running me, rather than me dominating them. Tonight a strange excitation took me out of myself. A desperate burning desire for life and love. A delirium, a desire for creation and destruction. I don't know what I would do if I had to return to prison – I don't know if I would be able to survive. Now, though, I want to survive and create new life. But with method – reorganizing the decisions of liberty rationally and gently . . . Paola did not arrive this evening. I was waiting for her, but she was not able to shake off the police who were following her. Quite properly, she didn't want to lead them to me. I was anxious while waiting for her . . . Franco and Emilio are pontificating from prison on what I should be doing, on what I should have done, etc., etc. It is pitiless on their part, but the prison gives them the right to speak out . . . Today I saw the request for an authorization to proceed against me in connection with the Campanile killing. It is really unbelievable! How can one defend oneself from this pack of raving dogs . . .? In *Il Manifesto* Pilenga launches a ferocious attack on Rossana. She describes her as a *chic* intellectual, a Parisian, an 'evil teacher' – with enormous vulgarity. The article is a heap of insulting commonplaces and cultural frustrations, really scary. The Italian provinces on the attack. 'Grunf, grunf.' A ferocious string of insults – which come from a *pentita*! They tell me that the letter was published because *Il Manifesto* came under a lot of pressure. I can believe it. They need to defame people so as to construct the perverse legitimacy of their power. The main fact is that the dirty spirit of *pentitismo*, intertwining with provincial vulgarity, has run through the whole of society – above all, through Italian culture – much more deeply than we ever thought possible . . . The hearings are beginning in the Rosso–Tobagi trial. Finally the socialists have found a little bit of courage and dignity, which has enabled them to launch a justifiable attack on Spataro and the Milan procurator. The latter have called for Barbone to be set free. Incredible! What disgusting horse-trading . . .! No, enough! New life. I want new life. I want to destroy these murky presences – the ghosts of those horrible memories. In defending myself, I put a maximum of rationality into the political struggle for liberation; I have somehow dislocated, displaced my contempt for the dirty origins of making justice in Italian style and for its tremendous effectiveness in debasing the spirit. No, enough. I have to produce a maximum of impassioned intelligence and disenchanted sweetness, so that I can also overcome the ghosts of this history. Within this very powerful chiaroscuro I define the new life which is due to me and which I want to rebuild. To clear out the chambers of my memory, to form hopes . . . I want to have a child. A material and irreducible sign of sweetness returning into life. (Paris – 2–3 November)

Folio 126

What we are constructing in our life is a system of values, concepts and relations. Sometimes it happens to us that the forward shifting of a value drags the whole ensemble with it to a higher level. Sometimes this does not happen. In that case we suffer the system of life as a pathology. At this moment I am experiencing the strongest ascesis that I have ever experienced – as a result of these months of huge passions and of very sincere imagination. Perhaps it is precisely the accumulation of the imaginative dimension, so repressed in prison and so suddenly liberated, which today permits me so much strength and hope. Maybe I succeed in bringing reason up to the level of the body which has been set free. There must no longer be a dilemma in living reason and body. I was thinking that I had become old, but I find that I have formidable energies. And I find that the delirium is sweetly conjoined with a capacity for balance and a strength of decision. I am working like crazy. I reiterate – in the long and subtle manner of letter-writing – an action of pressure on friends and enemies. I focus basically on the politicians. I defend my cause and my escape. This is underground work. I used to do it from prison too, and it was very fruitful. Before long, those who are denouncing me for the act of liberty which I undertook will be definitively isolated through the counterpoint of my untiring defence. There is nothing else that can be done. The comrades in prison are reproaching me for not conducting a campaign on their behalf – but it is not possible, because these foreign governments will not permit me, and because the links with Italy have collapsed after the campaign organized by the Guru and by the usual band of enemies. So the only possible solution is to find a line on which I can establish an initial relationship of power with foreign governments and re-establish links with Italy. But this means being capable of reconquering an internal equilibrium, matched to the highest level of the project, and being capable of setting in motion a maximum of animal spirits. And of bringing all our friends to this understanding of the project and to the strength of its realization. I know the technique of these radical shifts forward of the spirit. Everyone has to understand that it is only on this terrain that it is possible to achieve liberation. It is pointless to delay, and both useless and stupid to sit counting the column-inches and minutes devoted to you in the media. It is in the depths of relations of power that the situation resolves itself. How is it possible that the comrades – those in the prison community, those whose previous history and whose struggles have always been developed within this dialectic – how is it possible that they do not understand this? They will understand. I ask myself: 'Why don't you write to them, Toni?' Because it is useless. Here I make no appeal to anything other than my ability to understand, in all my uncertainties, their suffering, and to know how to resolve it into an operation for freedom. This, and only this, is what we have agreed. If I do not succeed in this operation, the responsibility will be mine and mine alone. For this reason, the whole schema of values, concepts and relations which constitutes my being must be brought to a very high tension: that of liberation. Of their liberation, which is also mine. Which means the possibility of resuming political work and reconquering the political space we need – these things which have been attributed to us by the history of the struggles. With how much pride and how much commitment I feel this task! The body can be free only if all the comrades are free. The struggle will be long. I must be capable of sustaining it. Here the supports are minimal, if compared to the ends; but they are not non-existent. We have to nurture the dimension of the struggle for liberation and fill it with a new programme. There are no alternatives to this plan. And there is no alternative to the fact that I myself assume – directly, in the first person – the weight of the work. But in order to keep it up I have to continue to rebuild myself too, and see to my wounds, and get them out of my system. Now, entering at last into a phase in which I feel my liberty to be balancing out, I can recognize the fearsome weight of the suffering of these past years. This weight has to be transformed into strength. I have to impose the imperative of liberation onto the whole system of my life. (Paris – 6 November)

Folio 127

The infamy of the characters in the courtroom is only a symbol of the infamy of public life in Italy as a whole. As I read the Italian newspapers, I am increasingly traumatized by what I read. It scares me how the degradation of everyday life and the barbarities of the judicial system go hand in hand. Having been educated *en bon marxiste*, I think sometimes that I should be more cynical in my reactions to this spectacle. But I cannot. Civil degradation and penal barbarism interweave to such an extent that you cannot get them out of your mind. It makes me want to laugh when I read moralistic journalists or high-minded judges declaring, with Protestant rigour, that our civil society and the state are shot through with Mafia and terrorism. And why not their own newspapers and their own courtrooms? In the business of ophthalmology, removing the beam is more important than seeing the mote – as someone once said who knew about these things. People often accuse me of having replaced humour with sarcasm, and they remind me that humour has an educative value – but how can one avoid falling into invective in situations such as these? A state which is founded on infamy. Law – their law – no longer has a place. I read and re-read the fierce outpourings of Leopardi on the ways of his Italy – I would like to do an edition of his writings. Ferocity is the least you can use against these clandestine gangs, which infect our society. Enough. Until large numbers of people are capable of saying 'No', there is no progress to be made. There is a place for moralism. Down with cynical reason and with the infamy of its articulations. Enough – in my spirit, I exit from Italy. Yesterday Patrick was telling me his theory about the suffix '-ship', which expresses the idea of 'community' in English, or community on board. A Viking theme: government within a framework of solidarity and discipline within a framework of needs, in the physical dimension of necessity. And, on the other hand, community as the original determination of big abstract themes such as peace, liberty and wealth. This etymological theory is fascinating – community against infamy, against the perversion of the final stage (unfortunately not of capitalism, but) of this imperfect and blocked democracy, mediating and corrupt – which operates so much as a straitjacket even on capitalism itself. With Félix and with Jean-Paul I talk a lot about politics. We are essentially in agreement over the fact that the broad themes of revolutionary reconstruction – of peace and Europe, of the breaking of Yalta and of commitment to a north–south axis – are today impinging on the edges of the European social democratic movement. It is therefore towards those forces, collaborating with their project of mobilizing participation and democratic decentralization, that we might direct ourselves, with a view to a campaign for the destabilization of the existing regimes and against their perversion. The insertion of these broad political themes as an explicit force implies an accumulation of contradictions which otherwise are unsolvable. The project of 'Lenin in England' can still be pursued. 'Yes to the Centre Left, No to Reformism' was the title we gave to an issue of *Classe Operaia* twenty years ago, in '63 I think. I am certainly not rediscovering the autonomy of the political here – at that time its dialectic appeared to us as an element which could permit a certain linearity of the project. Today all this has revealed itself to have been an illusion; only a radical overturning [*catastrofe*] can destroy the perversion of regimes that render us slaves. But the fact that dialectics is exhausted as a form of thought does not deny the allusion to an antagonistic thread of action. One can live innocently in a world of perversion. A 'mutant' is marked by the irreversibility, the irreducibility of the mutation which has taken place. The community is a republic of 'mutants'. So why should we fear a relationship with the great European social democracies? They are no better off than we are, and radical overturning is looming over them in the same way it has hit us. It will not be impossible to shift the debate from ideological trifles to the level of great denunciations, of great choices – the problem is posed only at the point where the possibility of this shift becomes actual. Community against perversion. I feel the political project to be growing. I am looking forward to meeting many friends, and the German comrades. It needs to be destroyed, it needs to be blown up, and then the terrain needs to be purged . . . it needs to be annihilated, that horrible Italian sewer, the antique symbol of a power which eternally renews the same old stereotypes. Damned Italy – the Italy of the judges, the sullenly filthy Italy of the prisons, perfidy and perversion. I would like to throttle you all with my own hands. But it is better to have the long work of reason and the torture that history and its radical changes impose on these people of infamy. The political line is disputed, over the radical overturning [*catastrofe*], between the capitalist reformism of the social democracies and the proletarian pressure against any law of so-called equilibrium at world level. It is played out on radical change, on the limit between reformism–restructuring and the new force of abstract labour power, on the reversal of the major axes of world development. The political line is played out on an overthrowing of you, you heinous and perverse torturers, and of your demented bestiality. (Paris – 10 November)

Folio 128

There is one thing in this whole business I am going through, something not fundamental, but for which (to put it mildly) I find it hard to forgive many comrades. This is the fact of their not considering – or of isolating, not mentioning and devaluing – the enormous investment that Paola has put into the 7 April case, both politically and personally. The trial, indeed our whole situation, would not have been what they are without her presence and commitment. A woman, a wife, a mother and an intellectual who, with enormous effort, has become an exceptional political figure. To the extent that she has become utterly political, people might say that she has been recognized as

such – the political terrain does not offer gratitude, and each of us is
repaid by the work they have done. To this I reply: true, were it not
for the fact that in our case the political has been the human – Paola's
political investment, her personal power, was the charge of humanity
and hope that managed to pass through the prison gates and gave us
life inside. Nobody, after my decision to escape, has been willing to
recognize this extraordinary human wealth in the huge work done by
Paola. For everyone, she has become purely and simply a wife – the
wife of the fugitive. I don't want to accuse anyone in particular. I just
want to accuse the political syndrome of cynicism, politics as such,
including that of our friends and comrades; its temptation and its
capacity to annul the human and to disaggregate every true ethical
investment. Apart from anything else it is stupid . . . I saw Paola
today. Her conversation oscillated between ethical commitment to
the continuation of the struggle and disappointment, extreme tiredness and feeling of the weight of our separation. But there is enough
energy left in her to make her raise the question of my return to
Italy. She tells me: 'As far as the media are concerned you are now
seen as an exile, for ever. The court will sanction your defeat, both
political and personal. But this is not true. Negri will return to Italy.
The battle is not over, neither at the political level nor in the courtroom.' She makes this point extremely passionately. She is right. I
have the impression that she sees me as a child, to be protected and
loved independently of myself – her maternal instinct has become a
great political force. So maybe from now on our relationship is a bit
incestuous, Paola? It won't be, if we both entrust ourselves to the
inspiration of love – to the freedom which comes from desire, to this
rebirth of feelings of love and to its passion – newly invented by the
long purgatory of prison. No holding on. No possessiveness. But a
love, a great love that extends over the whole of our life and opens
itself to the comrades, and is able to nourish itself with the abstraction of politics and the dream of revolution. Our children, Paola, are
all of this. Our life, Paola, is the sweetness of a project, of an intellectual and abstract project that has succeeded . . . Today Anna,
my daughter, arrived. She is pure Lombard sweetness – our origins,
re-found – along with an intelligence and an amazing desire for life.
With touches of egotism. She should not. She knows that. The game
is entirely within these tensions, which we have to understand before
quitting it. I experience a certain world-weariness when I see Anna
– she is too beautiful for my mediocre desire of living to be up to the
task of handling the provocation of her force of life. But it is in this
that I renew my nostalgia for struggle and my need to pull myself up

– up to their highest limits. We have the possibility of giving back to the world that youth which, in the struggle and in prison, we rediscovered as a heritage in all of us, as revolutionaries. The revolution has already happened, and I rediscover it fully and actually in the smiles of my children . . . Yes, Paola, I shall return to Italy . . . we shall return . . . and soon. (Paris – 13 November)

Folio 129

The tragedy of the 7 April trial in Rome continues, with cowardly behaviour on all sides. The president of the court does what he likes. Even the worm Tarsitano has found new courage. At least under Nazism there was the advantage that the trials were shorter. The traditional defenders, those of the 'lobby', say that they are overcome with a serious sense of guilt over my flight. Pessimism of the intellect and optimism of the will: they want good solid objects over which they can emote, these gentlemen! A sadism of pity, Petroniuses of penal judgement! What a disgrace! Such a court should be rejected out of hand. They are allowed to accuse me and my comrades of horrible crimes, and to launch infamies against comrades who have displayed a determined moral consistency in the courtroom of the Fascist Forum! No. The court's rejection of the proposal for house arrest (which the comrades have been calling for, for the past five years of their imprisonment) was inevitable. I have a huge bitterness about this. How is it that they are able to renew this monstrous strategy of insults and unwillingness to hear us, this juridical policy of 'everything as normal' within a mechanism which continuously overloads us with injustice and prejudice? Why this naïvety? If it is deliberately created it is even worse than pure stupidity. Today Rossana is taking a solid position in favour of a political solution to the Years of Lead, against the hypocritical and impossible proposal of an amnesty. A political solution for the restoration of a state based on right. But what forces does she have behind her? What possibility of really having an effect? I don't see how the problem can be solved. All the signs are pointing the other way. The Historic Compromise is again belching out its old stuff and trying to pass it for new. Firmness and the hard line are not only an ideology but a vice. Any political solution requires a force behind it – where is it? And will there ever be a force without a denunciation of the perversions of this trial and this regime? We have traversed it, this regime, from left to right, and viceversa. We have recognized all its contradictions, and we have gone into all the holes of this particular cheese – really like worms. But why theorize this traversing as the exclusion of the construction of a new force? As Ginzburg's miller teaches us, both worms and angels can dig into the cheese. Why does the pessimism of the intellect always want us as worms? Certainly this trial was born badly – it was constructed in the national unanimity of the Historic Compromise; and, for the best part of two out of the four years of the initial phase, we, from prison, saw no friends who were willing to lift their heads above the parapet and into the line of fire. Now our friends are murmuring that we have to be careful. Again. All right, we are cautious in practical terms; but why, for what reason, should we be cowardly in intellectual terms? How can we think, even minimally, that it will be possible to free the comrades outside of a political and civil movement that destroys the elements of structural perversion of Italian justice and of the Italian regime? I propose an outright onslaught on the court. I find myself facing a thousand articulations of prudence. But why so much cowardice? Why so much pessimism of the intellect? I see them here in France, the social democratic friends of our civil rights lobby, ruining the fruits of a tremendous victory and an exceptional state of grace through their absolute lack of liberating and political imagination. On our side the level is lower, but precisely for that reason it should permit a somewhat higher excitation of the will. And instead we have ruin. The trial is ploughing ahead and the execution squad is getting prepared. The court is a manipulated process and a guaranteed outcome. We have to fight back against this fearsome ferocity. At mass level, and in terms of hope. May this regime of torturers end its days in ruin and dishonour. But what is astonishing is the fact that people who are aware of all this, and who should be looking for new lines of attack, take refuge instead in alibis and despair. Why are the voices of freedom among us so few and so timid? Why is it that hope does not succeed in crying aloud? We find ourselves with oppositions that are simply oppositions of, and not against, the regime. The cruelty of the emergency laws is experienced as a necessity to be nibbled at, not denounced in its entirety. The tragedy of the Rome chapter of the 7 April trial, the horrible farce of injustice, is continuing. It makes me sick to think of it. It fills me with disgust when I see those faces. Not even sarcasm is possible any longer. I nurture a political dream of the destruction of these butchers and of the pleasure of bringing about this reality in practical terms. (Paris – 16 November)

Folio 130

I have been coopted as an overseas member onto the council of the Collège International de Philosophie. This decision, taken by my friends and colleagues, has made me very happy. I am well aware how little I deserve the honour. But I am young and capable of giving great commitment. I enjoy teaching. There are many things that I still have to say. Anyway, this opportunity to teach will involve me in the work, the hard work, of scientific rebuilding. The crisis of methods and models. And yet the disaster is not as deep as some people would describe it. There are too many positions hastily arrived at. As we know, time has a way of dealing with fashions. Time: this is now my philosophical theme, and I return to it often, continually. The antagonism of temporal values seems to me the only key for opening some of the doors which have been closed by the crisis of the theory of value and of Marxian ontology. In the Collège I sense a strong interest in the rebuilding of a philosophy of hope. It seems that, at last, the theories of disaster and epistemological nihilism are on the defensive – even in France, their land of choice. I do not know whether I shall manage this on the edges of being, on that terrain of pure and non-resolvable antagonism which I had constructed – to reopen a path of great ontological horizon. It is difficult. Nevertheless I want to make my contribution. Teaching is good. Memories come flooding back – the enthusiasm of my lessons in Padova, the seminars at the Institute, and then those meetings, either abroad or at other universities, where I was able to give bodily form to my thinking, speaking it aloud far more than writing it out. That profound emotion which, in discussions in class, pushes you into finding ways to be clear – almost an excavation you do into yourself, for others, driven by their need for understanding. And the spirit often trembles at the difficulties in store. Teaching is often, and can always be, a method of research. In communicating, you arrange in new ways the materials you have accumulated during your research. *Darstellung*, Hegel called it. But its high dignity is not accorded by the metaphysical thread which Hegel claims to unravel – rather, it is given by the intensity, by the corporality of communication. I have an incredible need to reconnect with this corporality of communication, to readjust the measures of the relationship with the real. In communicating you form concepts which criticism often does not register. Certainly, criticism is fundamental; but how can one exercise it if the concept is not constructed vividly within the complexities of communication? The years spent in prison have been a kind of intrusion, a raid into the void. Now I experience this void of communication as detritus and passivity. With a certain inertia. Teaching will force me to break the inertia and to locate myself in a living milieu. I have to have the courage to take the plunge and swim. For me, if I am to succeed in operating practically, at the political level and in life, restarting teaching is a precondition. How pleasurable is the tiredness you get from teaching! I remember the fear, the genuine tremors, which I faced during the period of my seminars on 'Marx beyond Marx' at Ulm. Before I went in I had to drink a Calvados. Today my uneasiness will be even greater. What I have to impose on myself is a new education of myself to begin with. Teaching demands great generosity – like a stripping bare of one's own scientific knowledge in order to show it, and then only slowly to re-cover it with its clothing. This moment of nakedness is fundamental. It is fundamental because in teaching only a pure subjectivity can accept open dialogue and the free development of discussion. When, in 1968 and after, the professors refused this naked condition of liberty, they were not defending the substance of teaching – they were reneguing on it. Now, in the difficulties of the situation where I presently find myself, returning to teaching seems like an act of hope. (Paris – 22 November)

Folio 131

From the Ministry of the Interior I have been informed that it is likely that I shall be granted a residence permit in a couple of months. Really good . . . We shall see. Among the Parisian intellectuals whom I meet, I continue to encounter kindness and brotherly feelings. Châtelet tells me stories about the university and anecdotes about intellectuals. Old Kojève, a Hegelian 'functionary of humanity' – as is clear from his conversation, half musing and half sarcastic. Castoriadis colours his discussion of the problems of war with a love for humanity in revolt which reconciles you to sectarian philosophy. Humanity and liberty. With all of them I experience a rebirth of hope. Yes, here too the miseries of academic life are visible to the naked eye. But here you don't have that courtier spirit which is the plague of Italian culture. The reference to the universal is never peaceably given; here it seems to be sought. I move with great pleasure in this world – I feel as if I have been plucked out of the destructive passions which have too often coloured my relations with academia. Memories of other friends come flooding back, in conversations that I would like to carry forward, in this anxious quest for the universal.

Rebuilding a life in which we can demonstrate this constructive and creative tension. It should not be impossible. (Paris – 26 November)

Folio 132

They have bombed the restaurant run by the Milanese comrades on Boulevard Saint-Michel. That's all we needed. I gather that they were accused of not having taken a position in favour of irreducibilism – and, on the contrary, of having distanced themselves from that position. The truth is that they had not even declared themselves in favour of dissociation. This is a really horrible thing to happen – the reminder of a horrible and persistent reality. I have broadly settled my accounts with the past – but how can I repropose the result of it in the face of this subterranean and cowardly reappearance of such ghosts? I think they may have been supported or covered by the secret services. Operations worthy of the OVRA fascist police. But saying this solves nothing – the problem remains. Ghosts from the past, flashes of violence. How to root them out of our existence and out of our history? I would like to succeed in this through a simple action of intellectual erasure. It is not possible. They keep coming back to you, like some of those ugly old songs you learned in your childhood. These kids who continue to plant bombs, they are certainly not members of any organization – they are splinters – but this is precisely what makes the whole spectacle so horrible. It is not possible to settle accounts with the past on this terrain. These ghosts can only be destroyed through a firm capacity to propose a future in political terms. Our accounts with the past cannot avoid a political debate about the future; they can be settled only through the opening of our accounts with the future. In the state of war that dominates this world there are always going to be uncontrollable breakaway elements. The scenario we face is one of war. But a forward-looking solution implies taking these dimensions into consideration. Every thought-out new constitution has to be a constitution of war. In other words, this is a recognition that the needs of transformation have to be imposed in a dynamic of constitution of war. The problem is not paradoxical, it is realistic. It is possible to resolve it in positive terms. Only on this condition – not avoiding the war, but organizing it and controlling it socially – only on this condition is peace possible. And, within these conditions, set up a debate and a political work which will also eliminate uncontrollable splinters. Soon we shall see a resumption of terrorism in Italy. Under two forms: one of revenge terrorism, oriented against the

repression, and one of international terrorism, for instance state terrorism and overdetermination of the conflict. Here in France only
the second type is present – I see no reason why it should not also
reach Italy. Having said this, what will enable us to intervene will be
a design that is no longer simply political but also constitutional. The
only way to deal with the horrible persistence of these old ghosts is a
deepening of the debate and a constitutional substantialization of the
project – for all of us. We have to operate a major shift in our terrain
of intervention. Only a struggle on the terrain of constitution (and
against the old constitution) can validate our thinking and make it
possible to eliminate the ghosts of the past. On the other hand, how
are we to resolve the problem posed by the existing counter-powers
– that of the corporations and of the disaggregation of the state into
separate bodies? How are we to destroy the compromising physiology
of the Italian state? Our accounts with the past will be settled in the
future – in the project of a new constitutional charter for political
struggle – in the organization and control of war. Here we have to
understand the ontological backdrop, namely the degrees of irreversibility of the Italian situation. Within the framework of a resumption
of revolutionary movement, the Left has to defend liberty and the
counter-powers, and not the existing constitution. The existing material constitution in our country produces terrorism. Enough of ghosts
– we want hope. (Paris – 25 November)

Folio 133

Farewell Italy! Goodbye, old witch. Today they set free Barbone, the
killer. The law of that state and its judicial corporation are exultant.
It is good to be proved right, to have understood that perversion was
inevitably going to triumph – but still, what sadness and what anger!
Injustice has an advantage over justice: the former is always absolute, the latter always relative. The murderer and his accomplices in
killing, informing and provocation have been set free. That has been
decided by a legal system which a great majority of the population
rejects. I literally feel like vomiting when I think about all this. Then,
in the next days, these vampires will be transferred to Rome, to spew
their infamies over my comrades and myself. Barbone, Morandi,
Ricciardi, the more the merrier . . . When this trial began, I wanted,
whatever the cost, to attempt a strong negotiation of this difficult
path of justice. It would have been a struggle, but I was committed
to it. But now everything in me is in revolt against that – against our

intention – and mine – to seek justice. What we have here is a festival of infamy! My anger is accompanied by feelings of nausea. We have a long road ahead of us before we can get out of the desert. Apart from anything else, it is inevitable that, in the conditions brought about by the Milan sentencing, the so-called armed struggle – in fact simply a series of killings and revenge crimes, now devoid of any strategic project – will resume. In the sentencing, the punishments are very heavy. It is inevitable that desperation will breed further acts of desperation. Justice no longer exists when it lives only in the last resort, as an ultimate refuge of constitutional illusion. I don't want to make improper comparisons, I am only addressing the problem of the conditions of consciousness at the outer limits: on this last edge of the desperate reaffirmation of a social and constitutional action, what difference is there between a Spataro and the last volleys of Salò? Goodbye, Italy. Goodbye to any hope of justice that your land might ever produce. Only a very deep-rooted constitutional change will make it possible for liberty and hope to flower again *chez nous*. I don't think that illusions are possible here. We have to destroy everything in order to be able to renew. People are calling for an end to all this. I watch in anger the delay in the comrades' initiative – they should have been ready for the upsurge of contempt for low-life *pentiti* and murderers such as Barboni, and ready to construct, on the basis of these elements, the destruction of the whole system of emergency legislation. Instead, small delays in forward thinking have combined with big illusions, to prevent this much-needed response. Not only is Italy's temple devoid of metaphysics, it is also full of shit. Tomorrow, I am sure, all the newspapers, as interpreters of public opinion, will protest against this incredible sentence; but, pharisaically, they will make a distinction between the law on the *pentiti* (which they will support) and the excesses occurring in its application! I am sure this is the way things will happen. And the intellectuals, now capable of swallowing everything, will protest – not too much . . . *adelante con juicio* – and that will be an end of it. The comrades placed in prison through the infamies of Barbone will remain there. An accommodation with injustice is part of the mindset of the petty bourgeois and of the sentimental and intellectual sphere of the Italic intellectual. And yet the falseness of the *pentito*, the dirty games played around him and around his family, the role of the PCI in this whole business, the dark manipulations of memory and mystification, the partiality, the stage management of the statements made by the *pentiti* – all this has been crystal clear in our trial. They have given him his freedom (and, before that, the licence to kill), in return for his denouncing

Rosso and substituting for Fioroni in the accusations against us. Why can justice not be done? Because there is no justice outside of revolution. We want independent judges, judges who are free. Only a big transformation can produce them. Each movement of the Italian justice system is like the flowing of a giant sewer. How will it ever be possible to block its disastrous effects? This peaceful radical change that we have to set in motion in order to succeed in all this – I can imagine it, but we are not succeeding in programming it. I promise, however, that I shall devote myself to this with all my energies. Do not tremble, Italy, you old witch, we are all sure that nothing will change. Unless . . . but more of this another time. For the moment, may only shit fall upon you – shit to the point of suffocating you, my dear red-white-and-green Italy. But other than that – and forever – long live Paolo Rossi! (Paris – 28 November)

Folio 134

Anaximander: 'The things that are perish into the things out of which they come to be, according to necessity, for they pay penalty and retribution to each other for their injustice, in accordance with the ordering of time.' It is not true. The history of mankind is a history of liberation. It has been improper, criminal, to superimpose onto the history of liberation the business of progress. Liberation is progressive; progress is not in itself liberating. It is not true that the things born and produced bow before the revenge of time, which annuls everything. We inherit and produce liberation. The idea of the eternal return is a myth and a reactionary ideology. Death to the reactionaries and freedom for the peoples! *Ça ira, ça ira, ça ira, les aristocrates à la lanterne!* Time moves within injustice; ontology forms against injustice. Only that which is alive has continued life. Liberation is not antagonistic law – or it is not only that. It is a dimension, the only progressive dimension of being. The obstacle is reduced to transparency. No, it is not Fioroni, Peci, Barbone and Savasta who produce the history of this Italic people of ours – no, these are monstrous superfoetations, symbols of the current material constitution, just as the Savoy monarchy and the republic of Mussolini were. No, the history of consciousness and ontology in Italy are phases of a process of liberation. A history of struggles, of vital enthusiasms, of great theoretical and practical anticipations. I have lived this great experience – I have no regrets for it. Far from it. When I look at them from near or far, these experiences seem to me to be enormous. A liberation that has traversed people's consciousnesses like a strong wind across the valleys.

It is only a question of months or years. It is impossible that we shall not see an avalanche of destruction of the old and the construction of a new landscape. The horizon is already there for the new. Today several tens of thousands of people marched through Paris. They were headed by second-generation Arabs who were protesting against racism, and to that end had organized a march from Marseilles to Paris. Now, the triumph of the march. A new labour power, a new political composition, an allusion to the future. It's hard to say exactly what I felt when I saw those people marching. A jumble of perceptions. But one overriding feeling – that the flowers of liberation are here, blossoming everywhere, mature and strong. They are still in their beginnings, but a mature force is preparing their explosion when the time comes. I live in restrained conditions of liberty – yet I have never felt so strongly the power of this clandestinity, so to speak. The clandestinity of the seedling sprouting beneath the snow, of the seed in its husk. Liberation is a state of the soul. We are discovering with horrible concreteness the channels of the new exploitation and of the restructured domination. Fear as humour, anger and sarcasm as rational denunciation, and a reproposition of hope: these mark us out as supermen. A collective superhumanity. A potentially realized degree of liberation. We really do not need to go back to Lenin's 'What Is to Be Done?' to point to ways of revolution. In those days, it was a little compact group of people who went hand in hand down the paths of revolt; here, instead, it is a whole world that can no longer abide its Time. This is the infinite, incredible force which we have to take from potential to action – to the action of radical change and hope. Today, following the march of the *beurs*, I was looking at the people's faces: serious old communist skilled workers and young smiling Arabs, bearded '68-ers and young whiter-than-white technicians, manual labour and intellectual labour – a new race, but really abstract and polyvalent, the only ones gifted with revolutionary imagination. The 'mutant'. Papageno. And my thoughts went back to our own struggles from '67 to '77 and to the incredible substrate of hope that underpinned them. Let us break the frozen earth, let us complete our crossing of the desert. The obstacles are becoming ever more transparent. The perversion is madness and dispersion: we can fight this perverse power. We can oppose the Time of power with a Time of hope. There is the strength to do it. Today they were tens and tens of thousands. It was the entry of the chosen people into Palestine. This diaspora of ours, in the clutches of the Time of repression, is at an end. The Messiah has already appeared – all we need to do is to realize, realistically and potently, his prophetic potentiality. In ordinary terms, we have this already; in ordinary terms, let us unveil it. We are all Peters, and on this rock we shall build freedom. (Paris – 29 November)

Folio 135

So it is true, I am expecting a child. It is good to grasp, in a real event, the reconstruction of hope in life. Love runs ahead and anticipates the realization of hope. We move within being, and these fruits of being can be determined by us. When we reconquer the capacity of giving life, only then have we returned to life . . . I wanted a child, a new child, a hope which grows – which increases and builds – and which can destroy my unease. A child for a new time, a child for the absence of memory. I was never satisfied by vitalistic and brutally realistic oneness – but rather by the complexity of the signs which can accumulate on this determination of existence. The threshold of life on which new hope can be built is narrow – prison teaches you this ruthlessly. However, from desperation there can emerge an animal in revolt, which is the sole antidote to dispersion of the spirit and to the trap of suicide. That's why I wanted a child; to me this seemed to be projecting forward a century. In prison I so much wanted to have a child . . . She was afraid that saying no would mean losing our friendship. I was afraid, too, that my pressing would have the same effect. Things got blocked there. Then there's the additional problem – the problem of my security, not only in the legal sense that I am in a foreign country; but, given the curious new habits of the secret services, also from a physical point of view. This is a powerful shadow to hang over hope. And yet my tension within myself is healthy: I think, I write, I have arrived at a new tenderness in my relationship with my intelligence. This business of the child can be a resurrection . . . Today she left, to try to solve some of these unresolvable problems. The child, her work, the relationship with me, and with her family. I also don't know if these pages of my diary will stop here, on this particular arc of my life which seems to be coming to a conclusion. Perhaps that would be good. I have done many things during these months, at the juridical, political and scientific level. That concrete revolt against injustice, which the start of the trial and the fact of getting my head out of the tomb of imprisonment had allowed me, is now composed on a horizon of new and general possibilities. Hope seems to be shaping itself afresh into life. Today she left, just as she entered my existence, on tiptoe. Will she come back? My mother used to tell me that only children stop the inexorable Time of death. Children and revolution. These very clear and simple things, which we need in order to confirm an ethical meaning for life. These years of imprisonment and escape, of struggles and study, have shown me the need to relate our hopes to natural rationality. To this second or third nature which the process of liberation has constructed for humanity. We have to rebel in order to reconquer nature, to carry forward the process of liberation. There is no difference between nature and liberty – there is a continuity of struggle and of continuous building, of the one and the other. The flaccidity of this desperate world which surrounds us – the solitude of man in the overbearing massification of life – this huge prison which embraces all of us and stands over us – just a few magic words of love, and the odd act of hopeful abandon can liberate us from all that. And strength, a collective strength, so necessary to the transformation of the world and to the process of liberation, nourishes itself on these fundamental acts. There is no artful or fierce alternative that can break the determinacy of this dialectic. The force we need to build in order to destroy hatred and repression, to found communism and peace, lives on justice – and justice lives and reproduces itself as an impulse towards life, in the dimension of nature and freedom. The strength to undertake a new cycle of revolution is a strength that we shall find by merging with the strength which the human collectivity puts forth every day in reproducing its own life, with love and with desire . . . What strength there is in the birth of a child. (Paris – 30 November)

Appendix

Quotations and translated phrases

Adelante con juicio!
Advance with great prudence!
 (Alessandro Manzoni, *I promessi sposi*, Ch. 12)

Avia Pieridum peragro loca, nullius ante
Trita solo. Iuvat integros accedere fontis
Atque haurire, iuvat novos decerpere flores.
I wander through the solitary places of the Muses, where no one
Has ever set foot before; I love to find unspoilt springs
And to drink eagerly; I love to pick up fresh new flowers.
 (Lucretius, *De rerum natura*, Book IV, lines 1–3)

Ça ira, ça ira, ça ira,
Les aristocrates à la lanterne!
It'll be fine, it'll be fine, it'll be fine
The aristocrats to the lamp-post!
 (Refrain from a popular song of the French Revolution, original
  version Ladré 1790)

Experientia sive praxis.
Experience or praxis.
 (Title of section in Negri's book on Spinoza, *The Savage*
  Anomaly, English translation 1981)

Hic Rhodus, hic salta!
Rhodes is here, here is where you jump!

(Hegel, Preface to the *Philosophy of Right*, (mis)quoting the
punchline from one of the fables attributed to Aesop)

Libertas philosophandi.
Freedom to philosophize [= free enquiry].
(Slogan first used in the full title of Spinoza's *Theologico-Politicus
Tractatus*, 1670)

Metus versus [ad] superstitionem.
Fear turned into superstition.

*Peu de gens devineront combien il a fallu être triste pour ressusciter
Carthage.*
Few people will guess how sad one must have been to bring Carthage
back to life.
(Gustave Flaubert)

Sine ira et studio.
Without anger and partis-pris.
(Cornelius Tacitus, *Annales*, i.1)

Vox in deserto clamans.
A voice crying in wilderness.
(Allusion to the Book of Isaiah first picked up in John Gower's
fourteenth-century poem *Vox clamantis*)

Index